COMINTERN ARMY

The International Brigades
and the Spanish Civil War

R. Dan Richardson

THE UNIVERSITY PRESS OF KENTUCKY

Copyright © 1982 by The University Press of Kentucky
Editorial and Sales Offices: Lexington, Kentucky 40506-0024

Library of Congress Cataloging in Publication Data
Richardson, R. Dan, 1931–
   Comintern Army.

   Bibliography: p.
   Includes index.
   1. Spain—History—Civil War, 1936–1939—Foreign participation.
2. Spain—History—Civil War, 1936–1939—Foreign participation—Russian.
3. Communist International.   I. Title.
DP269.45.R53   946.081   80-5182
ISBN: 978-0-8131-5446-6   AACR2

For Mary Alyce

Contents

Introduction   1

1 Spanish Politics and Comintern Strategy   3
2 Popular Front Militias   16
3 The Comintern Raises an Army   31
4 The Defense of Madrid   47
5 The XIII, XIV, and XV Brigades   68
6 A Military Overview   81
7 Comintern Politics   90
8 The Political Commissar   119
9 Comintern Propaganda Instrument   136
10 Dissidence, Desertion, and the Terror   159

Conclusion   177

Notes   181

Bibliographical Essay   217

Index   224

Introduction

When the first units of the International Brigades marched through the wind-swept and sparsely peopled streets of besieged Madrid in the early morning hours of November 8, 1936, a myth was born. This myth focused on the appealing idea that the men of those first International contingents, and the thousands who were to follow them into the whirlwind of civil war in Spain, represented the response of world democracy to the threat of fascism. These International volunteers were, so the theme ran, a band of modern Lafayettes and Garibaldis, the "cream of the progressive youth of the age" and "premature antifascists" who embarked on a "great crusade" to make the world safe for democracy.

The facts fail to support the myth. But since this myth meshed so neatly into the larger one that cast the Spanish Civil War as a clear-cut struggle between "democracy" and "fascism," so widely held at the time, it has exhibited remarkable staying power. Actually the Spanish conflict was, as many have shown, anything but a simple and straightforward contest between democracy and fascism. Both sides in the civil war represented a varied amalgam of mutually incompatible ideologies. To say that all who fought for the Loyalists were democrats is to stretch that term beyond meaningful definition. To say that all who fought for the Nationalists were fascists is to do the same. Once this is understood it becomes unnecessary to hold—as the myth within a myth would have it—that the foreigners who fought for the Loyalists were, by definition, fighting for democracy.

In fact, when civil war and revolution exploded simultaneously in Spain in July 1936, the explosion was the result of long-brewing and uniquely Spanish developments and had its roots deep in that distracted country's past. But because of the ideological power struggles then smoldering in Europe the Spanish conflict quickly assumed an international significance out of all proportion to its intrinsic importance outside of Spain itself. Spain had the misfortune to suffer a civil war at a time when it suited powerful states and fanatical ideological forces to use that war for their own purposes. Thus Spain, a land usually self-contained and remote from the dynamic forces of history north of the Pyrenees, became the arena in which the violent political passions of the time came to grips.

Germany, Italy, and the Soviet Union intervened actively in the war, using Spain not only as a pawn in their game of power politics but as a proving ground for their respective military and political techniques. The Soviet Union and its international apparatus, the Comintern, pursued a policy in Spain of organizing, unifying, and directing the Loyalist forces, both militarily and politically, while at the same time seeking to enlist the sympathy and support of a broad spectrum of world opinion for what they called the "defense of democracy" and "antifascism." That the Soviet-Comintern leadership saw fit to involve itself in the Spanish affair as it did resulted from a unique confluence of the stream of Spanish history with the larger currents swirling about Europe and the world in the tumultuous decade of the 1930s. It was that confluence also which spawned the International Brigades and accounted for a Comintern army fighting in a Spanish civil war.

The fame of the Brigades stems primarily from their military exploits, exploits certainly of significance and deserving of the recognition they have received. The Brigades were among the most effective military units on their side of the barricades and quite possibly made the difference between survival and defeat for Loyalist Spain during the critical winter of 1936–1937. But the Brigades were much more than simply a military force. They were a significant political, ideological, and propaganda instrument which could be—and was—used by the Comintern for its own purposes, not only inside Spain but on the larger world stage. No realistic understanding of the significance of the Brigades is possible without an appreciation of their intrinsically political nature and role, nor of the fact that they were, from beginning to end, an integral part of that interlocking directorate which was the Soviet-Comintern apparatus in Spain.

1 Spanish Politics and Comintern Strategy

On July 17, 1936, elements of the Spanish army raised the banner of revolt against the government of the Republic. The *pronunciamiento*, however, was not a complete success. Had it been so, the ministry would have resigned and a military junta would have assumed governmental powers.[1] What happened instead was the detonation of dual revolutions and a full-scale civil war in which each side sought not only the destruction of the other but the destruction of the Spanish Republic and the abortive experiment in "bourgeois democracy" which it represented.

The government against which the Spanish army rebelled was dependent upon the Frente Popular, an electoral coalition of leftist parties which had narrowly won the elections of February 1936. The cabinets that had held the executive power of the state since the Popular Front's victory in February had been composed entirely of left republicans because both the Socialist and the Communist parties refused to participate in a "bourgeois government." This reflected the fact that the "bourgeois republican" regime was supported only grudgingly, if at all, by those very proletarian political forces that accounted for the bulk of the Popular Front's electoral strength. Thus the left republican governments had been forced to walk a tightrope while performing a political juggling act in a frantic effort to keep their erstwhile political allies from pursuing a too blatantly revolutionary program while at the same time attempting to keep these same forces in harness behind the regime. Success in the former would jeopardize the latter. But failure in the latter would mean the political bankruptcy of a bourgeois republic dependent on the support of Marxist Socialists, Communists, and Anarchists.[2]

Perhaps the most immediate and obvious manifestation of the essential frailty of the Popular Front coalition as a base upon which to govern the Republic was the precipitous and vociferous radicalization of the Socialist party of Spain, the party that was the essential keystone of the coalition. The left wing of the party, led by the then-styled "Spanish Lenin," Francisco Largo Caballero, was demanding the Bolshevization of the party and the revolutionary road to the "dictatorship of the proletariat." Largo Caballero and his supporters had made it clear from the beginning that their adherence to the Popular Front was simply a matter of electoral expediency and implied no commitment to support the bourgeois republic. "With the Republic established, our duty is to bring about Socialism," said Largo Caballero. "I speak of Marxist Socialism . . . of revolutionary Socialism. . . . Our aspiration is the conquest of political power. Method? That which we are able to use. It [the Popular Front] is a circumstantial coalition, for which a program is being produced that is certainly not going to satisfy us."[3]

One of Largo Caballero's chief intellectual lieutenants, Julio Alvarez del Vayo, put it bluntly. The Popular Front, he said, was "an intermediate stage of common labor, in which the republicans dissolve the Fascist centres and purge the armed forces, so that the Socialists may soon install the dictatorship of the proletariat." In a speech in February 1936, Luis Araquistain, another of the Socialist intellectuals, poignantly pointed out the similarity between the revolutionary situation of Spain in 1936 and that of Russia in 1917. The weakness of the Republic, he concluded, set the proper condition for Spain to become the second country "where the proletarian revolution triumphs."[4] Presumably Manuel Azaña, the president of the Republic, was cast to play Kerensky to Largo Caballero's Lenin.

In April 1936 Largo Caballero said: "The present regime cannot continue,"[5] and, indeed, it would have been hard for anyone even remotely aware of the realities to argue with him on that. The government seemed incapable of governing the country or, indeed worse, of even trying. The most ominous result of the government's dependence on the sufferance of the proletarian parties was its reluctance to antagonize them by enforcing the law with vigor. Thus the period from February to July 1936 saw a breakdown in public order which was extreme even for Spain.[6] Speaking out bravely and honestly against the wave of political strikes, violent demonstrations, church burnings, and assassinations, Indalecio Prieto, a moderate Socialist, said: "What no country can endure is the constant bloodletting of public disorder . . . what no nation can bear is the attrition of its public authority and its own economic vitality through the continuance of uneasiness, anxiety and restlessness . . . that way does not lead to Socialism, it leads to an utterly hopeless anarchy."[7]

If an astute and dedicated Socialist felt compelled to speak out against Spain's decline into chaos, it was hardly surprising that moderate and conservative forces were agitated and alarmed. In a strange way the words of José Maria Gil Robles, a leading conservative spokesman, seemed to echo those of Prieto: "A country can survive as a monarchy or as a Republic, with a parliamentary system or with a presidential system, with Sovietism or with fascism; however, the one way it does not survive is in anarchy, and Spain today, unhappily, is living in anarchy."[8]

Against this background of governments that did not govern, strident revolutionary rhetoric and a rapid slide into chaos, action by the army, and support of or acquiesence in that action by a wide spectrum of Spanish opinion was hardly unexpected. When it came, the essential hollowness of the left republican regime became immediately apparent. Its already tenuous and feeble authority collapsed as the bulk of the forces of order normally at the disposal of any government —the army, the police apparatus, the bureaucracy—went over to the insurgents. "The state fell and the Republic remained without an army, without a police force," recalled a leading Spanish Socialist.[9] An astute foreign observer, Pietro Nenni, chief of the Italian Socialist party and an early participant in the Spanish Civil War, wrote: "The phenomenon most characteristic of the first phase of the Civil War was the absence of power, of a central direction.... The state did not exist, authority had collapsed."[10]

Within a few days after the *pronunciamiento,* the ephemeral Republican cabinets (there were three within as many days), faced with the collapse of the state apparatus, gave in to the demands of the proletarian parties for arms. From that moment the writ of the "government" ceased to count for much. Real power in Republican Spain passed into the hands of the proletarian parties—parties with frankly revolutionary aims.[11] The president of the Republic himself later testified to the utter collapse of governmental authority and the reality of revolution in Popular Front Spain: "The revolutionary excess [of the masses of Republican Spain] spread itself before the eyes of the astonished ministers. In view of this violent revolution, the cabinet was not able to choose between methods designed to halt or suppress the criminal agitation. The Government lacked the forces necessary to do it. And if it had disposed of some ... their employment would only have run the risk of provoking a second Civil War."[12] From the beginning then, the bulk of the elements actively opposing the *pronunciamiento* were essentially revolutionary forces motivated not by any desire to defend "bourgeois democracy," the "Republic," and the *status quo ante* July 17, 1936, but to "make the revolution."

While the facade of a regularly constituted Republican government remained in existence in Madrid, because it served the purposes of the proletarian parties to allow it to do so,[13] the reality of power lay in the regime of political committees which sprang into being throughout Popular Front Spain, committees dominated by the proletarian revolutionary parties. Despite the calculated denials of Popular Front propaganda,[14] the fact of revolution was starkly clear to anyone inside the Popular Front zone of Spain. Entering Barcelona in August 1936, Franz Borkenau felt as if he had "landed on a continent different from anything I had seen before." Later that year George Orwell wrote: "When one came straight from England the aspect of Barcelona was something startling and overwhelming. It was the first time that I had ever been in a town where the working class was in the saddle. Practically every building of any size had been seized by the workers and was draped with red flags or with the red and black flag of the Anarchists; every wall was scrawled with the hammer and sickle and with the initials of revolutionary parties; almost every church has been gutted and its images burnt."[15] The Cambridge-educated British Communist John Cornford felt awestruck and delighted at what he saw. "In Barcelona," he wrote, "one can understand physically what the dictatorship of the proletariat means. . . . Everywhere in the streets are armed workers and militiamen, and sitting in the cafes which used to belong to the bourgeoisie. . . . It's as if in London the armed workers were dominating the streets."[16]

Madrid made much the same impact. The government appeared little in evidence. The proletarian political parties and trade unions, acting with complete autonomy, dominated the city. Each wore its own insignia and maintained its own armed militia units and strongly fortified headquarters.[17] This Spain then, caught up in the throes of revolution and civil war, distracted, divided, and desperate, created one of the preconditions for the emergence of the International Brigades on the stage of history.

But in another and more critical sense the specifically Spanish issues were not the crux of the matter. To the men who brought the Brigades into existence and to the vast majority of those foreigners who fought in the Brigades, the issue was not really Spain and the Spaniards but the larger international and ideological forces of the day which simply found a convenient arena for combat in Spain. In this sense the International Brigades were both a by-product and an instrument of a Soviet-Comintern strategy of worldwide scope.

That strategy had been launched as early as 1934 and was a direct result of the fact that the view from the Kremlin had changed both rapidly and menacingly in the years immediately preceding. The threat posed to the Soviet Union by a resurgent Germany and an aggressive Japan had forced the men in Moscow to alter radically both the traditional Soviet foreign policy and the party line of the Communist International. The new Soviet foreign policy called for rapprochement and, if possible, alliance with any power that did, or might in the future, oppose German and/or Japanese expansionism. This, in effect, meant those traditional targets of Communist hostility, the nations of the "bourgeois imperialist" west. It also led to the Soviet Union's adherence to the previously despised League of Nations where its delegation immediately became the most vocal advocate of collective security. By 1935 the Soviet Union had concluded alliances with both France and Czechoslovakia and had apparently reversed her traditionally revisionist foreign policy to become a staunch defender of the status quo.

A second and complementary phase of the new Kremlin strategy was the Popular Front. The goal of the Popular Front policy was to secure as wide a spectrum of support as possible within the bourgeois democracies for foreign policies that would, in effect, support those of the USSR. Even with this new approach the Soviet leaders well knew that the vast majority of people and governments of the world would be little concerned with threats to the security of the USSR as such. Thus, a fundamental thrust of the Popular Front stratagem was directed toward making the threat to the Soviet Union appear to be only part of a general threat to all.[18] To do this the Soviet-Comintern interpretation of the world situation read that an international Fascist conspiracy, led by Germany and Japan, threatened the peace and security of the entire world. As the Soviet commissar for foreign affairs, Maxim Litvinov, put it: "The flame of war lighted by the aggressors on two continents threatens to set fire to Europe and then to the whole world. As always... it was the Soviet Union which was the first to raise its voice to the whole world... proclaiming the source of the danger... and pointing out the ways and means necessary to struggle against this bloody disaster into which fascism is ready to plunge humanity."[19]

Prior to the adoption of the Popular Front program the Communist line had stressed that the greatest enemies of the working class were the non-Communist proletarian parties: "The Fascist beasts were Fascist beasts," wrote Arthur Koestler, a member of the German Communist party at the time, "but our [the Communists] main preoccupation was the Trotskyite heretics and socialist schismatics."[20] On February 6, 1934, a leading French Communist, André Marty, wrote in *L'Humanité*, "It is impossible to struggle against fascism without struggling against social democracy." In that same year the Communist party of Spain took advantage of an abortive insurrection of Asturian workers to tell the working class that "the Socialist Party is the full manifestation of the impotence of social-democracy." The Communist's aim, wrote a leading member of the Spanish Communist party, was "to destroy the Socialist party."[21]

The new Popular Front policy began with a cessation of the more violent forms of abuse against the various socialist and democratic parties followed by efforts at seeking alliances with them. The slogan used to attract support for the Popular Front idea, by evoking an ideological image appealing to the widest possible audience, was "antifascism." Armed with the new ideological shibboleth, the Comintern undertook the task of making the Popular Front a reality. All talk of "social fascists" ended abruptly as did any hint that Communists were revolutionaries. "The notion that we [the Communists] had ever advocated violence was to be ridiculed as a bogey, refuted as a slander spread by reactionary war-mongers," wrote Koestler. "We no longer referred to ourselves as Bolsheviks, nor even as Communist ... we were just simple, honest, peaceloving anti-Fascists and defenders of democracy." American Communist party chief Earl Browder was simply parroting the Popular Front line when he later righteously declared. "The war in Spain is a part of the world-wide offensive against fascism of all peace loving and democratic peoples." Bourgeois democracy, which, as Koestler recalled, had a month or two earlier been castigated as "fascism in disguise," was now "praised as a guarantee of freedom." All revolutionary slogans were eliminated from the Communist vocabulary and replaced by the slogans of "freedom, peace and national unity."[22] An example of this was the adoption of the slogan "Socialist students, the most active upholders of peace, democracy and civilization," by the Communist-dominated Socialist Club at Cambridge University.[23]

A close reading of the Popular Front program as officially enunciated at the Seventh Congress of the Communist International of August 1936 showed that the Communists had not by any means given up their ultimate objectives of world revolution and the dictatorship of the proletariat. They were merely adopting a temporary tactic to meet the immediate threat posed by the rise of powerful enemies of the Soviet Union.[24] In clarification of the Popular Front line, Georgi Dimitroff, chief of the Comintern and the man most closely identified with that policy, wrote: "The flexible Bolshevik tactics, which are the application of the general tactical line of the Seventh Congress of the Communist International to a specific question arise of necessity from the whole present-day international situation." In his explanation Dimitroff made it clear that the real purpose of the Popular Front was the defense of the USSR. So also did the

German Comintern spokesman Walter Ulbricht. "No one can really fight fascism," he said, "so long as he does not contribute to the strengthening of its most important bulwark in this struggle, the Soviet Union."[25]

That a clear understanding of the true nature and purpose of the Popular Front policy was well understood by the various branches of the Comintern was demonstrated by an article signed by José Díaz, the top Spanish Communist, just prior to the Spanish elections of February 1936. "Our [Communist Party] struggle is for the dictatorship of the proletariat, for Soviets, we ... do not give up our aims. But ... the immediate task now is not the struggle for the dictatorship of the proletariat but the development of the anti-fascist struggle." Ulbricht, in a speech to the Seventh World Congress of the Comintern at which the new line was pronounced said: "In the struggle for Soviet power, it is possible—during a political crisis—to establish an anti-fascist popular front, so long as the masses are still not ready for a Soviet government. Later on, when conditions have improved, we can continue the struggle for a proletarian dictatorship. ... the goal of our fight is a Soviet Germany." Explaining the new tactic, he said, "We Communists fight for democratic freedom because it gives greater mobility to the working class and its organization [the Communist party], and permits them to prepare the masses for the battle for Soviet power."[26] The temporary and tactical nature of the new policy was not stressed outside the confines of the party itself.

Success for the Popular Front required a massive enlargement of the numbers of people who could be influenced by the Communist party. This was a task preeminently of propanganda which, to be most effective, must appear to be in large part of non-Communist origin. The Comintern had within its ranks a man who was something of a genius in just the type of work needed. Among the German political exiles living in Paris after 1933 was Willi Munzenberg, Comintern chief of agitprop (agitation and propaganda) for western Europe and Germany. Arthur Koestler, who worked with Munzenberg and knew him intimately, called him the "Red Eminence of the international anti-fascist movement." Munzenberg had been extremely successful since the 1920s in founding, editing, and marketing numerous magazines and newpapers which sought to popularize the Soviet Union and the Communist party in Germany. He invented and made use of the "fellow traveller," a new species which was to have a significant future, especially during the Popular Front period. He developed the organizational technique for making use of the "fellow traveller" as well as thousands of unwitting dupes in the ubiquitous front organizations clandestinely conducted by the party and designed to mobilize and direct public opinion in support of virtually any program or point of view. Of Munzenberg's multifarious propaganda activities, Koestler wrote: "He produced International Committees, Congresses and movements as a conjurer produces rabbits out of his hat."[27] As another ex-Communist put it, "The success with which the Communist line was propagated among Social Democrats and liberals during these years, ... the thousands of painters, writers and doctors and lawyers and debutantes chanting a diluted version of the Stanlinist line" vividly demonstrated the effectiveness of Munzenberg's efforts.[28]

Under the impact of one of the greatest propaganda barrages ever laid down, the new policy achieved rapid and widespread successes. Most apparent were those in France and Spain where Popular Front electoral coalitions with Communist participation put governments into power in 1936. But in England and the United States, too, the Communists had never been so popular or so successful.[29] The American Communists suddenly adopted and loudly supported the New Deal which just a short time before they had as loudly excoriated as "semi-fascist"[30] and Earl Browder, secretary of the party in the United States, posed as a great patriot, adopting the slogan "Communism is the Americanism of the twentieth century." In France the Communists attempted to widen the spectrum of the Popular Front far beyond the range of the political left. *L'Humanité* editorially called for the inclusion of the National Volunteers, a right-wing veterans organization, and the Catholic parties in the "anti-fascist front." All this seemingly strange benevolence toward those whom the Communists had formerly anathematized followed faithfully the policy laid down in the Kremlin. Stalin told the French ambassador that confidentially he did not care what a country's internal regime was so long as its foreign policy was anti-German.[31]

Against this background the eruption of civil war and proletarian revolution in Spain was highly unwelcome to Soviet policymakers. It exposed the contradiction in their new policy between the attempt to convince bourgeois democratic governments that the Soviet Union was no longer interested in exporting revolution on the one hand and their desire to continue to pose as the champion of the world proletariat on the other.[32] If the pre-Popular Front policy had been still in effect the Communists could logically have either favored proletarian revolution in Spain unreservedly or taken a hands-off, plague-on-both-your-houses, attitude since the whole conflict could have been written off as one between bourgeois capitalist factions or Fascists.[33]

Spanish Politics

But in the complicated world of July 1936 no such simple solution was possible.

At this difficult time the dual nature of the International Communist movement proved to be of value. While the Soviet Union's regular governmental apparatus remained, overtly at least, quiet and correct on the Spanish affair,[34] even to the extent of signing a British-sponsored nonintervention agreement designed to isolate the war in Spain,[35] the Comintern moved quickly and noisily into action. The immediate interpretation of events in Spain by the Comintern was that the *pronunciamiento* of the Spanish army was part of the worldwide fascist plot. The statement "Hitler is in direct control of the general staff of the [Spanish] Putschists" summed up this attitude as expressed in the first issues of the Comintern's official organ after the fighting broke out.[36] The first official Comintern reaction to the *pronunciamiento* apparently came at a meeting in Moscow of representatives of the Comintern and Profintern (the Communist labor organization). There the idea of aid to the Popular Front forces in Spain was agreed to in principle. Another joint Comintern-Profintern meeting was held on July 26 in Prague under the chairmanship of Gaston Monmousseau, Chief of the European office of the Profintern. There a program of financial aid to the Spanish Popular Front was adopted.[37]

At the same time Communist parties throughout the world quickly launched full-scale propaganda campaigns in support of Popular Front Spain. As early as July 26 Harry Pollitt, chief of the Communist party of Great Britain, declared to a rally in Trafalgar Square: "We must compel the national government [of Great Britain] to render every assistance to the Spanish peoples' front government . . . let us organize a mighty united movement of solidarity . . . organize meetings, demonstrations everywhere."[38] The Comintern also sought to use the Popular Front momentum to get united action from the Second International and other proletarian, labor, and liberal organizations on the Spanish question.[39]

Meanwhile Munzenberg's propaganda machine turned its full attention to Spain. A European Conference for the Defense of the Spanish Republic, called by the World Committee against War and Fascism, one of Munzenberg's front organizations, met in Paris on August 13, 1936, to mobilize opinion behind the Comintern's interpretation of the Spanish affair. That conference established an International Coordination and Information Commission in Support of the Spanish Republic, one of the first of the multitude of such commissions and committees organized and clandestinely controlled by the Comintern in relation to its policy in Spain.[40] On August 31 a meeting of the directorate of Secours Rouge, another of the Comintern's front organizations, convened in Paris. From that meeting emerged the Comité International de l'aide du Peuple Espagnol. A multitude of similar organizations for aid to Republican Spain mushroomed into being. Communist activists were ordered to "proliferate Spanish Defense Committees."[41] Most of these committees were directed by party functionaries who controlled them unobtrusively behind imposing lists of sponsors whose often well-known and respected names graced the organizations' letterheads and lent weight to their appeals for funds and support for their cause.[42]

On another front in the propaganda war Munzenberg dispatched party writers like Koestler to Spain to produce firsthand accounts of the situation there, all, of course, from a strictly defined point of view. Munzenberg relied on Otto Katz, alias André Simon, as his chief lieutenant for Spain. Katz, a longtime Comintern functionary, organized the Spanish Relief Committee, directed the Spanish News Agency, and dispensed Loyalist government propaganda funds to French newspapers and politicians. As Munzenberg's roving ambassador, Katz made trips to England and Hollywood to collect funds and organize antifascist committees.[43]

The Comintern also lost no time in intensifying its activity inside Spain, assigning Palmiro Togliatti, chief of the Italian Communist party, to the Spanish front.[44] Togliatti worked behind the scenes in Spain using the aliases Ercoli and Alfredo and played a key role in the direction of the Spanish Communist Party.[45]

At about the same time a full-scale Soviet diplomatic and military mission arrived in Spain. On August 27 the experienced diplomat Marcel Rosenberg presented his credentials in Madrid as Soviet ambassador. He was accompanied by a formidable staff, among whom was General Berzin, previously head of Soviet military intelligence. Berzin, along with General Goriev, commanded the staff of Soviet military advisers who virtually took over direction of the military operations of the Popular Front forces.[46] During the month of September additional Soviet personnel arrived in Spain. Among them was Michael Koltsov, *Pravda's* leading foreign correspondent and a man who clearly had more important duties than journalism.[47] About this time Alexander Orlov arrived with instructions to set up a branch of the NKVD in Spain.[48] Thus by the middle of September 1936 the Soviet Union and Comintern had a high-powered contingent in Spain covering all spheres of political and military operations.

Meanwhile, in an operation that demonstrated the meshing of official Soviet military intelligence apparatus with that of the Comintern,

Red army general Walter Krivitsky, then chief of Soviet military intelligence in Western Europe, received orders from Moscow on August 30: "Extend your operations immediately to cover the Spanish War. Mobilize all available agents and facilities for prompt creation of a system to purchase and transport arms to Spain." Krivitsky immediately began setting up "paper companies" in various countries of Europe for the procurement of arms for Popular Front Spain.[49] His orders stipulated that the operation must remain highly secret. The furnishing of military supplies for Popular Front Spain was to be a clandestine affair which could not be traced back to the Soviet Union. The Soviet-Comintern machine thus became progressively more deeply committed to the Popular Front cause in Spain. As yet, however, the Soviet Union's involvement remained limited, overtly at least, to diplomatic and propagandistic support. Comintern operations in Spain were not acknowledged as being sponsored or controlled by the Soviet government and Krivitsky's clandestine arms-buying did not officially exist.

Swiftly moving political and military developments in Spain soon brought more direct and overt Soviet intervention. In early September a new cabinet headed by the Socialist Largo Caballero had assumed governmental power in Madrid. On specific instructions from Moscow the Spanish Communist party officially participated in the new government, more clearly than ever tying Communist prestige to the Spanish Popular Front cause.[50] The Communists were thus in an increasingly strong position to push their own policies and viewpoints on the nature of the war and the methods, both political and military, by which it should be conducted. They sought to control the situation in Popular Front Spain in such a way that their intervention there would not wreck their larger policy of rapprochement with the bourgeois democracies. As the best way to achieve that end, the Communists adopted the position that the war in Spain (and thus their role there) was simply the defense of the democratic Republic against fascism and that it had nothing to do with revolution. An article, "Spain's Struggle against Fascism," which appeared in the official Comintern organ, succinctly summed up this position while at the same time making clear to the initiated the strictly tactical nature of it.

> Present task of the Communist Party is to crush the fascist revolt and save the republic. . . . The slogan of the defense of the democratic republic makes it possible to bring the widest masses of the people . . . into the struggle . . . creates a very wide basis

for the struggle ... assists its formation of a wide democratic front around the struggle ... throughout the world. The struggle ... in Spain ... is meeting with the sympathy of tremendous sections of the population in all the capitalist countries. ... The party understands that this growing wave of sympathy ... is a strong weapon which the workers organizations [Communist parties] of all countries must use ... therefore the party is against all irresponsible statements, against frivolous chatter as to projects for the future "reorganization of society" which in the present international situation can only serve to complicate the struggle.[51]

This stance by the Communists accounted for the paradoxical fact that they found themselves on the right of the political spectrum of Popular Front Spain and that many Socialists and virtually all Anarchosyndicalists and POUMists regarded the Communist role as counterrevolutionary. So also did many non-Spanish leftists.[52]

Despite everything that the new Popular Front government, the Spanish militias, and the Communists could do, the Popular Front's military position continued to deteriorate rapidly. Nationalist forces moving steadily toward Madrid from the south seemed unstoppable. The Soviet staff in Madrid, as well as most other foreign observers, concluded that unless substantial outside aid arrived quickly the Nationalists would take the city. Ambassador Rosenberg, General Berzin, and the influential Koltzov were all convinced that without rapid Soviet intervention the end could not be far off.

In addition to the urgent need for military materiel numerous observers stressed the need for a more effective fighting force than the Popular Front militias were affording. Ambassador Rosenberg reported that view to Moscow and, in addition, on September 22 Maurice Thorez, chief of the French Communist Party, flew to Moscow where he recommended that Soviet aid in the form of military supplies and equipment be dispatched to Spain immediately and that the Comintern undertake the organization of a military unit to be made up of foreign volunteers and directed by a Comintern political and military staff.[53] Under the pressure of these events and convinced that the Popular Front regime could not survive without significant military aid, Moscow made the decision to intervene more directly and decisively in the Spanish imbroglio, a decision that led to the appearance of Soviet tanks and planes on Spanish battlefronts in October 1936 and to the arrival of the first of the volunteers recruited by the Comintern for the International Brigades in the same month.[54] Thus the origins of the International Brigades are to be found in the working out of a Soviet-Comintern policy of worldwide scope and not, as some would have it, in the spontaneous response of world democracy to the threat of fascism in Spain. To put it differently, without the Soviet-Comintern decision to intervene directly in the Spanish War and, as part of that intervention, create a foreign volunteer force for use in Spain, the International Brigades would never have come into existence.

2   Popular Front Militias

Since the bulk of the army and heavy police forces of Spain either sided with the military revolt of July 1936 or were swamped in the proletarian revolution that followed hard on its heels, the only effective armed opposition to the *pronunciamiento* came from militia units that were organized and controlled by the various Popular Front political parties and labor unions. The Socialist and Communist parties had in fact been organizing workers and peasant militias for some time prior to 1936. Enrique Lister, after a three-year sojourn in the Soviet Union where he attended both the Lenin Institute and a Red army military school, undertook the task of building up units of the Communist MAOC (workers and peasants antifascist militia) as early as 1935.[1] The Italian Comintern agent Vittorio Vidali, who was to play a leading role during the civil war, arrived in Spain in May 1936 with orders to build the party militia into "the organizational basis for the future worker-peasant Red Army."[2] The Socialist party organ, *Claridad,* declared in headlines in April 1936, "The people's militia ... must be organized in every village in Spain."[3] And Jesús Hernández, a high-ranking member of the Spanish Communist party wrote just prior to the outbreak of hostilities, "The militia exists throughout the country."[4] The speed with which the more-or-less organized militia units of the Popular Front entered the fray against the insurgent forces in July 1936 could no doubt be attributed to the prior existence of such paramilitary organizations.[5] But the outbreak of fighting in July saw a rapid and widespread proliferation of militia forces.

The militia columns varied greatly from one another, forming as they did not parts of a single army but independent groups of armed men controlled by autonomous political factions. The Anarchosyndicalists recruited, organized, armed, fed, equipped, and commanded their militia columns while the Communists, Socialists, POUMists,[6] and others did the same for theirs. Indeed in the early stages of the conflict the militia units came and went as they or their party leadership saw fit without any direction by the impotent government in Madrid at all.[7] Even after a government more truly representative of the forces of the Popular Front was formed in September 1936, with the Socialist Largo Caballero as premier and minister of war, its authority over the militias was almost nil. Largo Caballero himself admitted privately that he had no control over the various political forces supporting the Popular Front cause.[8]

These militia columns were not motivated so much by a desire to defend the democratic-parliamentary republic of the previous period as to "make the revolution." As George Orwell, who was there, put it: "The fact is that the Spanish working class did not, as we might conceivably do in England, resist Franco in the name of 'democracy' and the status quo; their resistance was accompanied by—one might almost say it consisted of—a definite revolutionary outbreak."[9] When the Ascaso column, an Anarchist unit, left Barcelona for the front near Huesca on August 19, it was, according to a foreign participant, not an army but "an armed rabble," which, so far as the people in it were concerned, was "an armed demonstration for carrying the revolution to Saragozza."[10] A Dutch Communist who joined the militia and fought on the front south of Madrid echoed the same general impression. "Our regiments," he wrote, "are nothing but armed party groups."[11]

Three of the most militant and active forces on the Popular Front side of the barricades—the Anarchosyndicalists, the POUMists, and the left-wing Socialists—openly avowed their revolutionary aims and aspirations. For example, *Claridad,* the organ of the left-wing Socialists, declared in August: "The people are no longer fighting for the Spain of July 16 [the Republic].... The most powerful support for the war lies in the total uprooting of fascism, economically and in every other way. That is, in revolution."[12] The Anarchosyndicalist attitude was succinctly voiced to Franz Borkenau by an Anarchist militiaman who told him they were fighting "not for the legal government but in order to move swiftly toward the abolition of the state."[13] Not only were these groups positively oriented toward taking advantage of the collapse of state authority to "make the revolution" but they saw the militias as the vanguard and guarantee of that process. On the issue of retaining the militia forces or of trying to organize a regular People's Army under government control, *Claridad* declared on August 20: "Our army must be an army that is in keeping with the revolution.... To think of replacing the present combatants [militia] with another type of army which, to a certain extent, would control their revolutionary action is to think in a counterrevolutionary way." Eventually the Socialists came around to supporting the creation of a unified People's Army but only later and under the pressures of both the realization of its practical necessity for fighting the war and of the Communists' insistence that a unified army be created. The Anarchosyndicalists and POUMists never really accepted the change. The right-wing Socialists and the Communists usually claimed to be defending the Republic but for tactical reasons that concealed long-run revolutionary goals. Even though the Communists were normally the staunchest proponents, in public, of the defense-of-the-Republic posture, even they occasionally dropped the pose. For example, Dolores Ibarruri (La Pasionaria), a member of the Politburo of the CPS, said, speaking of the People's Army, that it must be like the Red army, not just the army of a nation but the "advance guard of shock troops of the world revolution."[14] Only the small and weak Republican groups could truly be said to be defending the Republic.

Each militia column represented a replica in microcosm of its particular ideological vision of the classless society and reflected the very different concepts held by the various ideologies to be found within the Popular Front spectrum of what constituted revolutionary organization and behavior. The Anarchist and POUM units were highly equalitarian and democratic organizations, at least in theory. Everyone from commander to private drew the same pay, ate the same food, wore the same clothes, and mingled on terms of complete equality. Frequently the troops elected their military commanders and no one considered it strange for a private to slap the commander on the back and ask for a cigarette or even to insist upon comradely discussion of commands and decisions.[15]

The POUM militia column in which George Orwell served was fairly typical of the general situation in the units in Catalonia. He joined the column at the Lenin barracks outside Barcelona and stayed there for about a week while a new unit was being formed. There were a thousand or so men and a few militia women at the barracks as well as a number of militiamen's wives who did the cooking. The Spanish recruits were mostly boys of seventeen or eighteen, utterly ignorant of matters military. Discipline did not exist. Chaos reigned. Uniforms and equipment were doled out piecemeal and the result was anything but uniform. After a few days the column was "still a rabble by any ordinary standard," but by Spanish militia standards it was considered fit to be seen in public. "Any public school O.T.C. in England is far more like a modern army," wrote Orwell.[16] The militia units were, as one would expect, hardly military in appearance or disciplined in action. They were rather, depending on one's point of view, an armed rabble interested primarily in murder, pillage, and the destruction of the social order or the heroic and picturesque advance guard of the revolution.[17] Regardless of how the militias were viewed, most observers agreed that they left much to be desired as effective military forces. Only the Communists had no philosophical qualms about demanding strict military discipline and obedience to orders in their militia units and, true to Bolshevik doctrine, did so. Even so, only in a very relative sense, and with much effort by their commanders and political commissars, did even their much-vaunted Fifth Regiment seem an example of military efficiency.

While the militia units were able to offer a certain amount of resistance to the forces of the *pronunciamiento* when they could fight from stationary defensive positions, a village or town, they could not stand in the open field against trained and disciplined troops. The rapid advance of the numerically weak Nationalist forces from the south during the early months of the war was a repeated story of sporadic tenacious defense by militia, an outflanking movement by the Nationalists, and panic and retreat by the militia.[18] One reason for this lack of effectiveness was that the military officers of the militia units acted only as technical advisers, all powers of decision being reserved to the party political leadership, often in the form of a committee. In the POUM unit in which Orwell served, the technical military command was exercised by a Belgian ex-officer, George Kopp, who was called "commandante," and a Polish Jew, Benjamin Levinski. Real authority in the column was exercised by the political chiefs of the POUM. The Englishman John Cornford wrote of the militia column with which he served for a time that the column's leader was an "admirable revolutionary" but had "no conception of the job of warfare." He also said that there was rivalry between the leader and his military adviser, a common state of affairs.[19] This was true even in the more disciplined communist Fifth Regiment where ultimate authority was exercised by the political commissars. Of course the problem was less apparent in the Communist militia because the military officers were almost always also party members and thus subject to the same political authority as the commissars.

In some cases Spanish officers from the old army or police forces acted as military officers in militia columns. But they were inevitably distrusted by the militiamen and in fact exercised no real authority. A report to the ministry of defense in September 1936 by a regular officer assigned to command a militia column called Tierra y Libertad showed the nature of the problem. The unit, he wrote, had fought on the preceding day with some success. "But today they left the positions which they were supposed to occupy, saying that they were not going to defend the socialists." The commander tried to oppose the retirement of the column, but the troops answered that they "did not obey any orders except those coming from their Committee."[20] In another such report a regular army officer, one Colonel Salafranca, gave vent to his frustration with the militia supposedly under his command. Their retreat, "or more correctly this cowardly flight, was not due to the thrust of the enemy, but to the absolute lack of spirit and morale of these forces," he said. The colonel protested to his commanding officer about having been given a command in "these extraordinary conditions of indiscipline."[21]

The militias even more obviously lacked effectiveness as offensive or assault troops, a weakness vividly demonstrated by the failure to break the resistance of the few hundred defenders of the alcazar at Toledo. Likewise in Catalonia the militia streamed out from Barcelona toward Huesca and Saragossa from the first days of the fighting with the objective of taking those important cities for the revolution. But these cities remained untaken throughout the war. Nowhere did militia units demonstrate any offensive prowess.[22]

Even in combat zones the militia units usually operated as completely autonomous units. Each held its own position at the front and took care of all its own replacements, administration, and logistics. The autonomous and highly political nature of the militia units, as well as the very real consciousness of ideological differences and distrust between the various proletarian parties, accounted for their occupation of separate positions and the incessant political discussions which seemed to be the chief pastime of the militiamen. Orwell wrote that from his unit's position at the front he could identify the various points held by the Popular Front units by the political flags each displayed. He was puzzled when, on reaching the front, the POUM militiamen pointed out the positions nearby. "Those are the Socialists," they said, meaning the PSUC. "Aren't we all Socialists?" asked Orwell. His attitude was, "Why can't we stop all the political nonsense and get on with the war?" This, as he said, was the "correct anti-fascist" attitude which "had been carefully disseminated by the English newspapers, largely in order to prevent people from grasping the real nature of the struggle." It was an attitude, he wrote, which no one could or did keep in Spain for very long. "No event in it [the war in Spain], at any rate during the first year, is intelligible unless one has some grasp of the interparty struggle that was going on behind the government lines." On the Madrid front conditions were much the same. "The spirit was bad," wrote Louis Fischer. "The soldiers played at war, and lay around discussing politics but not digging trenches. ... The antagonism between the Communists and the Anarchists was growing. The Communists blamed the FAI (Anarchist Federation of Iberia) for the loss of Toledo and called them 'Faiscists.'" The Communists declared that not a single rifle should be given the Catalans because they might fall into the hands of the Anarchists.²³

By far the most effective of the Popular Front militia units was the so-called Fifth Regiment organized by the Communists. A notable exception to the egalitarianism and indiscipline of the militia in general, the Fifth Regiment, true to Communist doctrine, stressed iron discipline and unquestioning obedience to orders. As early as July 22, 1936, the party organ, *Mundo Obrero,* was demanding "Discipline, Hierarchy and Organization." And in a manifesto of the central committee of the party dated August 18, 1936, the party demanded "that every act, that every rifle responds always to an organized plan, to a necessity of the war. If in all organization discipline is the fundamental base of power and strength, in the army discipline ... for high and for low, for the units and for the command, and only in the measure to which this discipline exists will it be possible to conquer an organized and disciplined enemy."²⁴ In the tradition of Bolshevik dictums on discipline in organizing the Red army, commanders and political commissars of the Fifth Regiment demanded "a discipline of iron" and at times exercised draconian measures to maintain it.²⁵

The Communist militia became active in Madrid on the very day the *pronunciamiento* took place and from the beginning provided a vivid example of the meshing of the various elements of the Communist apparatus as it operated in Spain. On July 18 two of the party's carefully cultivated adherents among the officer corps of the Spanish army presented themselves for duty at party headquarters in Madrid.²⁶ On the same day the party functionary Enrique Castro Delgado assumed direction of the militia, and very shortly the Italian Comintern agent Vittorio Vidali, using the *nom de guerre* "Carlos Contreras" in Spain, assumed overall authority as chief political commissar. Both Vidali and his wife, Maria Modetti, were old Comintern functionaries who, like others of their kind, had been assigned to work in Spain even prior to the outbreak of hostilities. As chief political commissar and the acknowledged representative of the Comintern, Contreras exercised supreme authority within the Fifth Regiment. Indeed he was untouchable even by members of the politburo of the Spanish party.²⁷

The Spanish Communists had the further advantage of the services of a number of cadres who had attended one of the Red army's training schools in the Soviet Union, including Enrique Lister, later among the most successful of the Communist's military commanders. They also enjoyed the services of a corps of non-Spanish Comintern functionaries who had military and/or political training and experience and, finally, they benefited from the expertise of the Soviet military mission in Spain.[28]

These trained leadership cadres gave the Communists' militia a tremendous qualitative advantage over any other element on the Popular Front side. The Fifth Regiment soon became a complete army in microcosm. All necessary branches, all essential functions—logistics, transport, commissary, quartermaster, medical—developed rapidly under the direction and guidance of the Regiment's military and political staff. The Regiment also proved to be by far the most successful and productive recruiting and training center on the Loyalist side, claiming some 60,000 to 70,000 men by January 1937.[29]

In addition to its important military function, the Fifth Regiment served Communist purposes in a number of political ways. Among the most important of these was as a spokesman for the party line on various important military and political issues such as the imposition of military discipline on the militia, the creation of a centrally controlled People's Army organized on a regular military basis, the institution of a political commissar system within that army, and various other concerns.[30] The Communist position on most of the above issues ultimately prevailed in part at least because the Fifth Regiment provided the nucleus for the People's Army of Popular Front Spain. Indeed the first brigades of that army were simply the old Fifth Regiment under a new name. This, of course, gave the Communists the important political advantage of supplying the new army with Communist officers and political commissars. Neither the speakers nor the words spoken at the propaganda rally staged to celebrate the conversion of the Fifth Regiment into the first units of the Popular Army left much to the imagination as to whose army the Regiment was. The major speakers were "Carlos Contreras," José Díaz, the chief of the Communist party of Spain, Dolores Ibarruri (La Pasionaria), a member of the politburo of the CPS and most effective of party speakers, and Gustav Regler, a German Communist then serving as a political commissar in the International Brigades. Among other things these spokesmen stated that "the Fifth Regiment was organized at the orders and decisions of the Communist party." La Pasionaria added the thought that the newly conceived Popular Army must be like the Red army, not just the army of a nation but the "advance guard of shock troops of the world revolution."[31]

From the first days of the war a sprinkling of foreigners fought in the ranks of various Popular Front militia columns. One of the more appealing myths that has been perpetuated about those early volun-

Popular Front Militias

teers is that they were the progenitors of the International Brigades. A second is that they were fighting to defend the Spanish Republic. Neither of these common and much-repeated assumptions is valid. There was no connection between foreigners in the militia and the International Brigades. The fact that some of the foreign militiamen were ultimately incorporated into the Brigades demonstrates rather that the Brigades were a new, different, and essentially unconnected development. Nor were those foreign militiamen fighting to defend the Republic. The overwhelming majority of them were adherents of some specifically proletarian revolutionary ideology and, as such, were fighting not for the "bourgeois republic" but for "the revolution."

That a significant number of foreigners were available and anxious to join the Spanish militia was due, in large part, to the extreme political polarization in Europe at that time. This resulted in a reservoir of men frustrated by the bitter life of exile who could see in the Spanish conflict a chance to strike a blow for their side or perhaps to find in a victory for the revolution in Spain a first step toward a similar victory in their own countries.[32] Such an attitude toward the Spanish conflict found clear expression in the words of many of those drawn to Spain. The Italian Carlo Rosselli, leader of the *Giustizia e Libertá* movement and a longtime political exile, coined the slogan "Oggi in Spagna, domani in Italia," a phrase that clearly indicated his hope that victory in Spain might prove a first step toward Rome. "Think, my dear wife," he wrote from Spain in August 1936, "of the great joy of your husband in being able to pass from a theoretical position to a practical position. Spain today, Italy tomorrow." Another Italian, Randolfo Pacciardi, leader of the Italian Republican party in exile, echoed Rosselli's thoughts. Of the Spanish struggle he wrote, "Easily, very easily, this could be the march on Rome and Berlin." Likewise, Hans Beimler, a member of the central committee of the German Communist party in exile, told a fellow German Communist, Gustav Regler, when they met in Spain, "The only way we can get back to Germany is through Madrid."[33]

The first foreigners to fight in the Spanish conflict came from among those living in Spain when the fighting broke out in July 1936. This included a number of political exiles who had found the atmosphere of Popular Front Spain to their liking. It also included, by a strange coincidence, a number of "red athletes" who were participating in the so-called Workers' Olympiad then being held in Barcelona.[34] A number of these visiting athletes and others associated with the event immediately entered the fray in Barcelona and subsequently joined one of the militia columns.³⁵ Barcelona became the principal focal point for men entering Spain from the outside who wanted to fight and by early September foreigners of diverse nationalities and political persuasions could be found scattered among Popular Front militia columns on numerous fronts.³⁶ Indeed, in several cases foreigners actually commanded militia units. The Italian Socialist Fernando de Rosa led a Socialist unit on the Guadarrama front north of Madrid until he was killed in September 1936. The Italian Communist Bassi, who went under the *nom de guerre* Nino Nanetti, entered Spain immediately after the outbreak of fighting and organized and led a Spanish unit. In addition, foreign Communists were heavily involved in the organization and direction of the Fifth Regiment.³⁷

While it is true that by August-September 1936 an occasional foreigner might be found in almost any militia unit, the three main concentrations of foreigners were in the Anarchist, the POUM, and the PSUC (Communist party of Catalonia) militia columns operating out of Barcelona. The partisan political nature of the various militia found expression from the beginning in the way in which foreigners wanting to join a given unit found themselves welcomed or refused admission on the basis of their political credentials. Those foreigners living in Spain prior to the revolution and those who came into the country armed with the proper political papers and recommendations reported to the party headquarters suitable to their respective brands of proletarian ideology. In Barcelona the Communists and those Socialists who were ready to accept Communist discipline found a welcome at PSUC headquarters at the Hotel Colón and the Karl Marx barracks. Anarchists, and others who preferred their credo, presented themselves at the Anarchist militia headquarters at the Pedrales barracks outside Barcelona, and the POUM operated from the Lenin barracks. In the Madrid area foreign Communists joined the Fifth Regiment, while others could find a number of Spanish Socialist militia units ready to welcome them.³⁸ The POUM and Anarchists were not so exclusive in their political screening as the Communists. Both accepted Communists into their columns, while the PSUC was more demanding of proof of orthodoxy. John Cornford, an Englishman who was in fact an English Communist party member but had no credentials to prove it, was denied entry into a PSUC column and had to settle for a POUM unit.³⁹ Orwell ended up in a POUM column because he "happened to arrive in Barcelona with ILP papers." Both the ILP (Independent Labor party of England) and the POUM were among those dissident Marxist parties that were opposed to the orthodox Stalinist line. As such they were anathema to the Communists in Spain.

Politics influenced not only the type of militia column a given foreigner would likely join but also the way in which he interpreted or rationalized what he was trying to achieve in Spain. All were, of course, "fighting fascism." But within that broad explanation many different attitudes and approaches existed. While there were isolated individuals among the foreign combatants, such as Rosselli and Pacciardi, who were not affiliated with any of the specifically proletarian revolutionary ideologies, the overwhelming majority of them were Communists, revolutionary Socialists, Anarchists, or adherents of various splinter Marxist groups which were in fact much more revolutionary than the orthodox Communist line was at that time. For example, a German militiaman wrote: "We are socialists and because we know that we have to achieve socialism from the struggle we are revolutionaries. ... We speak different languages but common to all of us is the language of the revolution. The workers of the world look to Spain not for the republic, nor even for democracy. ... The international comrades [foreign militiamen]—of whatever party fight for the victory of the Spanish proletariat ... for the total victory of the proletarian revolution. [They are] the pioneers of the world revolution."[40] John Cornford recorded in his diary and in letters to friends his conversation with a number of Germans in the same unit. Most of these men, he found, had left the Communist party not because it was too revolutionary but because "they genuinely believe the CI [Comintern] has deserted the revolution." Of these men Cornford wrote, "If anything is revolutionary, it is these comrades."[41]

Although practically every European nationality was represented among the militia volunteers, the bulk of them were French, Italian, and German. Widespread sympathy for Popular Front Spain existed among Frenchmen of leftist persuasions, and French sympathizers found it especially easy to cross the border and join the fighting in the northern area around Irun and San Sebastian. There a number of French ex-army officers, many with experience from the World War, played an important part in organizing the defenses.[42] In August, Nationalist troops reported finding the bodies of some thirty Frenchmen following one battle.[43] When the fight for Irun and San Sebastian was lost, those who wanted to go on fighting simply crossed the border into France, boarded trains that took them to the French-Catalan frontier, recrossed into Spain, and joined the PSUC militia in Barcelona.[44]

French Popular Front organizations began encouraging men to fight in Spain at an early date.[45] The prime mover behind this effort was the French Communist party.[46] On August 7 the party organ, *L'Humanité*, proclaimed, mistakenly, that "the French government authorizes the formation of volunteers to help the Spanish workers."[47] The French contigent under PSUC control in Barcelona, composed primarily of Communist party members, styled themselves the Commune de Paris centuria. Jules Dumont, an ex-French army officer and longtime Communist stalwart commanded the unit. In September the PSUC ordered the French centuria, along with other PSUC units, to Madrid where they came under Fifth Regiment control.[48]

The Italians were a more mixed lot, including assorted Socialists, a strong Anarchist contingent, a few Republicans, and the Communists. The Republican Randolfo Pacciardi represented one tendency among the Italians. He wanted to organize an Italian legion that would be nonpolitical, that is, at the disposal of the Popular Front government and not affiliated with any particular political party or ideology. Through the good offices of his compatriots, the Socialist Pietro Nenni and the Communist Luigi Longo, Pacciardi received a hearing from Largo Caballero in early September, but Largo Caballero was uninterested in Pacciardi's proposal.[49] Significantly, Largo Caballero did not change his mind on the idea of a foreign military unit until the Comintern decided to foster the organization of one in mid-October. Pacciardi later commanded the Italian battalion of the International Brigades, but this turned out to be not quite the nonpolitical legion he had originally sought.

In fact, the two major concentrations of Italians prior to the formation of the International Brigades were those who served with the Anarchist Ascaso column in Aragon and those with the Communist militia. A leading figure among the first of these groups was Carlo Rosselli. This group, composed primarily of Socialists and Anarchists, increased to some 250 Italians by October and remained with the Anarchist militia even when asked to coalesce with the Italian battalion of the International Brigade when that unit was organized in early November. The refusal of Rosselli and others among the Ascaso group to join with the International Brigades stemmed from their reluctance to put themselves under Communist authority.[50]

The second important Italian unit, the Gastone-Sozzi centuria[51] under PSUC direction in Barcelona, included combatants from several sources. One group had first fought in the northern sector. With the fall of Irun to Nationalist forces they, like their French counterparts, simply crossed the frontier into France, moved down the

French side of the border, and reentered Spain through Catalonia. Arriving in Barcelona, they placed themselves at the orders of the PSUC. Another small group came fresh from an abortive attempt by a largely Catalan force to capture Mallorca.[52] In addition, a number of Italians came directly from France where they had been recruited by the Italian Comintern functionary Giuseppe de Vittorio. Upon their arrival in Barcelona they reported to PSUC headquarters at the Hotel Colón and were quartered, along with other PSUC units, at the Karl Marx barracks.[53] In early September the PSUC ordered the Gastone-Sozzi centuria, along with other PSUC units, both foreign and Spanish, to Madrid where they came under the authority of the Fifth Regiment.[54] They remained at the Regiment's barracks in the capital for a few days during which time they were greeted by Nenni and Longo. The leaders of the centuria were all Communist stalwarts. The centuria paraded behind the red banner of the Communist party of Italy and their battle cry was "Italian Communists forward!"[55]

The Germans who joined Spanish militia came, like the Italians, from among the political exiles living in Spain, France, Switzerland, or elsewhere. They were primarily either orthodox Communists or Marxists who found the Stalinist line too restrictive and anti-revolutionary. The orthodox Communists naturally went into the PSUC militia where they formed the Thaelmann centuria of some 100 men and fought with PSUC forces in Aragon from August to October. Hans Beimler, onetime Communist Reichstag deputy and political chief of all German Communists in Spain, acted as the centuria's political mentor.[56]

In early October Ludwig Renn, a German Communist who had been living in exile in Switzerland, received the party's permission to go to Spain. Indeed, according to Renn, the German party actively encouraged its members who had military experience to offer their services to the Spanish Popular Front forces. On his arrival in Barcelona, Renn reported to PSUC headquarters. There he met Beimler whom Renn, as a disciplined party member, accepted as his immediate superior in Spain. Beimler took Renn with him next day to visit the Thaelmann centuria at the front. Renn recognized several members of the centuria as acquaintances made in pre-1933 Berlin, mostly through mutual Communist activities and organizations. The centuria was operating as a component part of a larger PSUC column. Renn, a former officer of the German army with World War experience, felt concern at the poor military disposition of the unit. The column commander, a Spanish trade-union leader with no military training, had all his troops in the line. When Renn asked him about his reserve, the commander seemed not to understand what he was talking about. Later Renn expressed his misgivings to Beimler about the military situation in the sector and his frustration at not being able to do anything about it. Beimler told him, in effect, not to worry about the situation in Aragon where nothing of a serious military nature seemed likely to occur anyway but to go to Madrid where his military knowledge would be of more value. But, cautioned Beimler, Renn should not accept any post less than that of battalion commander. Renn saw no more of the Thaelmann centuria until early November 1936, when the remnants of that unit transferred to Albacete to be absorbed into the International Brigades.[57]

The second major group of Germans in Spain, for the most part anti-Stalinist Marxists, found a more compatible atmosphere in the ultrarevolutionary POUM. John Cornford reported a number of Germans among the unit, as did Franz Borkenau. By December there were, according to Orwell, several hundred Germans in the POUM militia and they remained with that unit until it was broken up as a result of the internecine political struggle within Popular Front Spain in the summer of 1937.[58]

A relatively smaller contingent of Englishmen were to be found in the Spanish militia. Here too, the main concentrations were in the PSUC and the POUM. A group of English and Irish with the PSUC militia in Barcelona called themselves the Tom Mann centuria.[59] This group, which numbered only some twelve men, consisted almost entirely of Communist party members, the most dominant of whom was Lorrimer Birch, Cambridge graduate and Communist true believer. One of the Englishmen who joined this contingent, Keith Scott Watson, arrived in Barcelona in late September 1936. He came into Spain by train with some fifty French and German recruits from Paris. On their arrival in Barcelona the group reported to PSUC headquarters in the Hotel Colón. There, after enjoying a substantial meal in a dining room filled with militiamen, an officer took them upstairs to an office marked Department des Étrangers. There each man underwent a searching interrogation which included questions on their political affiliations and background. Next day Watson joined his fellow Britishers at the PSUC barracks at Sarrai, a village several miles out of Barcelona. Personality clashes within the English group finally led to a number of its members becoming so disillusioned with their political commissar, Nat Levy, that they sought to depose him. After drawing up an indictment of Levy's shortcomings and misdeeds, the malcontents sent it to party headquarters in Barcelona with the request that Levy be replaced. After a lapse of time and a second request for action,

Ralph Bates, the representative of the Communist party of Great Britain in Barcelona, arrived at Sarria. His authority to deal with the matter was accepted by all and he settled it by removing Levy and replacing him with Birch.[60] The other English group in Spain was affiliated with the POUM militia. It numbered between twenty and thirty men, most of whom were affiliated with the ILP, the English Marxist revolutionary, but anti-Stalinist, party.[61]

In addition to the French, Italians, Germans, and English, a number of other nationalities formed small units. The Poles, for example, most of whom had been living in France, formed the Dombrowsky centuria in the PSUC militia.[62] A few Czechs, Yugoslavs, and others were also present in these PSUC units.[63]

Despite the seeming ubiquity of the foreign elements in the ranks of the Spanish militias, they remained very few. Even the larger centurias, the Gastone-Sozzi, Commune de Paris, and Thaelmann, never numbered more than one or two hundred men each. The foreigners scattered through other Spanish militia units also amounted to only a few hundred. The total number of foreign combatants prior to the formation of the International Brigades was probably not more than one thousand.[64] Given the paucity of their numbers and the fact that they were scattered out singly or in small groups, the military significance of these foreigners was of necessity minimal. While it is true that in a few cases foreigners with previous military training and experience provided leadership for militia units, nowhere did foreign combatants, singly or in groups, achieve any important military results. Not until the entry of the International Brigades into the conflict in November 1936 did foreign combatants have a significant military impact on the war.

Of the thousand or so foreigners in Spanish militias prior to the organization of the International Brigades, there were probably more who were affiliated with Anarchist and POUM units than with Communist ones, and they remained with those columns long after the International Brigades were organized.[65] Indeed, as late as June 1937, the Popular Front government issued a decree dealing with this matter. It directed that all foreigners be incorporated into the International Brigades "except where in some other unit there exists a large nucleus of foreigners forming a unit, in which case the chief of the unit might ask for their continuance."[66]

Only those foreign units already under Communist control, the PSUC and Fifth Regiment centurias, were incorporated into the International Brigades when the Brigades were formed in late October–early November 1936.[67] The numbers involved in those centurias which did adhere to the International Brigades were insignificant in comparison to the influx of volunteers into Spain as a result of the system set up by the Comintern to recruit men for the Brigades. The first contingents of recruits for the International Brigades entered Spain in mid-October. By the end of that month some 3,000 to 4,000 men had arrived and by mid-November, probably between 7,000 and 8,000.[68] In contrast, the centurias that were assimilated into these Brigades amounted to only a few hundred men.[69] In fact only the French Commune de Paris centuria of about one hundred men was even included in the first (XI) International Brigade. The Thaelmann and Gastone-Sozzi groups were subsequently incorporated into the XII Brigade. When the numerical paucity of the contribution of the pre-International Brigade centurias is considered, the orthodox interpretation that they formed the nucleus or origins of the Brigades can hardly be maintained.[70] Although the veterans of the centurias furnished a number of experienced cadres, the International Brigades were in no meaningful way an outgrowth of those early foreign groups. To the contrary, the International Brigades, with their substantial numbers and their separate military and political structure, came into existence only with the decision of the Comintern to sponsor such a unit. It is therefore misleading and incorrect to say, as the myth has it, that those early foreigners in Spain were the originators, nucleus, or vanguard of the International Brigades, thus implying some direct connection or organic development. It is also misleading and erroneous to say, as the myth goes, that these early foreigners were fighting to defend "the Republic" or "for democracy" unless it is clearly understood that the definition of these terms was "proletarian revolution," "Socialism," "Anarchism," or "Communism."

3 The Comintern Raises an Army

In conformity with the Kremlin's decisions on its Spanish policy in September 1936, the Comintern launched a full-scale drive to recruit an international army to fight in Spain. Within the framework of the Comintern the major direct responsibility and role in the operation went to the Communist party of France. France's contiguous border with Spain, as well as the convenient fact that France had, at that time, a sympathetic Popular Front government and a large Communist party with members sitting in the Chamber of Deputies made that country the obvious choice for the concentration of recruits and their transportation into Spain.

Paris quickly became the focal point for a large Comintern delegation representing most of the nationalities of Europe. The well-known French Communist André Marty, a member of both his country's Chamber of Deputies and the Executive Committee of the Comintern, assumed direct control over the operation. He was ably assisted by the Italian Communist stalwart Luigi Longo ("Gallo" in Spain), an efficient operator who arrived in Paris directly from Spain in late September with party orders to help organize the recruitment of volunteers and a system for transporting them into Spain. In addition to Marty and Longo, the Italian Giuseppe de Vittorio, the Czech Clement Gottwald, the Yugoslav Joseph Broz (later called "Tito"), and numerous lesser-known Comintern figures directed their efforts toward developing methods for funneling men from various parts of Europe into France.[1]

Communist party offices and local branches of party-affiliated labor unions in France served as recruitment and processing centers, the central office being installed in the *maison des syndicats* on the Rue Mathurin-Moreau in Paris. The directors of the enterprise quickly established concentration points at Marseilles for those men slated to be sent to Spain by sea, and at Perpignan, a town in the southeast corner of France near the Spanish border, for those going in by land. Longo soon returned to Spain where, with the help and political support of the PSUC, he established a receiving center in the Spanish border town of Figueras for the recruits as they crossed the frontier from France.[2]

The Comintern assigned recruitment quotas to the various national Communist parties on the basis of their membership and sympathizer potential, and Communist parties throughout the world began using and expanding their existing organizational networks for recruitment and transportation purposes. The quotas tended to be higher than each party could reasonably hope to attain, but the party leaders made the most strenuous efforts to meet them, assigning party functionaries to the task of recruitment and impressing on them that successful performance was a party responsibility of the highest priority. Earl Browder, for example, emphatically stressed to United States party functionaries the necessity of providing "a constant stream of reinforcements and replacements" to the American contingent of the Brigade, and Harry Pollitt, Browder's British counterpart said, "We pledge ourselves" that the 750 British men in the Brigades will soon "become a thousand." The British Communist Charlotte Haldane, who became intimately involved in the recruitment process both in Britain and France, later wrote that the British party "had to make terrific efforts to raise their volunteers for Spain," and that although party leader Pollitt was reluctant to recruit young boys and married men he had no choice but to do so. "His quota had to be filled."[3]

During the first months after recruitment began, the Communists staunchly denied having any part in it. The party line propagated for public consumption ran that the Brigades represented a spontaneous movement of individual volunteers. As the British party writer and sometimes political commissar in Spain William Rust somewhat ambiguously put it in his book *Britons in Spain,* "The International Brigades arose spontaneously in the minds of men.... from the spontaneous movement of the volunteers there naturally arose the decision to form the International Brigade."[4] The explanation of spontaneity continued to be widely propagated to the general public long after the United States *Daily Worker* had openly admitted, as early as September 14, 1937, that the party was in the recruitment business, and after Browder stated publicly in December of that year that the party was recruiting men for Spain.[5] As late as April 20, 1938, for example, *Time* magazine reported: "European observers incline to believe that the Communist International and its section, the American Communist Party, were instrumental in creating the Abraham Lincoln–Washington outfit, but according to its members it arose spontaneously in Leftist Spain on Christmas Day, 1936. Around a campfire were some 90 U.S. Leftists who had simply gone to Spain as individuals and they formed the nucleus of the battalion."

Indeed the Communists (and others) have continued to put forth the spontaneity line when it suits their purpose to romanticize the Brigades or to picture them as a great ground swell of antifascist solidarity. A recent version of this approach by a Czech writer went: "The solidarity of all the workers, of the progressive and democratic men of all the world, found its highest expression in the formation of the International Brigades.... From all points of the globe men arrived in Spain to place themselves spontaneously at the service of the Spanish Republican Army."[6]

The Communists had good reasons for concealing their role as creator of the Brigades. For one thing, the operation entailed numerous possible risks for the party. No one could be sure how the venture would work out, or if it would work out at all. The military and political situation in Spain made it highly problematical that, even with Soviet aid and an influx of foreign fighters, the Popular Front regime would long survive. The Comintern thus sought to play a cautious role, just as the Soviet Union was doing in its direct intervention in Spain, in staking its prestige too openly on such a shaky venture. For another thing, the Communists wanted to camouflage their efforts at raising an army to fight in Spain in the subdued and chameleon tones of the Popular Front rather than the bright reds of International Communism. This meshed the enterprise smoothly into their general strategy of the time, as well as their specifically Spanish policy. Earl Browder was simply echoing the broad Popular Front, antifascist, theme of the party's efforts when he said, "the war in Spain is a part of the world-wide offensive against fascism of all peaceloving and democratic people."[7]

The Comintern hoped also to attract not only Communists into their army but a broad spectrum of antifascists. Thus they needed to cast a wider ideological net than Communism alone would provide. As one American party writer (and sometime political commissar in Spain) put it, "By the initiative of our Party we must draw in every anti-fascist to the movement ... must draw the Socialist Party into the movement ... must become the initiators of a new flow of men into Spain." Here too the Comintern's reasons were several. One stemmed from the desire to use the Brigades as an instrument for broadening and strengthening the Popular Front. Indeed the American journalist and active Loyalist sympathizer Louis Fischer was told by Georgi Dimitroff, then chief of the Comintern, that the party was anxious to recruit non-Communists in the United States into the Brigades as a way of strengthening the Popular Front. Yet another, and quite practical, reason for wanting to recruit non-Communists was that the party did not want to see its own ranks decimated by sending too many of its cadres to Spain. And, finally, party leaders stressed the value of getting nonparty men into the Brigades as a method of "politically educating" them into the party.[8]

As time went on and the successful defense of Madrid made the International Brigades a well-known and prestigious military unit, the Communists found it impossible to completely restrain themselves from taking their due credit. By the summer of 1937 tributes to the Comintern and its titular chieftain, Georgi Dimitroff, for their role as founders of the Brigades began to appear occasionally in the party press. For example, "Comrade Dimitroff mobilized the Communist party sections throughout the world so that it was possible for the International Brigades to come to Spain," said the Brigade's own *Boletín de Información* on August 7, 1937. And, in 1938, the official Comintern organ carried the statement: "The International Brigades are selected units formed . . . in reply to the call of the Communist International."[9]

Even then the party's stance remained ambiguous. The Communists tried to have it both ways: credit for the Brigades and their glorious exploits and, at the same time, the Brigades as a spontaneous effusion of antifascist solidarity. The approach actually taken at any given time depended on the audience being addressed. To an amazing degree the Communists succeeded in making the most of both worlds.

In their efforts both to broaden their appeal beyond the ranks of the party itself and to conduct the recruitment enterprise clandestinely, the Communists sometimes used various front organizations, controlled by the party but ostensibly unconnected with it. The Friends of the Abraham Lincoln Brigade, for example, a party front organization designed to afford propagandistic and financial support for the American contingent of the Brigades, served the additional purpose of recruitment agency. The party in the United States also set up the American Society for Technical Aid to Spain, a front organization designed primarily for recruitment purposes. The Society operated branches in various cities around the country which printed leaflets and ran advertisements in newspapers for men to go to Spain to "take the place of skilled workers who had gone to the front." A number of men were apparently recruited and sent to Spain, ostensibly to do skilled jobs, only to find themselves in the Brigades.[10]

The Communists also extended their recruitment efforts into the potentially productive areas of the universities and labor unions. According to one American who went to Spain, "The Communist Party has units ... in all the colleges and universities in the United States, and these and other Communist organizations have been very active in getting volunteers for the Spanish Army [the Brigades]." He stated, however, that "the Communist Party is careful to do nothing officially, but operates through agents who pretend to be acting entirely upon their own responsibility as individuals, and not in connection with any organization of any kind."[11]

The experiences of individuals going through the Comintern's recruitment and processing system naturally varied in detail, but the general pattern proved much the same. If the potential recruit was a party member he had to secure the approval of his party superiors. In the case of rank-and-file members such approval was usually readily granted. Indeed the party put great pressure on members to volunteer and in the case of functionaries sometimes ordered them to do so.[12] Despite the efforts to attract non-Communists, the majority of those who volunteered were party members.[13] As British party worker Haldane commented, "The vanguard were Communist Party members under discipline to show an example to their fellow proletarians."[14] In some cases the party ordered members to join the Brigade as a "control task," a disciplinary measure by which those in bad grace with the party could prove their loyalty and achieve forgiveness for their shortcomings.[15] On the other hand, party functionaries were sometimes denied permission to go to Spain because the party felt they could not be spared from their activities at home.[16] For example, an American Communist who had been assigned to party work in the waterfront section of New York City approached party hierarch, Fred Brown, and told him he wanted to volunteer for the Brigades. Brown replied that as a disciplined party member he would go only where he was sent and that he should return to his assignment on the waterfront. Later this same man was told by Brown that the party had decided the time had come for him to go to Spain, and he did.[17]

Nonparty men interested in joining the Brigades had, as a first step, to establish contact with a party recruiter. The recruiter directed the prospect to one of the party's clandestine enlistment offices where he was questioned by one or more party agents as to his reasons for wanting to join, his background, his politics, and so forth. In England, a "dour member of the Party leadership known as 'Robbie' " performed this task. He interviewed each would-be volunteer and "tried to weed out obvious adventurers, fascists, and spies ... he was also the contact man with the C.I. [Comintern] organization in Paris, to which all volunteers were sent."[18] The party investigated the political background of each prospective volunteer following this first interview. If approved, the recruit was sent for a physical examination from a "politically reliable" physician. If found satisfactory, he received instructions for proceeding to the next link in the chain which would lead eventually to Spain.[19]

The procedures and techniques for moving the recruits to the Comintern's central concentration point in Paris varied, depending on the different areas from which they were drawn. For example, Nick Gillain, a Belgian of no particular political persuasion, heard, in the fall of 1936, that foreign volunteers were being solicited to fight in Spain. Assuming that the Loyalist government was doing the recruiting and that the logical place to apply would be a Spanish consulate, Gillain crossed into France and presented himself to the Spanish consul in Lille. The consul received him courteously but informed him that the Loyalist government was not involved and that he knew nothing officially about the business of foreign volunteers. As Gillain walked toward the door on his way out, however, the Spaniard said quietly, "Go to the *maison des syndicats*. You will get what you want there." At the *maison des syndicats* Gillain found a scene of lively activity. "You want to go to Spain?" asked a "Comrade Burneton." Gillain answered affirmatively and, after a brief questioning, was assigned to a group of about twenty men and sent to Paris. On reaching Paris the group went to the central recruitment center, the *maison des syndicats* in Rue Mathurin-Moreau. He and his group quickly went through the induction process and soon left Paris with a contingent of some five hundred men bound for Perpignan, the last stop in France for those going into Spain by land. In Perpignan he and his fellow volunteers received identity documents covered with official looking stamps and Spanish names. "If they [the French border guards] ask you why you don't speak Spanish," a functionary told him, "say you left the country when you were a baby." That proved to be an unnecessary precaution, for Gillain's contingent crossed the frontier with no questions asked.[20]

Those men recruited in central and Eastern Europe, most of whom had no passports and whose movements were thus illegal, had to be smuggled into France via the underground-railway systems established for that purpose by the Comintern. The future Yugoslav strongman, Joseph Broz (Tito), was instrumental in creating the apparatus for transporting his compatriots and other Balkan nationals into France. Brotz himself seems to have been among the Comintern delegation in Paris, while direct responsibility for the system in Yugoslavia fell to Blagoye Parovic, a member of the Central Committee of the Yugoslav Communist party and subsequently a political commissar in the International Brigades.[21] Similarly, an "underground" route for moving volunteers from Poland to France via Czechoslovakia was directed by Leon Chajn.[22]

In most of the western nations Communist parties existed legally and, although the parties were careful not to admit officially that they were involved in the recruitment enterprise, at least in the beginning, they carried on the operation more or less openly. In Great Britain the party established its central processing center in an office in King Street, London. Recruits underwent an interrogation and investigation there and, having been accepted, waited until a new contingent had been collected and the party was ready to send them across the channel. The movement of the British into France presented a few problems. Passports were unnecessary since with the purchase of a forty-eight-hour return-trip excursion ticket British citizens could enter France freely. Each contingent traveled under the authority of a party-designated leader who, in most cases, returned to London after turning over his charges to party functionaries in France.[23]

Among the early volunteers from Britain, Peter Elstob and John Sommerfield later recorded their recollections of the Spanish adventure. Elstob went through a complicated and highly conspiratorial process in England, being shuffled from place to place and from person to person. First names only were used, usually preceded by "Comrade." After being questioned by numerous comrades in turn, Elstob finally received a letter of recommendation and the address of a bookshop in the Gare du Nord in Paris. There, as instructed, he asked for a "Comrade Le Gros," who subsequently questioned him and told him to sign some papers. The Englishman was then directed to yet another Paris address where, after presenting his credentials, he entered a large cellar room in which he joined some two hundred closely packed men whom he later described as "the choicest selection of Parisian sewer dregs that I had ever seen." A man stood on a table haranguing the audience. He finished with a "magnificent gesture, pointing upstairs," and "they all tore up the ladder ... singing the 'Internationale.' " At that time Elstob signed yet more documents and received fifty francs and instructions to report to the train station at ten o'clock.[24]

John Sommerfield, a young Communist, reported to the recruitment office in Paris with a small group sent over from England. They found a room filled with men talking in a Babel of languages. The majority seemed to be Frenchmen and Poles and some were, thought Sommerfield, "pretty tough." At one end of the room two harassed-looking men sat behind a table strewn with forms printed in French and Spanish. Sommerfield and the others filled out a number of questionnaires stating their ages and military experience, their jobs, and their politics. Then he and some friends went out and purchased small pistols, which, said Sommerfield, were "good for the morale." They left Paris for Spain within the week.[25]

In the United States the concentration point for the volunteers was New York City. Men recruited in various parts of the country received money or tickets for their transportation to New York and instructions on where to report upon arrival there.[26] The party used the quarters of various front organizations such as the Hungarian Workers Club as meeting centers where party functionaries, occasionally including Earl Browder himself and visiting Communist celebrities such as the Englishman Ralph Bates (fresh from Spain), entertained the recruits with political speeches and a perfunctory sort of military drill while they awaited their departure for Europe.[27] While in New York the Americans procured passports and bought clothing and other items that they were to take with them to Spain. Arrangements for the voyage to France were made by the party through Intourist, the Soviet travel agency.

The first group of American volunteers left New York aboard the S.S. *Normandie* on December 26, 1936. Typical of the recruiting procedures in the United States was the experience of a member of that first contingent, William Herrick. A member of the Communist party in New York, he offered his services to the section organizer at party headquarters in lower Manhattan. After an interview the section organizer told Herrick that he would be contacted. A short time later he had a second interview, this time in the presence of Paul Brown, a Comintern agent.[28] The section organizer vouched for Herrick's reliability, and Herrick began reporting regularly to a hall in Manhattan where, along with a growing group of recruits, he engaged in a perfunctory sort of drill and heard numerous addresses from party luminaries.[29]

Other members of the first American contingent were Robert Gladnick and Morris Maken. Gladnick, a member of the Young Communist League, was working at the time for the party on the New York waterfront. He applied directly to Paul Brown for permission to go to Spain. After being accepted he, like Herrick, attended drills and listened to speeches at the hall. When party member Morris Maken approached his section organizer about going to Spain the section organizer directed him to Bill Lawrence, a party functionary active in the recruitment operation in New York. After being cleared by the party Maken too attended drills and training sessions which he later characterized as "a joke."[30]

Others went by a somewhat more circuitous route. On a night in March 1937, the wife of William Ryan brought home a leaflet issued by the American Society for Technical Aid to Spain. Ryan, a Communist, "recognized the party's style in the leaflet" even though it mentioned neither the party nor fighting in Spain. The following day Ryan called at the offices of the Society in Milwaukee. When asked for references Ryan gave the name of a lawyer who was a member of his party section. When asked about political affiliation, Ryan said he was a member of the Communist party. The representative then asked if Ryan's skills included "an ability to handle a rifle?" Ryan said, "This is, of course, for the army, isn't it?" The answer was yes. Ryan returned to the office a few days later and the Society's representative directed him to a physician for a medical examination. The doctor gave him a "very cursory" check and said, "Well, comrade, you will go into the trenches." Having cleared the preliminary hurdles, Ryan received instructions to come to a "little send-off party" at which some "fellow travelers and liberals would be present." The party functionary warned him and his fellow volunteers not to use "radical phrases" but to talk only about fighting fascism. The party proved a success. Ryan and other recruits made short speeches and a collection netted part of the money needed to "get the boys to Spain." Next day Ryan's group took the bus for New York. There they reported to a hall where they saw "a couple of hundred men from all over the country, and Canada, Mexico and Puerto Rico." They left New York on the S.S. *Manhattan* under the orders of a student from the University of Wisconsin who gave them tickets and distributed the fifteen dollars per man necessary to enter France. Later during the same month William McCuiston sailed for France with another contingent. McCuiston, once a Communist, had become disenchanted with the party and sometime in 1935 had dropped out. He wanted to go to Spain, however, so he contacted the party section organizer in New York City. Three or four weeks elapsed before he learned that he was to be allowed to go.[31]

By July 1937 the party in the United States was apparently finding it difficult to find enough recruits. During that month John Seacat, an agent of the Friends of Abraham Lincoln Brigade in Milwaukee, approached William Harris, a non-Communist, asking if he would be interested in going to Spain. Seacat informed Harris that a dire need existed for volunteers. Harris accepted the idea and Seacat gave him money for transportation from Milwaukee to New York. After going through the usual procedure in New York, Harris sailed on the S.S. *Washington* within the month. At about the same time party member Edward Horan approached a section organizer for the party in Chicago about the possibility of going to Spain. The section organizer welcomed Horan's offer to volunteer and told him to "recruit as many men as possible to go to Spain who were not Communist." He emphasized to Horan that the party wanted to recruit as many nonparty members as possible for the Brigades. Horan himself, as a party member, had to get the party's approval before being allowed to go. He reported first to Eugene Berchtold, the party organizer for Illinois (and also Chicago secretary of the newly organized front organization, the Friends of the Abraham Lincoln Brigade). Berchtold sent Horan to see Irving Herman, a party organizer in Chicago who was handling the recruitment operation there. Herman told Horan that since he, Horan, was already doing important party work in the Food Workers Union, the matter would have to be checked out with party leaders to see if Horan could be spared. Later Horan received the word that the Cook County party leaders had decided that he should go to Spain. Herman then arranged for Horan's physical examination and gave him money to obtain a passport and to travel to New York where he was to report to a party official at the Hungarian Workers Club. He sailed for France on the S.S. *Laconia* in late September 1937 with a group of eighteen men.[32]

The aura of secrecy surrounding the entire enterprise no doubt added to the sense of adventure of the men involved, but its effectiveness may be doubted. In both England and the United States the police authorities were well aware of what was going on. Although both countries had statues against recruitment for, or enlistment in, foreign armies within their sovereign jurisdictions, the laws were not, in the case of the Spanish affair, enforced. It would have been difficult to make a case that would stand up in court since no official enlistment documents existed. And, perhaps more important, the strong passions aroused by the Spanish war would have made any serious attempt at suppressing the recruitment operation unrewarding politically. At any rate, no serious efforts were made to halt the operation and no prosecutions were attempted against those who fought in Spain.[33] Nevertheless, the clandestine nature of the enterprise continued to be emphasized by the party functionaries in control. On the voyage from New York to France group leaders ordered the men to maintain complete secrecy as to their destination, to avoid contact with the other passengers, and to try to act like tourists. At the time of disembarkation onto French soil the effectiveness of the conspiratorial tone of the enterprise seemed dubious to some. Maken, for example, had his first doubts about the "much vaunted efficiency of the Communist party" when he noticed that "every single man carried precisely the same . . . kind of imitation leather suitcase. Ninety of us pretending not to know each other. . . . going [according to their passports] to Austria . . . Poland . . . and all the four corners of the earth with identical baggage." That situation evoked comment also by the American volunteer John Gates who arrived late in February 1937. "The French customs inspectors took one look at our suitcases and our fleece-lined coats and congratulated us," he said. Identical baggage was still in style a full year later when Alvah Bessie arrived in France.[34]

In France all volunteers came under the jurisdiction and authority of the French party. Numerous representatives of other national Communist parties worked within the apparatus in France and exercised a special responsibility for the men coming in from their own countries. One such person was the Englishwoman Charlotte Haldane. Her ability to speak French, a rarity within the ranks of the British party, led to her being asked to work in Paris to handle the contingents that arrived from England. On her arrival in Paris she reported to an address in the heart of what she called the "red" working-class district. This, as it turned out, was the headquarters of some of the French labor unions. On entering the designated room she saw several men seated around a table. Asking for Comrade Max as instructed, she was told to wait outside. After a time Comrade Max approached her. He came from Prague, was "a prominent member of the Czech C.P. and branch of the C.I.," spoke fluent French with a strong Eastern European accent, and was acting as "the chief responsible comrade for the I.B. [International Brigade] organization in Paris, under the general direction of the French Party."[35] After satisfying himself that her party credentials were valid, Max told her that he hoped she would stay in Paris indefinitely to help with the English. "We've asked London again and again, but all the comrades they've sent have been quite unsuitable," he said. "If they're any good they can't be spared from London, and those they can spare are useless. And none of them know French." Haldane agreed to stay. On their way to a restaurant Max complained of the difficulties they were having keeping the recruits out of the many drinking dives and brothels in the district, especially the English and Americans who usually arrived with more money than the others. At a large working-class restaurant, Max led her upstairs where she saw many men seated at long dining tables. The men were all recruits for the Brigades and spoke "every European language . . . from Finnish and Latvian to Dutch and Walloon." Max led her into a smaller room at the rear which, as he told her, was reserved for the "responsibles." Entering the room, Max introduced her to a number of men, among whom were a German, a Belgian, a Pole, and an Italian. All were introduced by first names only, the three Americans being Jack, Eric, and Lee. Later Max informed her that she would be paid 300 francs a month from the coffers of her own party. When she later tried to refuse the money, which she did not need, her party superior insisted that she take it. "It's not a matter of who gets it," he said. "That's what we pay, and you earn it."

Settling rapidly into her work, Haldane became well acquainted with the Americans on the staff. She described Jack[36] as "a professional Communist, a Marxist missionary . . . a trusted lieutenant of the American leaders, Earl Browder and Robert Minor." He had been "among the first chosen to go to Spain" and had led one of the first contingents of Americans to France. He had been bitterly disappointed when the party ordered him to remain in France rather than go on into Spain. Party orders, however, were to be obeyed unquestioningly and he had remained to head the American delegation in Paris. Jack told her of the difficulties he had had with the French party bureaucrats. Apparently all was not proletarian brotherhood and international solidarity between the French Communists in charge of the operation and the various other nationalities, especially the Americans. The French, according to Jack, had bullied the Americans, as they did all the others, until Jack arrived on the scene. He had had several heated arguments and had "put the French in their place," always making sure to "base all his arguments with them strictly on the Party line." In the final analysis, however, there could be no question but that ultimate control lay with "the dogmatic edicts of the French Party Executive," which had been delegated final authority by the Comintern. Haldane summarized her observations and feelings on this subject by writing of the "positive hatred felt by all the foreign internationals for the French Party bureaucrats under whose domination they were obliged to work."[37]

Haldane's work entailed receiving the English contingents as they arrived in Paris, seeing to their lodging (in "shabby unobtrusive hotels in the quarter whose owners' discretion and loyalty could be relied on"), and in general overseeing them during their usually brief sojourn in France. Specifically this included lecturing the recruits on the dangers of drunkenness, brawling, or visiting the brothels. So that

Comintern Raises an Army

none of these temptations would become overwhelming to the English, the party leaders decreed that the recruits' money should be confiscated and that each man should be given ten francs a day, enough only for a pack of cigarettes and a beer or two. Her duties also included giving the recruits a "political peptalk," speaking with each one individually and then reporting to Max on their "political and personal reliability." Finally she acted as interpreter for them when the guides, who were to take them through France and into Spain, gave them instructions concerning the trip.

Among the most controversial and unpopular rulings of the Comintern directorate of the recruitment enterprise was the policy of confiscating passports. Many of the volunteers had no passports to begin with. But among those who, like the Americans, did have passports, the demand that they be surrendered caused much dismay and discord. Haldane wrote that in the cases where British passports were taken she made sure they were returned to England via a British party functionary. Whether in fact the passports ever got back to England she had no way of knowing. She recounted an episode in which she accidentally took an attaché case belonging to Max and found it filled with passports taken from Czech volunteers. The Soviet intelligence officer Krivitsky said that the policy on passports came from the NKVD who took advantage of the opportunity to acquire legal passports which, with a little expert doctoring, would serve their needs in moving agents in and out of the countries involved, and that many of them were actually used in this way.[38]

The NKVD also apparently exercised a direct role in the policing of the recruiting process. The Comintern apparatus clearly attempted, through interviews, interrogations, questionnaires, and investigations, to screen out what from its point of view were undesirable or unreliable individuals. According to some who were in a position to know, including General Krivitsky and the onetime German Communist hierarch Ruth Fischer, this operation fell under the purview of the NKVD.[39] That various interviews, interrogations, and checks were made on the volunteers in their own countries, in France, and in Spain was amply borne out by the experiences and testimony of many who went through the system. The American volunteer Hecht, for example, after having been screened by a party review board in the United States went through another interrogation by a committee that included two Americans at recruitment headquarters in Paris. The same procedure applied to the American volunteer Horan, a party functionary who had been appointed leader of his contingent while en route from the United States to France. He was questioned in Paris by a panel that included an American called Jack (probably the same Jack reported by Haldane) as to the political reliability of the men in his contingent. And, on arrival in Figueras, he was questioned once more by Tony De Maio, an American later reputed to have been an NKVD agent in Spain.[40]

While most of those who left records of their experiences in going through the recruitment process mention the various interviews and interrogations involved, they have not mentioned anything about the NKVD. This would be as expected. Few, if any, of the rank-and-file volunteers would have had any reason to know that they were under the watchful eye of the Soviet secret police. The interrogations were usually conducted by ordinary party functionaries, sometimes even under the camouflage of one of the party's front organizations. Indeed a few of the recruits, at least among the non-Communist ones, seem never to have realized that they were dealing with a Comintern apparatus, much less one under NKVD surveillance.[41] Highly placed party functionaries who may well have been aware of the NKVD's role would not have mentioned it publicly. British party writer Rust, for example, brushed all this off lightly by saying simply, "After a political and medical examination in London, recruits went on to Paris, where they were again examined." Those less highly placed, even when they were part of the recruitment system, quite probably never knew of the NKVD role. Charlotte Haldane, for example, had among her various responsibilities in Paris the task of reporting to her superiors on the "political and personal reliability" of the recruits who arrived from Britain but apparently had no idea of NKVD involvement.[42]

If we consider the all-pervasiveness and the virtual omnipotence of the NKVD in Communist affairs during the period of the Spanish war (the great purges were under way in Russia and the NKVD was certainly active in Spain), it would be stranger to think it was not involved in the Comintern's recruitment activities than the contrary —especially since the Communists were particularly affected during this period with a hypersuspiciousness regarding any type of "left deviationism." They were also very worried about persons with these opinions slipping into and corrupting their army in Spain. An obvious step would have been to try to eliminate such persons before they ever got in the Brigades at all, and for an operation of that type, what better instrument than the NKVD.

The actual movement of men from France into Spain proved relatively simple. By December 1936 the Comintern apparatus was putting several hundred men per day into the country by the overland route. Train number seventy-seven, which left the Quai d'Orsay station in Paris in the evening and arrived at Perpignan the following morning, became widely known as the "train of the volunteers," or the "red express," because of the large numbers of volunteers it regularly carried.[43]

Elstob's journey from Paris to Figueras was fairly typical. He left Paris with a contingent of some two hundred volunteers whom he characterized as "one hundred and ninety-seven Apaches, two German doctors and I."[44] During the train ride through France, the Frenchmen sang wildly and waved to the people along the way, many of whom returned the clenched fist salute,[45] making it clear that they knew who the men on the train were and where they were going. The party functionaries who met them upon their arrival in Perpignan stressed the necessity of secrecy and instructed the men to stroll casually, in groups of twos and threes, to the buses waiting to take them across the border into Spain. That advice, however, was ignored by numbers of the Frenchmen, some of whom had brought their own supply of liquid refreshment along and were in high spirits. Fifty or so formed up in a column and marched down the street with clenched fists held high and singing the *Internationale* at the top of their voices. The leader of the marchers, a huge Frenchman called Jean, who had been "pleasantly pie-eyed since leaving Paris," scorned the idea of secrecy. He seemed to want all southern France to know where they were going. As it turned out the stress on secrecy proved unnecessary. The local gendarme carefully turned his back on the whole affair.[46]

The buses carrying them to Figueras on the Spanish side of the border pulled out of Perpignan that evening. When they approached the frontier the driver turned out the lights inside the bus and the men became quiet. The French border guard carried out a perfunctory inspection and asked no embarrassing questions. Indeed, as the bus rolled past, he smiled and gave the clenched fist salute.[47] On their arrival at Figueras they were welcomed by what Elstob called a "lively little man" who mounted a large stone in the courtyard of the Castello de San Fernando where they were to be quartered, raised his clenched fist in the familiar salute, and shouted, "Camaradas, Salud!"[48] Pandemonium followed. Then the little man who, it seemed, was the commander of the fortress, gave a short speech of welcome, concluding with the announcement that they would soon be fed. After eating, the men settled down in their sleeping quarters in the fortress which proved to be so filthy and vermin-invested that Elstob ended by sleeping outside on the grass. The Castello de San Fernando was an ancient fortress with massive walls enclosing numerous buildings and a number of courtyards of various sizes. During the five or six days they remained there, the men had no duties assigned and their favorite pastime quickly became drinking in the cafe in the village of Figueras and admiring the charms of the waitress, Rosita.[49]

The second route into Spain, by sea, led from Marseilles to a Spanish Mediterranean port, usually Valencia or Alicante. The English volunteer Sommerfield left Paris with a contingent of several hundred men, among whom were French, Polish, German, and Italian. Their train arrived at Marseilles the next morning and the recruits spent the day hidden in the back rooms of cafes and cellars in the working-class district. That night taxi cabs picked them up and took them to the waterfront where they boarded a Spanish ship. The ship, carrying some 800 men, steamed out of Marseilles that same night. The next morning they passed Barcelona, faintly visible along the horizon, and continued down the Spanish coast. On the following day they made port at Alicante in southern Spain. The recruits disembarked and marched, singing the *Internationale,* through cheering crowds.[50]

Another Englishman, Esmond Romilly, also went to Spain via the sea route, having signed up for the Brigades in Marseilles. He embarked on the Spanish ship *Mar Caspio,* along with some six hundred other recruits, mostly German and French. The group included a number of what Romilly called "very tough guys—ex-foreign legionnaires." The ship put in at Valencia where the recruits marched, also singing the *Internationale,* to a barracks where they assembled in a courtyard and listened to a welcoming speech from André Marty, the political chief of the International Brigades. Marty told them that they would soon depart by train to join the International Column.[51]

Later, in February 1937, the French government officially closed the frontier with Spain in compliance with the nonintervention agreement. From that time, moving men into Spain became more difficult. Now they had to slip across the border through rugged Pyrenees trails, often at night, to elude French border patrols and some landed in French jails when apprehended trying to cross illegally.[52] The official closing of the frontier, however, proved no insurmountable obstacle to the Comintern in moving men into Spain. Except for sporadic outbursts of efficiency the French police and border patrols showed a general lack of interest in stringent enforcement. Indeed, through its hastily improvised but steadily improved apparatus, the Comintern moved some 6,000 to 8,000 men into Spain by the end of November 1936 and between 25,000 and 30,000 by mid-February 1937.[53]

4 The Defense of Madrid

The inexorable advance of the Nationalist columns toward Madrid throughout the month of October created widespread pessimism among Loyalist supporters. The fight seemed to have gone from the militia. Most observers agreed with Pravda correspondent Koltsov who lamented to his diary, "How is it possible with such troops, and with such commanders . . . to defend Madrid."[1]

And yet, not all the advantages lay with the Nationalists. Their military position was, in fact, extremely vulnerable. Not only were they numerically weak and physically exhausted from the rigors of their long campaign from the south, but their long and exposed flanks presented a constant threat.[2] The Loyalist forces, on the other hand, were not only more numerous but had the advantages of occupying the ready-made fortress afforded by the city itself. What they needed to make these advantages effective was firm direction, determined will, professional military expertise, and modern technology. Beneath the surface of continued defeat and spreading pessimism, these requirements were gradually being supplied by the Soviet Union and its Comintern apparatus.

The Soviet decision to intervene, in late September, had brought a widely publicized message from Stalin to the prime minister, Largo Caballero, which contained the much quoted phrase, "The cause of Spain is the cause of all advanced and progressive mankind." More important, the decision had brought Soviet tanks and planes, a corps of Red army advisers and technicians, and, ultimately, the International Brigades.[3]

During that period, too, preparation of the defense of Madrid became the chief business of the formidable Comintern contingent in the capital and its faithful servant, the Communist party of Spain.[4] Fifth Regiment headquarters became a beehive of activity, the focal point for the party's campaign to defend the capital. Propaganda designed to stir resistance poured forth. Instructions, slogans, commands, exhortations bombarded the people of Madrid through the party press, colorful wall posters, loudspeakers, mass meetings, and street corner harangues.[5] As early as October 10 Comandante Carlos (Vidali), chief political commissar of the Fifth Regiment, declared: "We give the guarantee that Madrid is unconquerable. . . . Madrid will not be taken by the enemy come what may."[6] The regiment's propaganda stressed that city street fighting was a different thing entirely from fighting in the open country and that if every house were turned into a fortress, every window were a gun port, the city could not be taken.[7] The Communist party hierarchs, Ibarruri, Díaz, and Checa, made the grand gesture of personally helping to build fortifications so as to inspire the people of Madrid to emulate them. On a more practical level the party functionary Enrique Castro Delgado organized special squads to terrorize and suppress, through nightly arrests and liquidations, any potential fifth-column activity in Madrid. Meanwhile the party issued manifestos exhorting the people of the city to "Make Madrid the tomb of Fascism," and while André Marty wrote of "Madrid—The Verdun of Democracy," the slogan "No Pasarán" became the watchword of a good part of the world.[8]

Despite all that, however, the Nationalist columns continued to drive relentlessly forward. By the first days of November they were within five miles of the center of the city and the end seemed imminent. Indeed so desperate did the prospects appear that, on November 6, the Loyalist government fled to Valencia, leaving the fate of the capital in the hands of a hastily composed Junta de Defensa.

When the Largo Caballero cabinet left Madrid it did so with little hope that the city could be held. An episode reported by the Communist commander Lister indicated that the Loyalist high command had decided to abandon Madrid to the Nationalists and that it was the Communists who determined otherwise. On November 6 Lister received orders from General Pozas, recently appointed commander of the central zone (which included Madrid). According to Lister these orders were pursuant to the decision of the Loyalist government to withdraw its forces from Madrid. Lister refused to carry out the order and reported the situation to Communist party headquarters in Madrid. José Díaz, general secretary of the party, countermanded the order of Pozas and told Lister that the party was assuming responsibility for defending Madrid on its own authority. Lister then proceeded to ignore the commands of his military superior and to act on the orders of the Communist party.[9]

As for the Junta de Defensa, virtually all observers agree that it was thoroughly dominated by the Communist apparatus in Madrid.[10] The Communists, after all, had the organization, the discipline, the will, and the determination to defend the city to the last drop of Spanish blood. Moreover, they had control of most of the effective military power at the disposal of the capital's defenders, the Fifth Regiment, the Soviet tanks and planes and guns, the technical proficiency of the

Red army advisers, and, finally, the International Brigades. The old Spanish general in nominal command of the Junta, José Miaja, provided a convenient figurehead for the Communists. Their propaganda cast him as a hero, the doughty old defender of the Republic. This myth served their purpose at the time, but they have since been less kind, as have others, in their evaluation of the old general. The still loyal Communist Lister, writing in the 1960s, agreed with defector Castro Delgado in this, if in nothing else.[11] The military command in the Madrid sector devolved, in fact, almost entirely on the Soviet staff headed by General Goriev.[12]

It was against this background of chaos and confusion that the first of the International Brigades entered the Spanish war as combatants. Just who was responsible for ordering the Internationals into action has remained obscure, as has much else about the defense of Madrid during that chaotic period. But the evidence clearly points to the Communist apparatus which was in de facto control of the capital. Brigade hierarch Luigi Longo did not say from whom the order came. Rather he said that "the comrades of the Spanish Communist Party made an urgent appeal to the International volunteers to come to the aid of imperiled Madrid." The Spanish Communist Castro Delgado also recalled that it was the Communist party (and more specifically himself and Vittorio Vidali) who were responsible for the Internationals coming to Madrid's defense.[13]

Others have held that it was General Goriev, the Soviet officer directing the military defense of the city, who ordered the Brigade to Madrid.[14] This conclusion seems most reasonable, considering the real relationship between Goriev and Miaja and the real relationship between Goriev (representing Soviet authority) and the Brigade command. The organization and command of the International Brigades dovetailed neatly into the larger Soviet-Comintern machinery in Spain. Also, it is quite reasonable, assuming that the decision did come from Goriev, that his orders to the Brigade command would be accompanied by an appeal from the Spanish Communist party as a convenient smokescreen for the somewhat dubious procedure of a Soviet general issuing orders against the directives of the government that he was supposed to be serving as an adviser. Regardless of the source of the order to commit the Internationals to combat, the Brigade directorate did move the first contingent of its troops (the XI International Brigade) into the Madrid area immediately. That such troops existed and were available for use resulted from the strenuous efforts of the Comintern apparatus in general and of the Brigade hierarchy in particular over the preceding few weeks.

As soon as the Comintern recruitment and transportation systems had been set in motion in France, Luigi Longo returned to Spain. There, in early October, through the influence and efforts of various components of the Communist apparatus, he rapidly put together the essential necessities for receiving, feeding, quartering, and clothing the first contingents of volunteers coming in from France. Working through the Communist party in Catalonia (PSUC), Longo received permission to use the fortress at Figueras as the concentration point for the men coming into Spain by land. Then he hurried on to the Spanish capital where he conferred with leading Communist party figures. José Díaz, chief of the Spanish party, assured Longo that he and the other Communist members of the Popular Front cabinet would use their influence to see to it that the needs of the Internationals would be met. Díaz also suggested that Longo go directly to see the prime minister, Largo Caballero, in order to offer officially to the government the services of the arriving volunteers. Longo, however, thought it would be better to put that off until later, when he could lead a delegation for that purpose.[15]

The first and most pressing requirement facing Longo at that point was to find a satisfactory location for a base of operations for the Internationals. The Comintern had no intention of seeing its army based in Catalonia and Aragon, strongholds of Anarchosyndicalism and Catalan separatism. Madrid was the focus and fulcrum of Communist strength in Spain and the Comintern was determined to establish their Brigades in that zone of operations. Longo solved his problem with the aid and advice of Enrique Lister and Vittorio Vidali, commander and chief political commissar respectively of the Fifth Regiment. The regiment had a base in the town of Albacete, a location well situated to the Brigades' needs along the main railroad line between Madrid and Valencia. Lister and Vidali offered to make their organization there available to Longo and the Internationals. With that problem solved and a letter of introduction to the Fifth Regiment commander in Albacete, Longo left Madrid and arrived at Albacete on October 12. The chiefs of the Fifth Regiment in Albacete, including one Barneto, a Comintern functionary whom Longo had known previously in Moscow, cooperated fully in placing their facilities and personnel at Longo's disposal.[16] This personnel included a number of non-Spanish Comintern men who had been active in the organization and direction of the Fifth Regiment and who now transferred part or all of their activities to the Brigades.[17] It also included several Red army officers who, while maintaining a low profile, directed their expertise toward the Brigades.[18]

Meanwhile, the Comintern organization in France had performed its function successfully and the first contingents of volunteers were on their way to Spain. The Spanish ship *Ciudad de Barcelona* landed the first of the volunteers who came via the sea route from Marseilles at the Spanish Mediterranean port of Alicante on October 13. That group, some 500 strong, entrained for Albacete that night and arrived there on the following day. On October 15 the first contingents from Figueras marched into Albacete and new groups of from 200 to 300 each came in almost daily thereafter.[19]

With the arrival of the Internationals in Albacete, a Comintern political directorate took control. Chief among these party stalwarts was André Marty. Marty, a charter member of the Communist party of France, had, as a young seaman, played a role in the mutiny of the French fleet operating against the Bolshevik regime in the Black Sea in 1919. By that action, for which he served four and one-half years in prison, he established himself with the Bolshevik leaders and became a Communist folk hero. He had lived for a period in the Soviet Union where he had been lionized and a number of Soviet factories were named for him. A devout Stalinist, he never showed the least inclination to deviate from the party line as laid down in Moscow and he seems to have been one of the few non-Russian Communists in whom Stalin had any confidence. An official biographical sketch of Marty, which appeared in the party press in December 1936, stressed the fact that Marty had always been a "staunch Leninist" and had never shown either "Right opportunism" nor "Left deviationism." As a member of the executive committee of the Comintern, it continued, Marty was "taking part in the leadership of the whole world Communist movement" and was among the first to "organize aid for his Spanish brothers."[20]

By the 1930s Marty had become a leading member of the Communist party of France, a member of the executive committee of the Comintern, a member of the French Chamber of Deputies, and a Comintern agent working for the Soviet military intelligence apparatus.[21] Placed in direct political control of the International Brigades by the Comintern, Marty became one of the most hated men in Spain. He cowered in the presence of Soviet military and political representatives but played the iron-fisted autocrat in his dealings with subordinates and colleagues. He was suspicious of virtually everyone and highly sensitive about any imagined threat to his position or his absolute authority in the Brigades.[22] His reputation as a brutal disciplinarian and his proclivity for having International Brigade men shot for "political dissidence," an offense categorically labeled "Trotskyism" by orthodox Communists during that period of the great purges in the Soviet Union, won him the unhappy sobriquet "Le Boucher de Albacete."[23] He demanded the same kind of public adulation within the Brigades that Stalin was receiving in the Soviet Union and the Brigade press missed few opportunities to praise Comrade Marty. For example, the organ of the mainly French XIV International Brigade declared, "In the sorrowful history of the people the name of André Marty will always be remembered, the friend and the organizer of the International Brigades." And another Brigade journal pointed out that "from the first moments our great comrade André Marty was the founder, the organizer and motive force of our glorious International Brigades."[24]

With Marty came a high powered contingent of leading Comintern functionaries, or, as Longo referred to them, "professional revolutionaries."[25] An interesting recent listing of the organizers of the Brigades by a Communist writer included Marty, François Billoux, Longo, de Vittorio, Swierczewski, Copic, Zeisser, Beimler, Stern-Kleber, Mate Zalka, Togliatti, Dahlem, Codovilla, Stefano, Nenni, and "other militants of the international workers movement."[26] Significantly, of this list only Nenni was not a Comintern stalwart, and the fact is that Nenni had only an indirect connection with the Brigades.

The most important of these "professional revolutionaries" in direct relation to the International Brigades was Longo. The leading politico in the Brigades from start to finish (except for Marty himself), Longo ultimately assumed the title of inspector general of the Brigades. As the Brigade press itself put it, "next to [Marty] Comrade Luigi Gallo [Longo's *nom de guerre* in Spain], secretary general of the Italian Communist Party, Inspector of the International Brigades in Spain, was able to channel the entire movement of solidarity which flowed to our nation, being an exemplary commissar."[27]

Among the German contingent of Comintern stalwarts who played a part in the political apparatus of the Brigades were Walter Ulbricht, Franz Dahlem, and Heinz Neumann. While Ulbricht's role in Spain remains somewhat obscure,[28] Dahlem became the chief political commissar for the Germans in the Brigades and a leading member of the political commissariat. Neumann, another seasoned Comintern agent, was apparently involved in the NKVD-controlled police apparatus in Spain which dealt in part at least with maintaining the political purity of the International Brigades.[29]

A Communist municipal counselor from Paris and trusted lieutenant of Marty's by the name of Gayman ("Vidal" in Spain) acted as the first military commandant of the base at Albacete.[30] Vidal, who had been an officer in the French army in the World War and a reserve officer since, impressed some as a man of organizational ability and military knowledge.[31] Vidal remained base commandant until replaced by the Bulgarian Colonel Bielov in July 1937.[32] In direct charge of the first arrivals at Albacete was an old French noncommissioned officer who had long military service behind him. Known as Commander Jean Marie, he demonstrated proficiency in the rough language of the barracks and loudly announced to all that they would "crush the fascists" in a couple of weeks.[33]

The basic problems of organization, supply, discipline, and training challenged the abilities of the leaders, who set to work with determined zeal. They immediately requisitioned numerous buildings which they converted into offices, barracks, supply depots, and training rooms and set up an improvised system for processing the recruits as they arrived from France. After mustering each group of new arrivals a clerk read off the list of names and asked if there were officers, noncoms, cooks, stenographers, artillerymen, or machine gunners among the contingent. That the great majority of the recruits had some previous military training and, in many cases, combat experience was a great help in all this. Eventually each man reported to the office of the political commissariat where he was once more interrogated regarding his name, age, political party affiliation, and reasons for coming to Spain. The answer to the last question was easy, recalled one volunteer. "The poster on the wall answered it: 'To Smash Fascism.'"[34]

The quartermaster service operated, in the early period at least, in an extremely erratic way. The American journalist Louis Fischer, who claimed to be the first American to enroll in the International Brigade, filled the post of quartermaster for a brief period in early November 1936. It was not long, however, until he quarreled with Marty and left the Brigade (a privilege the rank-and-file brigader did not enjoy) to resume his journalistic activities.[35]

The recruits usually received uniforms and equipment on their arrival in Albacete. The uniforms, supplied in the beginning mainly by French Communist sources, consisted of heavy khaki coats, full-cut brown corduroy trousers that strapped around the ankles, boots, a black or brown beret, a helmet, a mess kit, and a blanket. In many cases during the early period, however, the men received no weapons until virtually the time of departure for the front. The arrival and distribution of rifles was an event provoking an almost mystical excitement for some. John Sommerfield, a young and fervent Communist, recalled the emotions fired in himself on that day. "We were in a state of tremendous impatience; we wanted to see them, to handle them, to know what type they were; we wanted *ours,* to hold it and test the sights and the bolt and the trigger action. And when my turn came, I experienced a pang of delight." The rifles delivered to Sommerfield's unit were American-made Remingtons, model 1914, still coated with the grease in which they had been stored and shipped. They were good rifles, probably as good as any and better than most to be found in the Spanish war at that time.[36]

The task of quickly transforming a multinational group of diverse individuals into an effective military unit or, as one participant put it, "to transform militant revolutionaries into obedient soldiers"[37] was not easy. It was especially difficult to establish the kind of automatic obedience to officers essential to military efficiency when the officers themselves were improvised, often without experience and always without that authority supplied by custom, tradition, and habit so much a part of the pattern of discipline of a normal army.

In those early days of the Brigades there was much talk among the rank and file of a "democratic army." The illusion that a Communist army was a democratic organization ended quickly, however, as the Comintern hierarchy established firm control. The necessity of absolute discipline, "revolutionary discipline," and the appointment of military and political officers from above, quickly became the order of the day in Brigades and, even as in "bourgeois" armies, fatigue duties and the guardhouse punished slackness and indiscipline.[38]

In fact, Communist party discipline provided the otherwise missing ingredient and thus the basic sinews of authority within the Brigades. Party discipline worked effectively because, as Brigade hierarch Franz Dahlem put it, these first contingents were "almost exclusively Communists, mainly party functionaries and Red Front Fighters."[39]

From the very beginning political commissars, almost invariably selected from among tried and true party stalwarts, played a key role in the life of the Brigades, and political propaganda quickly became a regular feature of life at Albacete. On the walls of the barracks the political commissars pinned each morning a copy of *Mundo Obrero,* the official organ of the Communist party of Spain, and, often, translations of articles from Soviet newspapers. The first German contingents at Albacete posted a placard that proclaimed, "Discipline, We Exalt Discipline," while a French poster exhorted the comrades not to render themselves unfit for service by contracting diseases in the brothels.[40]

Meanwhile all roads led to Albacete for the foreign recruits who continued to pour in at the rate of several hundred a day. Albacete itself was what one volunteer called "one of Spain's most unpleasant towns." A dirty little railroad and manufacturing center and the capital of the province of Albacete situated on the windswept plateau of Don Quixote's La Mancha, the town sat astride the railroad line between Madrid and the important Mediterranean port cities of Valencia and Alicante. Thus it had undoubted advantages as a base of operations for the Brigades. Devoid of charm, the town boasted two main industries—the manufacture of knives and a thriving brothel district—to the latter of which the men of the Brigades brought booming prosperity. The climate, typical of La Mancha, produced burning, hot, dry summers and cold, wet winters during which Albacete's unpaved streets became rivers of mud. Others retained somewhat fonder recollections of Albacete. A devout young English Communist found deeply moving such evidences of the revolution as the gaily painted and initialed automobiles which sped wildly about, the ubiquity of working-class dress, and the atmosphere of excitement and "slightly hysterical gaiety."[41]

By early November the town presented a strange spectacle, filled as it was with men from all over Europe speaking a babel of languages. The Brigades even boasted a few Russians, exiles from their homeland since the revolution, who were attempting to demonstrate their good faith toward the new regime in Russia and thus win their eventual return home by fighting for the Comintern in Spain. Those unfortunate people (who, needless to say, never achieved their goal) were the only Russians in the International Brigades. Indeed the one European nationality most significantly not represented among the Brigades was the Soviet.[42]

With the continued influx of recruits (3,000 to 4,000 by the end of October),[43] Albacete became overcrowded. To cope with this, the Brigade chiefs ordered the organization of four battalions, based as nearly as possible on linguistic lines, and their dispersal into training quarters in the outlying villages. The first official document issued by authority of the International Brigades was an order for the concentration of troops in the towns of Mahora and Tarazona de la Mancha on October 29, 1936. The document, typewritten in French, was signed by Commander Jean Marie and base commander Vidal. The Italians went to Madrigueras, the Poles and other Slavs to Tarazona de la Mancha, the French to La Roda, and the Germans to Mahora.[44] In the countryside around their cantonments the newly formed squads, companies, and battalions stood morning parades, marched over the dusty roads, and carried out elementary maneuvers in the surrounding fields. Through the desperate efforts of officers and political commissars, the rudiments of a military organization began to emerge. As an article published in the Brigade press on the first anniversary of the formation of the Brigades put it, "Under the resolute direction of our great Comrade André Marty... and... Comrade Vidal... Albacete became a hub of seething activity, the birthplace of the International Brigades."[45]

Despite all the efforts of the Albacete directorate, their forces were far from ready for entry into action when the order (or appeal) came from Madrid. Although four battalions had been formed, they had had little time to organize or train. Further, no higher military command structure had as yet been created. Nevertheless, faced with the call to commit their troops to battle, Albacete put together a necessarily weak and incomplete Brigade structure within which three of the four available battalions would operate.[46]

The first battalion of the newly founded XI International Brigade was a predominantly German unit which called itself the Edgar André battalion in honor of the well-known ex-chief of the Roten Front Kämpfer Bund, the Communist party's paramilitary organization in Germany (the Red equivalent of the Nazi SA). News of André's execution by the Nazi regime reached the Germans in Spain just as the battalion was forming.[47] Appointed to command the André battalion was Hans Kahle. An ex-German army officer with combat experience in the World War, a longtime member of the German Communist party and the Roten Front Kämpfer Bund,[48] Kahle was a big tough man who in his bearing retained much of the appearance and manner of the Prussian officer. Although he was a thorough Communist and disciplined party member who obeyed orders without question, Kahle concealed beneath a rough exterior certain human characteristics which expressed themselves in an ironic sense of humor and periodic flings in Madrid during which he indulged himself with large doses of wine, women, and song. He spoke fluent Spanish and was one of Hemingway's favorite characters in Spain.[49]

The André battalion consisted almost entirely of devout German Communists, most of whom, prior to volunteering for the Brigade, had been living as political émigrés in France. The battalion included a large number of World War veterans and, like Kahle and the battalion political commissar Arthur Dorf, most were party activists who had a long history of political, military, and/or revolutionary activity behind them. They had all experienced the frustration of seeing their party, their friends and associates, and their aspirations crushed in their fatherland since 1933. They were, as militants in a party forged in the heat of struggle, a highly disciplined group. And, as embittered losers in their struggle at home, they proved to be fanatical combatants in Spain. A very high percentage of those who marched through the streets of Madrid on Sunday, November 8, 1936, died before the year was out.[50]

The French battalion of the XI Brigade adopted the name of the Commune de Paris centuria, which had recently joined the French recruits at La Roda.[51] The battalion commander, Jules Dumont, was an ex-captain in the French army and veteran of Verdun where, a widely circulated story went, he had faced Hans Kahle across no-man's-land. A longtime Communist stalwart and one of the earliest of the foreign combatants in Spain, Dumont had fought at Irun in July and August. As the commander of the Commune de Paris centuria when it arrived at La Roda and as one who combined military experience and political reliability, he was the obvious choice to command the French battalion.[52] Pierre Rebiere, a member of the central committee of the French Communist party[53] and a member of Longo's delegation to the Largo Caballero government, filled the post of battalion political commissar. The battalion consisted chiefly of those Frenchmen and French-speaking Belgians who had been among the first volunteers to come into Spain through the Comintern recruiting system. They, like their German comrades in the André battalion, were predominantly Communists.[54] While perhaps less anxious to die than their German counterparts, having lost less and having, therefore, more to lose, they too were to die in large numbers in the days and nights of November and December 1936.

The third battalion of the XI Brigade called itself the Dombrowski. It was made up predominantly of Polish Communists, most of whom had been living as political émigrés in France and Belgium. The commander of the Dombrowski battalion was Bolek Ulanovski and its political commissar, a Comrade Matuczacz. Both men had fought with the Polish Dombrowski or General Woblewski centuria alongside the Italian Gastone-Sozzi with the Fifth Regiment prior to the formation of the International Brigade.[55] Small South Slavic groups were attached to both the André and Dombrowski battalions and some twenty Englishmen, mostly of the old Tom Mann centuria, were assigned to the Commune de Paris battalion.[56]

The XI Brigade, composed of these three battalions, was commanded by the Soviet army officer who passed in Spain under the *nom de guerre* "General Emilio Kleber." Kleber, a vigorous man of some forty years of age whose ruggedly handsome face was topped by a full shock of iron-gray hair, was to gain worldwide fame as the "Savior of Madrid" for his role as commander of the International Column during the defense of the capital in November and December 1936.[57] The propagandists presented him to the world as a soldier of fortune, a naturalized Canadian, a man of Austrian birth who had been taken prisoner in the World War by Russian armies and had subsequently been converted to Bolshevism.[58] Geoffrey Cox, a British Communist journalist, embellished the story further by saying that Kleber's family had taken him to Canada as a child and that he was a naturalized British citizen whose English showed "only the faintest traces of foreign accent in addition to its Canadian tone." Cox further wrote that Kleber originally went to Russia as a member of a Canadian army of intervention in 1919. From there he made his way across Siberia to Moscow and joined the Red army with which he served throughout the Russian civil war. "After that was over he went to Hamburg (Germany) where he organized Communist shock troops. In 1927 he was in China, leading one group of the Red armies against Chiang Kai-Shek. From there Kleber went north to Manchuko and played his part there. He had been a revolutionary since 1914. The Spanish civil war is the third in which he has fought."[59]

That picture, according to Krivitsky, who was well acquainted with Kleber, was fabricated by the NKVD which supplied Kleber with a Canadian passport and complete biography. In fact, Kleber had never lived in Canada. The elaborate fiction, laced as it was with vagueness and mystery, served simply as a smokescreen for covering the fact that Kleber was an officer in the Soviet army. It provided a plausible background for his sudden emergence as the commander of the "spontaneous" troops of the International Column. Kleber remained a mystery man even to many in important positions in the International Brigades. On meeting him for the first time and being informed that he was the general in command of the International Brigades at Madrid, Pacciardi asked rhetorically, "Who is this General Kleber? They say Canadian yet he speaks Russian. But he is not Russian. Who has made him a general?"[60]

Actually, the mysterious General Kleber was General Lazar Stern, a native of Bukovina, a territory that prior to the World War was within Austria-Hungary but was after the war in Rumania. Stern-Kleber, an officer in the Austro-Hungarian army during the Great War, was captured by the Russian army and interned in a prisoner of war camp. After the revolution in Russia he joined the Red army and fought throughout the civil wars. Later he attended the Soviet

Defense of Madrid

military academy, graduating in 1924. In 1927 Kleber became a member of the Red army intelligence department and was assigned to the military section of the Comintern.[61] In that capacity he performed numerous assignments in various parts of the world, including China, Germany, and the United States.[62] By assigning Kleber, and men of similar status and background, to the military command of the International Brigades, the Soviet Union was able to use a reservoir of trained and experienced military technicians completely under Soviet control without at the same time compromising the USSR's officially neutral status in the Spanish war.[63] Acting alongside Kleber as political commissar of the XI Brigade was the Italian Communist Giuseppe de Vittorio ("Nicoletti"), the third-ranking Comintern politico in the International Brigade directorate.[64]

The sudden order for the departure of the Internationals from their training bases produced both high excitement and barely controlled chaos. In the morning the troops remained confined to barracks with kits packed, a situation that led, inevitably, to a rash of rumor and speculation as to when and where they were going. Some struggled with pocket dictionaries to decipher three-day-old Madrid newspapers for a clue to the situation. A member of the Commune de Paris battalion recalled the departure as "a kind of rout."[65] In the afternoon the troops formed ranks on the parade field while trucks rolled in loaded with crates of ammunition. Each man received two or three cloth slings containing fifty rounds each. Then they marched to the La Roda station and boarded a waiting train which soon began making its slow way across the quiet, night-shrouded, countryside. The train carried them as far as the village of Alcazar where the troops transferred to Russian-built trucks. The trucks bounced over rough roads through the night, arriving the next morning at Vallecas, a town some ten miles east-southeast of Madrid. That night the men slept in the fields around Vallecas and heard the far-off rumble of artillery fire for the first time. It rained and turned cold and the men shivered as they stood two-hour stints on guard.[66]

The next morning as the men of the Commune de Paris battalion were eating breakfast, the André battalion marched past singing a German Communist marching song and waving a big red banner at the head of the column. "It was a brave sight," recalled a member of the British machine-gun section of the French battalion. "All the glamour and excitement that governments can use to make men forsake their homes and die on foreign soil for foreign markets, but it was *ours*, it was our army, and the glamour was real."[67] The men of the French battalion stood saluting with clenched fists raised as the

André battalion marched past. Later that morning the French battalion held a brief commemorative ceremony in honor of the nineteenth anniversary of the Bolshevik revolution. Short speeches in French, Spanish, and English were followed by singing of the *Internationale* in several languages. Not long thereafter they entrained for Madrid and the celebrated march through the streets of the beleaguered capital. That march saw the birth of the legend of the Internationals. The march itself inevitably was seen in sometimes startlingly different ways by different observers and described in even more startlingly different ways by some who observed it not at all.

Geoffrey Cox, the British Communist acting as correspondent for the *London News Chronicle* in Madrid, wrote of it:

> Up the street from the direction of the Ministry of War came a long column of marching men. They wore a kind of corduroy uniform, and loose brown Glengarry caps like those of the British tank corps.
>
> They were marching in excellent formation. The tramp, tramp of their boots sounded in perfect unison. Over their shoulders were slung rifles of obviously modern design. Many had scarred tin helmets hanging from their belts. Some were young; others carried themselves like trained, experienced soldiers.
>
> Each section had its officers, some carrying swords and revolvers. Behind rolled a small convoy of lorries stacked high with machine guns and equipment. At the rear trotted a squadron of about fifty cavalry.
>
> The few people who were about lined the roadway, shouting almost hysterically, "Salud! Salud!" holding up their fists clenched in salute, or clapping vigorously.[68]

The book *La Quatorzième,* published by the commissariat of the International Brigades in 1937, said of the Commune de Paris battalion on that march: "By the word battalion one imagines some hundreds of men dressed and armed uniformly. These men did not resemble that image. One was in a military blouse, the other in civilian, a third in khaki trousers, the fourth a beret, the fifth a forage cap. The rifles were Remington, Mausers, surplus of the Swiss Army."[69]

Arturo Barea, a Spanish Socialist, working at the time for the government press bureau in Madrid wrote: "On that Sunday a formation of foreigners in uniform, equipped with modern arms, paraded through the center of town: The legendary International Column which had been training in Albacete had come to the help of Madrid.

Defense of Madrid 61

After the nights of the 6th, and 7th, when Madrid had been utterly alone in its resistance, the arrival of those anti-fascists from abroad was an incredible relief. Before the Sunday was over, stories went round of the bravery of the International Battalions in the Casa de Campo."[70] And John Sommerfield, one of the marchers, recalled it this way: "Ours was no triumphant entry; we were a last desperate hope and, as tired out, ill equipped, and hungry, we marched through the wind-swept streets.... I thought that the hurrying people on the pavements looked at us as if we were too late and had come only in time to die."[71] Some of the Brigade units went directly into the lines with the Spanish militia troops in the Casa de Campo, a large park in the southwestern outskirts of Madrid.[72] There they set to work digging trenches and making use of natural cover, elementary military techniques of which the Spanish militia troops were either unaware or disdained to practice as beneath the dignity of brave men. The military efficiency exhibited by the Internationals, which by Spanish militia standards was phenomenal, was seen by many as one of their most important contributions to the defense of the city. "The militiaman learned. He acquired the habits of a soldier. Each international converted himself, without thinking of it, into a teacher."[73] The Internationals had not come to Madrid to teach, however, but to fight. And in the days and nights that followed their entry into Madrid they were to have ample opportunity to do so.

On November 9, as the troops of the XI Brigade were experiencing their first taste of combat, the Madrid command called on the Albacete directorate for the immediate commitment of all troops still available to it. The result was wild improvisation and an even more chaotic situation than had been the case with the XI Brigade's departure several days earlier. For Albacete had only one organized battalion, a few barely formed companies of diverse nationalities, and the merest outline of a Brigade structure available. The directorate's efforts to organize a military unit and simultaneously to move it into combat produced, as Marty put it, "what the bourgeoisie calls a miracle." He credited that miracle to the "highly qualified military cadres" and the "antifascist consciousness of the rank and file of worker soldiers, above all the Socialists and Communists."[74]

The one organized battalion available to the Albacete directorate at that moment, the Italian Garibaldi, had been among the first formed, along with the André, Dombrowski, and Commune de Paris. But it had been held out of the XI Brigade to serve as a nucleus for the organization of a second Brigade. Its commander, Randolfo Pacciardi, had arrived at Albacete and taken effective command of the

Italian contingent on November 3. On the following day the Garibaldis, who had recently been issued uniforms and rifles, moved to the village of Madrigueras where they established a base and began serious training. On November 6 Ludwig Renn, an ex-officer in the German army, observed the Italian battalion holding a mock attack on a hill outside Madrigueras and came away favorably impressed. Here, thought Renn, were the troops who might really accomplish something.[75]

The Garibaldi battalion stood out in a number of ways as unique among the units of the International Brigade. For one thing, its first commander, Pacciardi, was not a Communist but the leader of the Italian Republican party. Although Pacciardi and his party had adhered to the Popular Front in 1935 along with the Italian Socialists and Communists, he saw the Spanish conflict chiefly in terms of the Italian situation, feeling that a defeat for the Right in Spain would be a defeat for fascism in Italy. He felt, as did numerous other antifascist Italians, that Italian participation in a victorious struggle in Spain would be an important step on the road to Rome. Pacciardi thus favored the formation of a specifically Italian combat unit in Spain which, he felt, would serve as a living example to the Italian people. Italians, he wrote, should form a combat "legion" in Spain which would be a symbol of the vitality of the antifascist cause to Italians, a legion that would "be honored with sacrifice" and pass from "the era of martyrs to the era of heroes." Such a force would forge in the fire of combat the cadres of the revolution and move the Italian people with their "strong deeds."[76]

The Italian legion visualized by Pacciardi would be nonpolitical, not tied to nor directed by any particular political party but at the service of the Spanish government and general staff. While interested in aiding the Popular Front forces in Spain, Pacciardi saw his legion above all as a demonstration to the Italian people that they could fight and die for their own liberty. He felt that the knowledge that Italian democracy in exile was fighting in Spain would rouse the Italians at home and rally them to "the tradition of Garibaldi."[77]

Pacciardi's earlier attempts to interest the Largo Caballero government in his Italian legion had proved unsuccessful. But he continued to work for the idea through the Italian Popular Front committee made up of representatives of the Communist, Socialist, and Republican parties of Italy and headquartered in Paris. That committee, dominated by the Communists (since Pietro Nenni, secretary of the Italian Socialist party, consistently followed the Communist lead),[78] had not favored Pacciardi's plan for creating an Italian military unit.

But that attitude changed abruptly following the Soviet-Comintern decision to organize an international military force for service in Spain, and the Italian committee's endorsement of Pacciardi's plan followed quickly. The parties represented on the committee formalized their agreement to create an Italian legion in a document that set forth the juridical basis of the legion and named Pacciardi as its commander.[79]

The reasons for a Communist-dominated committee appointing a man from outside the party's ranks as commander were several. Pacciardi had, for one thing, better qualifications from a military standpoint than most. He had been an officer in the Italian army in the World War and had been decorated several times for valor. Politically, his antifascist credentials were impeccable. An early and consistent opponent of Mussolini and the Fascists, he had gone into exile in 1926 and had remained active in anti-Mussolini politics ever since.[80] As leader of the small but influential Italian Republican party and as one who supported the Popular Front program he seemed eminently fitted, from the Communist point of view, to represent a Popular Front organization. Longo explained it by saying that the Communists wanted to show the spirit of unity and not take all the command positions just because they were in the majority. His fellow International Brigader and Italian party comrade Giacomo Calandrone agreed, saying that in order to emphasize the unitary, broad antifascist, as opposed to narrowly party, character of the Garibaldi battalion they had a Republican commander and a Communist and a Socialist political commissar.[81] While there is an element of truth in both statements, both are also after-the-fact rationalizations. The Communists were content to have a known nonparty member in a conspicuous position in the Brigades so long as he remained completely amenable to their control. But if he showed any signs of political unreliability, they spared no effort in getting rid of him as, in fact, they did with Pacciardi later.

The contractual document creating the legion, dated October 27, 1936, was clearly executed not only after the Comintern decision to form an international army in Spain but subsequent to the concentration of a large number of foreign recruits at Albacete. The agreement made no mention of the fact that the legion was to be part of a larger international organization, and Pacciardi did not know anything about the International Brigade until he arrived at Albacete on November 1 to find, to his surprise, not only Italians but men from most of the countries of Europe. Longo later claimed that none of the people on the Paris committee knew of the prior formation of the

International Brigades.[82] This seems extremely doubtful so far as the Communist members were concerned and certainly Longo himself knew all about it. At any rate, Pacciardi's efforts to bring his legion into being proved successful only after those efforts came to coincide with the policy of the Comintern, and, in fact, the legion was incorporated into the Comintern-controlled International Brigades from the beginning. The Italian legion, which became the Garibaldi battalion at birth, provided a good illustration of the fact that the Popular Front only operated with any real effect when following the lead of the Comintern.

When Pacciardi found that the Italians were to constitute part of a larger international army, he said: "We Italians had no interest in a mysterious and unavowed legion. We wanted on the contrary to popularize it in our country, as an example to the sleeping and a reprimand to the cowards. We did not want to be lost in the anomymity of internationalism." The Brigade directorate reassured him, however, that the Italians would be organized in a specifically Italian unit to be called the Garibaldi.[83]

By early November the Italian contingent at Madrigueras numbered some five to six hundred men. Although composed predominantly of Communists, including the remnants of the Gastone-Sozzi centuria, the Garibaldi battalion contained a larger percentage of non-Communists than any other unit in the Brigades at that time, a fact recognized symbolically by having two political commissars, Antonio Roasio, a Communist, and Arnaldo Azzi, a Socialist.[84] The Italian volunteers were largely middle-aged men, many over forty, a fact attributable to the long tenure of Fascism in Italy and the early date of the effective purging of the country of active antifascist elements. In organizing the battalion and nominating officers, Pacciardi took the previous military experience of each one into account. The commanding officers of companies were all men with military experience, either as officers or noncommissioned officers. Most of the original Garibaldinis were veterans of the World War. Pacciardi proved to be not only a capable military commander but a successful and respected leader of men.[85] His only fault was that he would not render unquestioning obedience to the Brigades' Comintern political chieftains and for that he would eventually pay.

The second battalion incorporated into the new XII Brigade took the name Thaelmann, in honor of the chief of the German Communist party. Its commander, the German writer Arnold Vieth von Golssenau, who used his pseudonym, Ludwig Renn, in Spain, had served as an officer in the German army in the World War. During the 1920s he had joined the German Communist party and had been a member, along with Hans Khale, of the Roten Front Kämpfer Bund. Renn had been imprisoned in 1933–1934 by the Nazi regime and on his release from prison his party superiors ordered him to leave the country. He crossed the border into Switzerland where he joined the growing ranks of the German Communist party in exile.[86]

When the Spanish war broke out Renn contacted KPD headquarters in Paris for recommendations and papers to allow him to enter Spain. Arriving in Barcelona in early October 1936, he reported to PSUC headquarters where he met an old acquaintance, Hans Beimler, who was a member of the central committee of the German Communist party and political chief of the German Communists in Spain.[87] The next day Renn visited the Thaelmann centuria on the Huesca front with Beimler and requested that he be allowed to join a military unit. Beimler told him to go to Madrid where his military experience would be put to better use. When Renn reported to party headquarters in Madrid both the Spanish Communists and a representative of the German party's central committee assured him that they would find a suitable military post for him. He remained in Madrid, however, still without a command, as late as November 6, when he left the capital for Valencia with a group of foreign journalists. When that group went through Albacete on November 6 Renn learned for the first time of the existence of the International Brigades and offered his services to the Albacete directorate.[88] That an available party member with Renn's military background should have been ignored, as it seems, by the Comintern directorate in Spain was an example of the way in which the Comintern generally tended to ignore the party's intellectuals in its plans for staffing the International Brigades. Both Renn and Gustav Regler, another German Communist intellectual, came to Spain, according to their reports, without any particular assignment from the party and only by coincidence or accident became affiliated with the Brigades. This bears out the general disdain, contempt, and distrust in which the intellectuals were held by the party hierarchy in general. The intellectuals, most of whom were renegades from bourgeois backgrounds, were considered unreliable. While the party astutely used the intellectuals for its own ends, and especially in appealing to the bourgeois liberals of western Europe and America as part of the Popular Front policy, they never really fully trusted them.[89]

Renn's chance arrival at Albacete almost simultaneously with the urgent mobilization order from Madrid, coupled with the severe shortage of trained officers available to the Albacete staff, led to his being offered command of a new battalion (the future Thaelmann) then in the process of formation. Renn accepted and plunged into the chaos engendered by the attempt to organize a multilingual mass of individuals (Germans, Slavs, Hungarians, British, and more) into a military unit.

The political commissar of the battalion, Fritz Vehlov ("Louis Schuster" in Spain), a German Communist who had previously fought with the Thaelmann centuria and who had arrived in Albacete with the remnants of that unit a few days prior to Renn's arrival, explained to Renn that disorganization reigned supreme. Not a single company had been organized, and the harried Schuster, desperately trying to bring some order out of the chaos, could not (since he spoke only German) even communicate with many of those assigned to the battalion. Renn and Schuster called on each of the nationality groups to pick a political delegate, if possible one who could speak German or Russian, and in some cases this linguistic factor became the criterion by which unit commanders were chosen. The thirteen men of the English-speaking group attached to the battalion, for example, sent forth their only German-speaking member, Arnold Jeans, as its political delegate. Having gotten this group together, Renn, who spoke Russian as a result of having lived in the Soviet Union for several years where he wrote propaganda for the Comintern, could communicate with each of the delegates either in German or Russian. Each group, Renn informed them, would have to organize itself as best it could for the time being. The battalion would be going into battle before its officers had a chance to know one another.[90]

The battalion, as roughly organized, consisted of a German company, a German-English company, a Polish company, and a polyglot company composed of Bulgarians, Yugoslavs, Hungarians, and others. The last of those companies had as yet neither a commander nor a political commissar since no one could be found among them who spoke Slavic and Magyar as well as German or Russian. A representative finally came forward who could communicate with Renn in a half-German, half-Russian patois. The companies were divided into "zugs" of thirty men each and the zugs into groups of ten. The English, now numbering some twenty men, made up, along with a few Flemings and Germans, the third zug of the first company. Their zug leader, recalled a young Britisher, was a tall, tough Prussian called Paul, and the company commander was "even more of a Prussian" called Max.[91] The third battalion of the XII Brigade, the so-called Franco-Belge or André Marty was even less organized than the Thaelmann, lacking even a commanding officer upon departure for the front.[92]

A Soviet army officer of Hungarian origin, Mate Zalka, known in Spain as General Lukacs, assumed military command of the XII Brigade.[93] Renn and Lukacs, old acquaintances from their days in the Soviet Union, had run into each other in Madrid on November 3. At that time Lukacs had told Renn that he had been sent to Spain to organize partisan groups for work behind the enemy lines, a task for which Lukacs was qualified by experience. When Renn arrived at Albacete on November 6 and offered his services to the Brigade directorate, he found to his surprise that Lukacs had become the commanding general of the new XII Brigade. Lukacs explained that the partisan assignment had been called off.[94]

General Lukacs was a man of many talents and one whose qualities of humanity and warmth set him apart from most of his colleagues among the Soviet-Comintern hierarchy in Spain. He became the best liked of the International Brigade commanders.[95] A cavalry officer in the Austro-Hungarian army before and during the World War, Lukacs had been captured by the Russian army. When released as a result of the Russian revolution, he had joined the Bolshevik party and fought in the Red army during the civil war. He continued to live in the Soviet Union and remained in the Red army serving at one time with Cheka troops in the suppression of "banditry." He had been decorated with the Order of the Red Banner for his services to the USSR.[96] Communist propaganda, aimed at liberal sentiment in the western nations, inevitably stressed that he was an author.[97] The Communists recognized the value of claiming as many intellectuals as possible as supporters of their cause in Spain. To have an intellectual general was too good a thing not to make the most of. That Lukacs was a Red army officer who had come to Spain directly from the Soviet Union was not mentioned publicly. Longo himself assumed the post of Brigade political commissar while one Lukanov, a Bulgarian who used the *nom de guerre* "Bielov" in Spain and had reputedly been an artillery officer during the Balkan wars, took the post of Brigade chief of staff. With this makeshift arrangement the XII Brigade moved out for combat.[98]

5 The XIII, XIV, and XV Brigades

While the first two International Brigades fought on the Madrid front, new recruits continued to stream into Albacete at the rate of 500 to 1,000 a week. Because of the heavy casualties sustained by the XI and XII Brigades at Madrid, the Albacete staff posted many of the new recruits to those two Brigades as reinforcements during November and December. At the same time, they organized new battalions slated for a third (XIII) International Brigade. One battalion, composed primarily of French and Belgians, trained at Mahora; another, also predominantly French, at Villanueva de la Jara and Quentinar de la Orden; a third, composed of Germans, Poles, and various Balkan nationalities, at Tarazona de la Mancha; and a fourth, predominantly Italian, at La Roda.[1] One of these battalions, later dubbed the "Chapaiev" for the popular partisan hero of the Russian civil wars, was the most international of all the International Brigade units. It contained Poles, Germans, Hungarians, Swiss, Jews, Czechs, Austrians, and small groups of Dutch, Swedes, Danes, Norwegians, and Yugoslavs.[2] The companies and squads of the Chapaiev battalion took names of national heroes like the Polish Mickiewicz company, or of antifascist heroes like the Czech Gottwald zug. The two predominantly French battalions of the Brigade were later combined to form the Henri Vuillemin battalion, named in honor of a Communist killed in the riots in Paris in February 1934, an occurrence that had become part of the mythology of the Popular Front.[3]

The formation of the command structure, staff, and service units for the new Brigade proceeded in a much more orderly way than had been the case with XI and XII Brigades.[4] The man chosen to train the new Brigade and then to command it, known in Spain as "General Gomez," was in fact Wilhelm Zeisser, a German Communist and longtime Comintern functionary. He had served as a lieutenant in the German army in the World War. Stationed in Russia when the revolution broke out, he joined the Bolshevik party, became a Soviet citizen, and remained a devoted Communist from that time on. He received specialized training in Moscow which made him an expert in the methods and techniques of insurrection and civil war. In the 1920s and 1930s Zeisser functioned as part of the Soviet military intelligence and espionage apparatus in Germany and also on occasion as a Soviet agent in China and Manchuria. His mysterious appearance in Spain as General Gomez followed the pattern set by Kleber, Lukacs, and the other Brigade generals. Zeisser was a classic example of the type of professional revolutionary who performed the Comintern's work throughout the world.[5]

As chief of staff of the XIII Brigade the Albacete directorate chose another German called Schindler, a Communist who, so the popular story ran, had once served a prison term for his participation in the *Spartakusbund* in the early days of the Weimar Republic. He had since occupied himself as a journalist specializing in military affairs and, prior to the Spanish conflict, had been living in France. Schindler had entered Spain immediately after the outbreak of the conflict in July 1936. He was prominent among the earliest foreigners to fight in Aragon where he participated in the formation of the original Thaelmann centuria and became its first commander. Later he went to Paris to help in the recruiting of volunteers for the International Brigades. On his return to Spain in early December he was appointed first chief of staff in the XIII Brigade.[6]

The Brigade chiefs assumed that the XIII Brigade would join the other International units in the Madrid sector. But in the first days of December the Albacete command received orders to rush all available troops to Valencia. The reason given for that unexpected turn of events, a turn that subsequently vitally and dismally affected the entire future of the XIII Brigade, read that a seaborne invasion by Italian military forces was imminent.[7] Knowledgeable and reliable sources have since contended that the real reason behind this move was not fear of an Italian invasion but of a rising by the predominantly Anarchist population and militia units in Catalonia and the provinces to the south against the Popular Front government itself.[8]

Whatever the reason, the Brigade did go to Valencia where it remained for several weeks. Then, in the last week of December, the XIII Brigade saw its first combat in an attack on the city of Teruel in Aragon. Writing long after the event, Longo claimed that the original purpose of the XIII Brigade's being ordered to Valencia was to make this attack on Teruel.[9] That about three weeks elapsed between the time the Brigade was ordered to Valencia and the beginning of the Teruel campaign and that Teruel was some 140 kilometers from Valencia cast strong doubt on this explanation. More likely the Valencia regime saw the use of the Brigade in an attack on Teruel as a good method of making a show of strength in an area largely under

Anarchist control and prone to a dissident attitude toward the government. The attack on Teruel proved to be a costly failure. The Chapiev battalion suffered over 50 percent casualties and the two French battalions lost so heavily that they were subsequently merged into a single battalion. One factor in the poor showing at Teruel was the "barely concealed hostility" of the local Spanish command toward the Internationals. Also, according to Longo, the Spanish troops involved, mainly Anarchist militia forces, showed a distinct hostility toward the Internationals. Whether or not this was merely a rationalization for failure by using two well-known Communist scapegoats— the non-Communists among the Loyalist military command and the Anarchists—or whether it was a real factor in the defeat is hard to say. Certainly the Anarchists distrusted the International Brigades as a Communist force which many of them undoubtedly believed was being used as a counterweight to the Anarchists themselves. The fact that the non-Communists among the Loyalist army command in general looked with suspicion and ill-concealed dislike on the Internationals was attested to by others.[10]

The XIII Brigade remained in the southern zone of operations for the next five months. As a result it was the only International Brigade that did not participate in the central epic of the war during that period, the battle for Madrid.

With the departure of the XIII Brigade for Valencia in December, the Albacete directorate set to work organizing three more battalions and a fourth Brigade. Appointed commander of the XIV Brigade was Karol Swierczewski. Known in Spain as "General Walter," Swierczewski was, like Kleber and Lukacs, a Soviet army officer. Of Polish origin he had joined the Bolsheviks during the revolution and fought with the Red army during the civil wars. He remained in the Soviet army thereafter and served as one of that group of non-Russian Red army officers widely used by the Soviet government through its Comintern apparatus in operations throughout the world. A rugged appearing man, he had received the Order of the Red Star for his services to the Soviet Union. Walter had served for a time as a professor in the Soviet military school in Moscow and on the staff of the Chinese Red army.[11] He ultimately commanded a division in Spain and appeared much later as vice-minister of defense of the Communist regime in Poland following World War II.[12]

André Heusler, a functionary of the French Communist party, filled the post of Brigade commissar while Ralph Fox, a prominent member of the small but vocal clique of Communist intellectuals in

Great Britain, served as his assistant.¹³ A graduate of Oxford's Magdalen College, Fox had worked in the colonial department of the Comintern in Moscow in 1925 and had remained a dedicated party member ever since.¹⁴ The Italian Communist Aldo Morandi served as the Brigade chief of staff.¹⁵ Vincenzo Bianco ("Krieger" in Spain), an ex-deputy of the Italian parliament from Trieste and a charter member of the Italian Communist party also held a post on the Brigade staff.¹⁶ A French Socialist called Putz commanded one battalion of the Brigade. Putz, a soldier of courage and popularity with his troops, but not a Communist, ultimately left the International Brigades to command a regular Spanish brigade.¹⁷ Boris Guimple, a Communist who had been an officer in the French army until shortly before his arrival in Spain, commanded a company in Putz's battalion. He later took command of the battalion and eventually became XIV Brigade chief of staff.¹⁸ Another battalion commander was an ex-officer of the French army, Delasalle. Delasalle quickly became unpopular with a number of people in the Brigade hierarchy including Marty himself.¹⁹ He was soon to meet the same untimely end that awaited many another who provoked Marty's ire in Spain. George Nathan commanded the British company of Delasalle's battalion. Nathan, who had been an officer in the British army in the World War, succeeded Delasalle as battalion commander and eventually became chief of staff of another (the XV) International Brigade. He quickly gained a reputation for great coolness and courage under fire, a reputation that lasted until he was killed in action in July 1937. One of the few nonpoliticals who attained relatively high command position in the Brigades, Nathan was among those who most clearly fitted the description of the Internationals as a "bohemian military society." He commonly led troops in combat with no weapon more potent than a cane and, in an army not noted for punctilious care in matters of dress, Nathan stood out as a one-man exhibition of spit and polish.²⁰

One of the battalions of the XIV Brigade was commanded by a Bulgarian Communist called Stomatov, a man whose political activities had cost him seven years in prison in his native country. A Serbian Communist called Petrovich, who was, as Marty remarked in his inevitable speech to departing troops, "a young man, but an old revolutionary,"²¹ served as its political commissar. Commanding the Italian company was one Bocchi, a Communist who had been living in Paris prior to the Spanish conflict. As political commissar, the Italians had the services of a comrade Locatelli, a party stalwart who had arrived in Spain but a few days earlier direct from the Lenin School in Moscow.²²

The XIV Brigade had hardly been formed when it was dispatched to the Cordova area where it received a scorching baptism of fire in an action around the town of Lopera. This action turned into a thorough debacle for the Brigade. The resultant high casualties and general breakdown in discipline brought both Longo and Marty to the scene and led to the execution of battalion commander Delasalle for treason. With order more or less restored, the XIV Brigade was moved into the Madrid zone of operations where it participated in the ongoing battles there.[23]

In late December 1936 the Albacete directorate launched the formation of the fifth and last of the International Brigades. The new Brigade, the XV, consisted of four battalions, a British, a French, an American, and a Slavic-Italian one.[24] The Brigade's military commander, a Red army officer named Janos Galicz, used the *nom de guerre* "General Gall" in Spain. The Brigade newspaper pictured him as "a true son of the people," a Hungarian, a "simple soldier" in the Austrian army in the World War. Freed by the revolution in Russia he joined the Bolshevik party and the Red army where he "advanced militarily." He had been involved, so the story went, in the Bela Kun affair in Hungary in 1919 following which he returned to Russia and adopted Soviet citizenship. Subsequently Gall performed various services for the Comintern including military work in China.[25] Virtually all sources except official Communist ones agree that Gall was a vain, egotistical, brutal man and the worst of the International Brigade generals.[26] Possessed of a harsh personality he quickly gained a reputation for complete disregard of the lives of the men under his command. Despite this he ultimately moved up to a divisional command in Spain as did his colleagues Kleber and Walter.

A Croat Communist, Vladimir Copic, served as Brigade political commissar. He too had become a member of the Bolshevik party in Russia after being freed from a prisoner of war camp by the revolution. Immediately after the World War he returned to his homeland where he became a charter member of the Communist party of Yugoslavia.[27] As fervent in his Communism as his colleague Gall, Copic appeared to have been cut from a different mold. A man with rather wide cultural interests, he spoke, in addition to his native language, Russian, German, and English and could get along in several others including Italian and French. He had traveled widely, been a professional opera singer, and served briefly as a member of the Yugoslav Chamber of Deputies. Prior to Copic's entry into Spain he had been instrumental in organizing the recruitment system in Yugoslavia for the International Brigades. On his arrival at Albacete in February

1937, he assumed the post of political commissar of the XV Brigade. Copic eventually became commander of the XV Brigade upon Gall's being posted to command of a division.[28] The picture of Copic as a cultured cosmopolitan may well have been in large part a propaganda image. It seems somewhat tarnished by the tone of the following statement by him: "It is a month since you have come to this point of Jarama face to face with the fascist enemy and received your baptism of fire. The fascist hordes have not succeeded in cutting off and surrounding Madrid, thanks to the heroic stand of the fighters of the XV Brigade. We withstood the mad attacks of the enemy and inflicted heavy losses on him. Yet we have even greater and ruder tasks in front of us. We must crush completely the fascist reptile. The commanders and men of the XV Brigade will strive to make their Brigade second to none and to deal with the heaviest blows to the fascist robbers. Forward to the complete victory of the People's Front."[29]

The French Communist Jean Chaintron ("Barthel" in Spain) served as assistant Brigade political commissar. A longtime functionary of the French party, Barthel had served in various party posts in France and had been, just prior to his coming to Spain, secretary of the Communist party of Algeria. Upon Copic's assumption of command of the Brigade, Barthel replaced him as chief Brigade political commissar. George Nathan, who had commanded the British company in the XIV Brigade in its first action at Lopera, became the first chief of staff of the XV Brigade.[30] One of the few non-Communists who achieved a relatively high military post in the International Brigades, Nathan was promoted to major upon his appointment as chief of staff. Following Nathan's being killed in action an ex-regular German army officer, Lieutenant Colonel Klaus, filled that post. Klaus, a member of the German Communist party since 1927, had been living in exile in France since 1933 and arrived in Spain in July 1936.[31]

Following the pattern set by the earlier Brigades, the new battalions were based and trained at villages in the vicinity of Albacete. The British battalion began formation at Madrigueras on December 27, 1936, with a nucleus of about 150 men. Following the return of the XIV Brigade from its unhappy experience at Lopera and its brief period of action in the Madrid sector in January, the remnants of the British company of that unit joined their compatriots at Madrigueras. By January 1937 the British battalion had grown to some 500 men. The battalion, which included a number of Scots and Irishmen, first adopted the name "Saklavata" in honor of an Indian Communist who had once been a member of the British parliament. But the name never took firm hold and the unit became generally known simply as the British battalion.[32]

The men in charge of training and organizing the British at Madrigueras were Wilfred Macartney, Tom Wintringham, and D.F. Springhall.[33] Macartney, in command of the battalion during its training period, was a "flamboyant journalist of the Left" who though not a member of the Communist party had once served a prison term for giving military secrets to the Soviet Union. Macartney had served as a British officer in the World War and proved to be an effective organizer of men and formulator of a realistic training program at Madrigueras. His most formidable problems involved the maintenence of a modicum of discipline and sobriety among what a fellow officer and subsequent commander of the battalion called "a mixed mob—ex-servicemen, hunger marchers, political enthusiasts, and honest toughs and queer'uns."[34]

Just prior to the battalion's going into combat in early February, Macartney was shot in the leg by Peter Kerrigan, a functionary of the British Communist party and at that time chief British political commissar at Albacete. The British party hierarchy apparently did not want Macartney, a nonparty member, to lead the battalion into combat. He was being relieved of command when the shooting, presumably accidental, occurred.[35] As a result of Macartney's incapacitation, Wintringham assumed command of the battalion. A graduate of Oxford's Balliol College and more recently editor of the Communist *Left Review* and military editor for the British *Daily Worker,* Wintringham was a charter member of the clique of intellectuals who found a home in the British Communist party. He had been among twelve British Communists who were convicted and imprisoned in 1925 for violation of the Incitement to Mutiny Act.[36] Although he had served in the British army in the World War and had read Clausewitz and Liddell Hart, his views on war were based, as he put it, less on their theories than on "those of Frederich Engels, and on the general Marxist idea of the connections between war and politics."[37]

The first political commissars of the battalion were D.F. Springhall and George Aitken, both functionaries of the British Communist party.[38] Fred Copeman, an ex-British navy man who had been court-martialed as a leader of a mutiny in 1931 and had been a member of the Communist party since 1932, quickly came to occupy a leading position in the battalion. Another longtime party member who later assumed command of the battalion when Wintringham was wounded was Jock Cunningham, a man who had been imprisoned for his part in a mutiny of British troops in Jamaica in 1920. By the end of January the British battalion, by then numbering some 600 men, most of them Communist party members, was organized into four companies plus auxilliary units and stood ready for combat. The battalion had received a longer period of training and organization than any previous International unit.[39]

The French battalion called itself the "6 Fevrier" in honor of the political riots in Paris on that date in 1934. The battalion trained at Tarazona under its military commander, Captain Fort, a French Socialist who had served as an officer in the French army in the World War and as a reserve lieutenant since that time. The first political commissar of the battalion, a French Communist who went by the name "Galli" in Spain, was later replaced as political commissar of the battalion by the French Communist Durbecq. Durbecq had been a functionary in the French party's labor union work prior to the Spanish war, a position he had used to recruit large numbers of Frenchmen to fight in Spain before arriving in Albacete himself in January 1937.[40]

The fourth battalion, composed of Slavs and Italians, had some difficulty in deciding on a name. The Yugoslavs in the battalion wanted to call the battalion the "Diura Diakovich," in honor of the leader of the Yugoslavian Communist party and member of the executive committee of the Comintern. Due to the large number of other nationalities in the battalion, however, they finally settled on the name of the chief of the Comintern, Dimitroff. The Dimitroff battalion trained at Mahora and included four companies of different national composition. The first consisted of mixed Slavic and Balkan elements including Yugoslavs, Bulgarians, Czechs, and Rumanians; the second was predominantly Polish; the third, Italian; while the fourth, the machine gun company, contained a mixture of nationalities.[41]

The commander of the Dimitroff battalion, a Bulgarian Communist called Grebenaroff, came from among that numerous group of European Communists who had been living in the Soviet Union prior to the Spanish conflict and whom the Comintern used as cadres for the International Brigades. Grebenaroff, a man of twenty-eight years of age, had attended the Soviet military school in Moscow. He proved to be both a fervent Communist and a courageous combat commander until killed by enemy fire in the first action of the Dimitroff battalion. The political commissar of the battalion, a German called Furman, had a brief and stormy career in the Brigades. A Communist fanatic who resented anyone outside the party being placed in any position of authority in the Brigades, he soon became the source of a near mutiny among some of the officers in the Dimitroff battalion over the appointment of a non-Communist to command. Although Furman, like Grebenaroff, came to Spain directly from the Soviet Union and therefore had a certain aura of sanctity about him, he was subsequently demoted and ultimately shot for his lack of discipline.[42]

Giorgio Anillo, an Italian Communist who had previously been commissar of the Italian company of the Dimitroff battalion, succeeded Furman as battalion commissar. A Bulgarian Communist and Comintern functionary called Tabakoff who had been imprisoned for his role in a Communist insurrection in Bulgaria in 1924 later succeeded Anillo as commissar of the Dimitroff battalion when Anillo and the other Italians were transferred to the Garibaldi battalion. The Croat Communist Vidakovitch commanded the Yugoslav company of the battalion, while a Montenegrin Communist, one Arsenovitch, acted as the company's political commissar. Commanding the Italian company of the Dimitroff battalion was Carlo Penchienati, a former officer in the Italian army and a man of no specific political affiliation. Penchienati later also joined the Garibaldi battalion with the other Italians of the Dimitroffs.[43]

The first contingent of American recruits for the International Brigades arrived in Spain on January 5, 1937, and proceeded through Albacete to their training base at Villanueva de la Jara. Composed primarily of Communists,[44] the American battalion included a large number of Jews, several blacks, and a contingent of Cubans and Puerto Ricans. A number of Irishmen who had fought at Lopera with the British company and had become ruffled because the British *Daily Worker* failed to mention the fact that Irishmen had been among those killed there also joined the American battalion.[45]

The American battalion, in line with the Communist party's Popular Front policy of identifying itself with the historical and patriotic traditions of the various countries, adopted the name "Abraham Lincoln." In the same vein a second American battalion, which had a brief existence later, called itself the "George Washington," and a Canadian battalion, also organized later and which was in fact predominantly American, called itself the "MacKenzie-Papineau."[46]

The American volunteers differed in a number of ways from their European counterparts. They were as a group younger. Only a handful had seen service in the World War. In fact, very few had done any military service at all although a few had received some rudimentary military instruction in college ROTC programs.[47] Strong leadership cadres among the Americans were also notably lacking, partially because of the youth of the group, partially because of its lack of military experience, and partially, and most significantly, because the Communist party in the United States was reluctant to part with its older and more experienced cadres at home. As a result the American contingent not only suffered from poor leadership but was completely at the mercy of the Albacete directorate, since the Americans had no one of sufficient stature in the Communist party of the United States to represent their interest in Spain.[48]

Another difference was that the Americans, even though composed predominantly of Communist party members, were unaccustomed to the strict discipline accepted as a matter of course by their European confreres who had been tempered in the heat of revolutionary and military struggles of which the boys from across the Atlantic had only a vague and romanticized conception. The situation was not made happier by the fact that the Americans were viewed with unrelieved contempt by the Comintern hierarchy of the International Brigades as little more than adolescent dilettantes and were treated accordingly. In fact, the Brigade chieftains originally intended to use the Americans as piecemeal replacements for other units rather than form a separate American battalion.[49]

As a result of these shortcomings the Americans experienced serious disciplinary problems from the beginning. In the absence of any real military or political leadership or clear authority on the part of any of the Americans at Villanueva de la Jara, the men attempted to operate on the lines of the Communist party at home. The problem remained, however, that while at home everyone knew where authority lay, at Villanueva de la Jara no one did. Since the Americans in Spain came largely from the same low to middle status in the party, none of them could clearly assume policical control as an established higher party functionary could have. Phil Bard, ex-cartoonist for the United States *Daily Worker,* acted as political commissar of the first contingent of Americans and was apparently intended to serve as American base commissar at Albacete. Bard soon returned to the United States, however, and never functioned effectively as political representative of the Americans at Albacete. He was followed in that post by George Brodsky, a minor functionary in the party who proved completely unable to cope with the job. As a result of all this the Americans at Villanueva de la Jara spent most of their time and energy in political meetings. Cliques and dissension developed to the point where arrests and counterarrests were being made by the various factions on one another's members. In the delicate phraseology of a recent apologist: "They were not properly oriented to the exact nature and need of a 'People's Army.' "[50]

United States party headquarters in New York, concerned by reports of the chaos in Villaneuva de la Jara, sent over Sam Stember, a second or third echelon party bureaucrat, to try to instill some kind of political discipline into the sad disarray of Americans in Spain. Commissar Stember had his problems too as can be seen from the following somewhat hysterical statement signed by him in the Brigade journal:

> Those who challenge the military or political authority of . . . commanders are self seekers who are no less guilty than the deserters who have been sentenced to hard labor in the Labor Battalion at a recent trial.
>
> The challenge manifested itself in the formation of committees which make demands on the Brigade as if they were framing demands against the Capitalist Class; in a form of disruption that tends to demoralize the ranks of the honest soldiers who volunteered and have a mandate from the working class at home to defeat fascism at all costs. . . . In the American Battalion, such a committee flared up recently and for a short time demoralized the Battalion until finally order and discipline was reestablished. But these traiterous elements are waiting for still further opportunities. . . .
>
> Our slogan must be, no traitors in our midst; absolute discipline; one unified, single command.[51]

The military command picture in the American battalion was as bleak as the political. Jim Harris, a party member who claimed to have had long experience in the United States Army, had been appointed military commander of the first group of Americans sent to Spain by Fred Brown, a Comintern representative in New York, and Alan Johnson, allegedly a former United States Army officer, who later played a role in the Brigades himself.[52] On January 11 an American named Robert Merriman arrived at Villanueva de la Jara directly from the Soviet Union.[53] Merriman, who had received ROTC training during his college career at the University of Nevada (and, according to some sources, further training at the Lenin Institute in Moscow), immediately began to assume a leading role in the battalion.[54] Shortly after his arrival, Merriman, accompanied by Stember, went directly to International Brigades headquarters at Albacete where they spoke with Marty and Vidal.[55]

Marty, furious with the Americans, vented his spleen, calling them "spoiled cry babies" and threatening to send them all back home.[56] Marty finally calmed down and Merriman and Stember returned to

The Brigades

Villanueva accompanied by Vidal, who informed the Americans bluntly that they were in an army in which discipline and authority were of paramount importance and must be accepted. He then confirmed Stember as political commissar and Harris as military commander and appointed Merriman battalion adjutant. It seems most likely that Merriman was slated to take over the military command of the American battalion from the beginning. Vidal may well have been governed by the assumption that since Harris had been appointed "military commander" by the American party hierarchy it would be impolitic to dismiss him summarily, especially in view of the already delicate situation in the battalion. Whatever the original intention, Merriman, virtually from the time of his arrival, did assume de facto command.[57] After having settled down under the triumvirate of Stember, Harris, and Merriman, the Americans engaged in some rudimentary military training and instruction. In fact no planned program of training existed in the International Brigades at that time. Each unit had to improvise its own.[58]

During the first week in February Marty and a contingent of Albacete chieftains arrived at Villanueva de la Jara to review the Americans. The battalion, which had by then grown to some 400 men, received approval from Marty on its progress. He told the troops that they would soon be moved to the new International Brigade camp at Pozo Rubio. That, however, never came to pass.[59]

The battalion, as then organized, consisted of two rifle companies and a machine gun company. The first company, which contained a Cuban-Puerto Rican section, an Irish section, and an American section was commanded by Inver Marlowe, a British Communist who had been on the editorial staff of the London *Daily Worker* and more recently on the staff of the American *Daily Worker*. Marlowe went under his pseudonym, John Scott, in Spain. Stephen Daduck, a man who had previously flown a fighter plane for the Loyalists, commanded the second company, and Douglas Seacord, who had once served in the United States Army, commanded the third.[60]

On February 12 the American battalion received orders to move out for Chinchon, a town located in the area in which a large-scale battle then raged. Just prior to their departure Vidal appointed Merriman and Harris to the rank of captain and issued them revolvers and binoculars. Meanwhile the battalion paraded in the bullring at Albacete and received weapons, equipment, and the usual pep talk from Marty.[61]

Sometime between the battalion's departure from Albacete and its entry into combat, the Albacete chieftans removed Harris from command and replaced him with Merriman. The explanations of how and why this happened vary. According to one story Harris became unnerved upon the battalion's being ordered into action, displayed unstable and irresponsible characteristics, and had to be replaced. According to others the Brigade staff concocted this story about Harris as a justification for getting rid of him and appointing Merriman to command the battalion, something they had intended to do all along.[62]

At any rate Vidal named Merriman commander and the battalion saw its first action under Merriman's command. Upon their arrival at Chinchon, General Gall ordered the battalion into reserved positions near Morata. Somewhere between Chinchon and Morata, Merriman stopped the convoy long enough to allow each man to fire five rounds from his weapon into a hillside. For many that was the first time they had fired a rifle although they had been in Spain for over a month.[63]

6 A Military Overview

The entry of the XI Brigade into combat on November 8, 1936, opened a five-month period in which the Internationals played a crucial, perhaps decisive, military role in the Spanish war. While a detailed treatment of the campaigns of the International Brigades is beyond the scope of this study, a brief synopsis and overview of the military developments in the Madrid area and the role played by the Internationals in them will serve to illustrate a number of factors of importance in understanding the politics of the Brigades, both then and subsequently.

The battles in and around Madrid lasting from November 1936 to March 1937 can be most easily visualized as three phases of a five-month-long campaign in which the Nationalists sought to conquer and the Loyalists sought to defend the Spanish capital. The first phase, opening in the first week of November and lasting until November 25, saw the Nationalist effort to take the city by direct frontal assault. The second phase, opening on November 29 and lasting until January 10, involved the Nationalist effort to envelop Madrid on its western flank. The third and final phase, lasting from February 6 to March 15, was the effort to achieve the same objectives on Madrid's eastern flank.

Phase one entered its most critical stage when, on the night of November 14–15, Nationalist forces succeeded in forcing a crossing of the Manzanares River and quickly pushed up the hills into the University City on the southwest outskirts of Madrid where they occupied several buildings. The Madrid command rushed in reinforcements including the XI and XII International Brigades.[1] The fighting in the University City quickly developed into a bitter and relentless struggle at close range with no quarter asked or given on either side. The combatants converted the university buildings into fortresses, sandbagging and barricading windows and doors with whatever could be found. They mounted machine guns to cover open approaches, dug communication trenches between buildings, burrowed tunnels under streets swept by enemy fire, and attacked for limited objectives. At times both sides occupied parts of the same building and fought for floors and even rooms. The battle raged until on November 25, after some twenty days of furious fighting, the

Nationalist command gave up the attempt to storm Madrid by frontal assault.[2]

During the University City fighting several changes were made in the Brigades' command structure and organization. Among the more important of these was the elevation of Kleber to command of the entire Madrid battle sector, a position he had in fact filled since his arrival with the XI Brigade in early November. He now commanded not only the XI and XII International Brigades but a number of Spanish units assigned to that area, a total of some 18,000 effectives.[3] Hans Kahle moved up from command of the André battalion to replace Kleber as commander of the XI Brigade, while Ludwig Renn moved over from command of the Thaelmann battalion to become Kahle's chief of staff. The German Communist Richard Staimer replaced Renn as commander of the Thaelmann. At the same time the Thaelmann battalion was shifted from the XII Brigade to the XI and, in exchange, the Dombrowski went from the XI Brigade to the XII. Thus, the XI Brigade consisted of the two predominantly German units, André and Thaelmann, and the mainly French Commune de Paris, while the XII included the Italian Garibaldi, the French André Marty, and the Polish Dombrowski. Several changes in the political commissar hierarchy also took place. The Italian Nicoletti, who had been XI Brigade commissar, moved up with Kleber. Both Hans Beimler, the leading German politico, and Louis Schuster, commissar of the Thaelmann battalion, were killed at the front during the fighting. Albert Denz, a German Communist, became XI Brigade commissar. Longo, who had filled the post of XII Brigade commissar, reassumed his role as number two man in the overall Brigade political hierarchy with the title of inspector general of the Brigades while the German Gustav Regler filled the post of XII Brigade political commissar.[4]

Phase two of the battle for Madrid opened on November 29 and lasted, with but brief respites, until the middle of January. The Nationalist command hoped that by shifting the action away from the congestion of the immediate Madrid area the advantages of better organization, tactical maneuverability, and firepower, which had been so important in their earlier successes, would once again prove decisive. The Nationalist thrusts followed one another in regular succession, swinging in ever wider arcs in the effort to outflank the capital's defenders. But the attackers were to be denied. For, as these events showed, the forces now defending Madrid were not the disorganized militia that had been handled so easily in the march toward the capital. The hardheaded Red army professionals, the Soviet tanks,

A Military Overview

artillery and aviation under their direct command, and the International Brigades, also commanded by professionals, proved quite a different matter.

The last and most powerful thrust of this second phase of the campaign came on January 3. The Madrid command threw the XI Brigade into the breach and, at the price of its virtual destruction as a fighting unit, it broke the momentum of the onslaught.[5] Meanwhile the XII and XIV Brigades were moved in and, supported by substantial artillery and armor, brought the offensive to a halt. With this move, the Nationalist effort to envelop Madrid on the west ended.[6]

In all these battles the International Brigades played the major role. Viewed by the Madrid command as the most reliable troops at its disposal, the Internationals were consistently thrown into the most critical point of battle and, as consistently, absorbed the Nationalist blows at the price of extremely high casualties. Of the XI and XII Brigades, *Pravda* correspondent Koltsov wrote, "Both have fought incessantly for more than a month.... They have lost almost forty percent of their effectives."[7] The Nationalists would try to take Madrid again, from another direction, but for the present they, as well as their adversaries, needed time to lick their wounds, restore their strength, and gird themselves for future efforts.

The third and final phase of the battle for Madrid opened on February 6. The Nationalists struck hard in a new attempt to envelop Madrid, this time to the east of the city. The assault broke the front wide open and, as usual, the Madrid command looked to the Internationals to save the day. The XII Brigade was rushed in first to blunt the thrust and the XI Brigade was ordered out of its rest quarters in Murcia. Despite the Loyalist command's efforts to contain the assault, the Nationalists succeeded in forcing a crossing of the Jarama River on the night of February 10 and rapidly extended themselves along its east bank.

On February 12 the recently formed XV International Brigade moved into the battle. Its British and Dimitroff battalions arrived at the front that day and both were quickly decimated in the severe fighting that followed. The British occupied a ridge called, from then on, "suicide hill." When the battalion withdrew that night only some 125 effectives remained of the 600 who had gone up in the morning. Most of the officers and political commissars had been killed or wounded. The Dimitroffs, too, paid a high price for their first day of combat, suffering some 350 casualties.

The last of the International Brigades to enter the battle, the XIV, arrived on February 14. By that time the Nationalist offensive had lost its momentum. Indeed, for the Nationalist the fourteenth was "el dia triste de la Jarama," the sad day which "extinguished totally the illusions of all who participated in the battle." Nationalist officers were impressed by the fighting capabilities displayed by their opponents. "The machine-gun and rifle fire is intense. The enemy fights with a tenacity unknown until now.... The Russian tanks appear constantly, firing machine-gun and cannon, and disappearing before anti-tank pieces can be used.... The numbers of our fallen is impressive."[8]

Not the least of the reasons for the Nationalist defeat was the expertise of the Soviet general Pavlov ("Pablo" in Spain) in directing the defense and especially in his tank actions which repeatedly smashed Nationalist drives. As the Spanish Communist commander Enrique Lister, who participated in the Jarama campaign, put it: "General Pablo was the true organizer of the Republican resistance during those days.... The role played by the tanks was at times decisive. Their rapid counter-attacks often broke the carefully prepared enemy attacks." Of this the Soviet general Voronov, who devoted his talents to commanding the Loyalist artillery, recalled that during the Jarama fighting his colleague Pavlov said to him: "Destroy with your artillery the anti-tank guns and my tanks will give the enemy a blow like they never had."[9]

Indeed the role of the Soviet-Comintern combine reached its highest level during that period. On February 15 the Madrid command carried through a reorganization of its forces in the Jarama area into four divisions and a tank corps. The XII and XIV International Brigades along with a Spanish brigade formed Division A commanded by General Walter (Swierczewski). Division B, composed of the XI and XV International Brigades and a Spanish brigade was commanded by General Gall (Galicz). A third division, all Spanish, was commanded by the Spanish Communist Lister, and the tank corps by the Soviet general Pavlov. Thus the Soviet-Communist command role in this army of the Jarama was almost complete, with two of the four divisions commanded by Comintern generals and composed primarily of the International Brigades, a third division commanded by a Communist stalwart, and the tank corps commanded by a Soviet general. In addition, all units, International and Spanish, had Soviet advisers. The brunt of the fighting was borne by the International Brigades and the chief direction of the defense came from the Comintern-Soviet officers.[10]

Following the reorganization of its forces, the Madrid command, by then with a superiority of manpower in the area, sought to retake the ground lost to the Nationalists. The major thrust of the counterattack focused in the area of the Pingarron heights. Chosen to spearhead the attack was the recently arrived American battalion. This, their first taste of combat, proved to be yet another bloody debacle. Aerial and artillery preparation was weak and ineffective and the promised tank support failed to materialize. The Spanish battalion on the American flank moved out of its trenches on schedule only to be met by such a hail of enemy fire that the troops immediately returned to their positions. At that point the XV Brigade chief of staff, Lieutenant Colonel Klaus, ordered the Americans to attack. Battalion commander Merriman, seeing that the heavy enemy fire would make the attack suicidal, contacted General Gall by telephone and attempted to explain the situation. Gall demanded that Merriman attack at once and, using one of his favorite expressions, "at all cost." At the same time, Springhall, the British political commissar, and Lieutenant Wattis, a British officer attached to the Brigade staff, arrived at Merriman's side with orders for the Americans to advance.

Merriman then ordered the attack. As the men moved out they met the same deadly fire that had driven the Spaniards back. Many were hit the instant they left the trenches. Merriman was shot through the shoulder as he gave the signal to advance and Seacord, the recently appointed battalion adjutant, was killed. Seeing the massacre, a number of the Americans refused to leave the trenches until forced to do so at pistol point by Wattis. The untouched Nationalist machine gunners cut the poorly trained Americans down by the score. The attack stopped dead. The men, wounded and unwounded, remained pinned down behind whatever bit of cover they could find until the dark of night allowed them to crawl back to their trenches. At nine o'clock that night Morris Maken, who had survived for nine hours in no-man's-land and was the only officer in the battalion still alive and unwounded, found less than 120 men of the battalion who could answer roll call. Later counts showed some 120 killed and 175 hospitalized for wounds. Less than 125 effectives remained of the 400 men who had composed the battalion that morning.[11]

Following the debacle of February 27 the Madrid command abandoned its efforts to dislodge the Nationalists, and the dawn of February 28 broke cold, windy, and strangely quiet over the Jarama. The losses sustained by all four of the International Brigades that participated in the Jarama fighting were extremely heavy. Many of the battalions suffered on the order of 75 percent casualties. Included among the killed and wounded were a high number of the International's military and political cadres including Grebenaroff, commander of the Dimitroff battalion, Wintringham, commander of the British battalion, Fort, commander of the 6 Fevrier battalion, Merriman, commander of the American battalion, Pacciardi, commander of the Garibaldi battalion, Rebiere, political commissar of the XI Brigade, Azzi, political commissar of the Garibaldi, and Galli, political commisar of 6 Fevrier battalion.

Militarily the battles of the Jarama resulted in another inconclusive standoff between the opposing armies. The Nationalists had maintained their initiative in the war, had taken ground, and successfully held most of it. But they had failed to achieve the strategic goal of the operation, the envelopment of Madrid. The Loyalist had succeeded in containing the Nationalist drive, thereby ensuring Madrid's (and perhaps Loyalist Spain's) continued existence. They had not, despite superiority in numbers and the large-scale assistance of the Internationals and the Soviets, been capable of launching an effective counteroffensive or of retaking the lost ground. In the longer view, and in retrospect, the failure of the Nationalists to break Madrid's defenses at the Jarama signaled a decisive watershed in the war. Before that became clear, however, Madrid's defenders faced one more challenge.

It came on March 8, when Mussolini's expeditionary force in Spain, the Corpo di Truppe Voluntarie (CTV), launched an offensive from the northeast toward Guadalajara. The plan envisioned the establishment of contact between the Nationalist forces on the Jarama with the CTV, thus achieving what the Jarama offensive had failed to accomplish. The Madrid command reacted by committing the best of the units at its disposal to the new front, chief among which were the XI and XII International Brigades.

Forward elements of both the XI and XII Brigades made initial contact with advancing Italian troops that morning. Heavy fighting ensued with the attacking forces making but little headway against stiff opposition from the Internationals. Meanwhile the Madrid command continued to commit all the troops it could muster to the sector. By March 11 the defensive line stood fairly firm and was supported by increasing numbers of reserves. The weather too came to the aid of the defenders when rain began falling and continued for several days. The mechanized units of the CTV bogged down in the mud while fog and overcast skies effectively deprived them of air cover. By March 13 the Italian offensive had clearly failed of its purpose and the CTV's commander, General Roatta, made clear to the Nationalist high command his desire to withdraw his forces and have them replaced by Spanish units.

A Military Overview

At the same time the Madrid command began preparation for a counteroffensive. On March 14 General Ivanov, one of the Soviet officers who had participated in the Guadalajara fighting, spoke to the staff of the XI Brigade. In high good humor the general informed them that having stopped the Italian offensive, they would now strike a strong counterblow. Renn and Kahle looked at him in astonishment. Calling him "Comrade General," Kahle said that the Brigade had not recovered from the past days of severe fighting. Nevertheless, said the general, the offensive would be made.[12] It began on March 18 spearheaded by the XI and XII Brigades. Despite the general disorganization and demoralization of the CTV forces, however, the Loyalist offensive soon lost its momentum and within a few days the fighting virtually ended. The long and bloody siege against Madrid came to a close.

Clearly, between November 1936 and March 1937 the defense of Madrid depended heavily on the efforts and the manpower of the International Brigades. If we take into consideration replacements and reinforcements, the number of International troops involved in the Madrid fighting by the end of December was in the vicinity of twelve thousand and must have reached between fifteen and twenty thousand by February. These units were consistently used as shock troops to be thrown in wherever the fighting was most intense and the situation most critical. The undeniably significant role of the Internationals in the defense of the Spanish capital led many to see the Brigades as the "saviors of Madrid." To take just two examples, the Italian Socialist Pietro Nenni, who was intimately involved in Spain at the time, wrote: "The contribution of the International Brigades was, without exaggeration, decisive." And the American journalist Louis Fischer, a close supporter of both the Brigades and the Loyalist cause, wrote of the Internationals: "They saved Madrid."[13]

Others have objected to this view, feeling that it ignores the essential contribution of the Spaniards themselves in defending the capital. The point remains debatable. It seems safe to say, however, that while the Internationals did not, and probably could not have, defended Madrid alone, Madrid would not have been defended successfully without them. Thus, while giving due weight to the essential Spanish contribution, the role of the Internationals was probably decisive. But, in stressing the role of the Brigades, a larger and even more crucial point is often overlooked. That is that the Brigades were only one component of a larger, and even more surely decisive, effort in the defense of the Spanish capital, namely, the multifaceted enterprise of the Soviet-Comintern organization.

Following the battle of the Jarama and its immediate but much less sanguinary sequel in Guadalajara, the nature of the Spanish war changed. The Nationalists gave up on their effort to take Madrid and end the conflict quickly. Instead they settled down to building a large army composed chiefly of Spanish conscripts and, girding for the long war, shifted their main attention to conquering the northern provinces. The Loyalist regime likewise concentrated on building a strong central government and a large People's Army based on conscription and under that government's authority. This meant an end to the heavy fighting in the central (Madrid) area (for several months at least) and, for the Internationals, a prolonged period of relative surcease from major combat.

It also meant a qualitative change in the relative importance of the Internationals in the war. With the development of an army of several hundred thousand men by the Loyalist regime, the participation of a few thousand foreigners as rank-and-file troops could no longer make a fundamental difference as it had earlier. In addition to the relative decrease in the military significance of the International Brigades, the actual number of foreign combatants steadily declined after the spring of 1937. This resulted from both the high casualty rates among the Internationals and from the decrease in the numbers of new men who could be recruited. That ready reservoir of political émigrés and Communist militants which had supplied the bulk of the early Internationals had been, by the spring of 1937, substantially exhausted. Once that limited resource had been drained it became more and more difficult to recruit men for the Brigades. No doubt also the reports of disillusioned Brigade men who had managed to get out of Spain, the reports of the Communist terror, and the generally growing awareness that joining the Brigades was less a romantic adventure than a good way to die young played a part in reducing the numbers of men who might otherwise have been tempted to join.

Both the relative and the absolute decline in the military significance of the Internationals was clearly shown by the so-called Brunete offensive launched by the Loyalists in July 1937. Employing 50,000 first-line troops organized into army corps and divisions, the offensive proved without doubt that the Loyalist regime had succeeded in creating a substantial army. Less encouraging, to some at least, the offensive had been designed chiefly by the Soviet military staff, and the command structure of the key combat units remained heavily Communist and foreign. For example, the five International Brigades which participated in the operation all served under Comintern divisional commanders: the XIII and XV with General Gall's Fifteenth Division, the XII and CL[14] with General Kleber's Forty-fifth Division, and the XI with General Walter's Thirty-fifth Division. While the International Brigades continued to be among the best of the new People's Army's combat units they were clearly no longer so crucial to Loyalist military strength as before. The numerical weight of the International Brigades in the Brunete campaign, some 15,000 effectives, amounted to only about a fourth of the total and even this figure included large numbers of Spaniards within their ranks. The progressive filling of the ranks of the Brigades with Spaniards had in fact been going on for some time as the only way of replacing casualties. It was a process that could not help but alter fundamentally the nature of the Brigades. After Brunete, 60 to 70 percent of the XII Brigade were Spanish.[15] The percentage was as great or greater in the XI and XIII Brigades. The process continued throughout the Brigades' sojourn in Spain and gradually transformed even the XIV and XV into predominantly Spanish units with a foreign command. "The XV Brigade is so diluted with Spanish soldiers that the Internationals are acting mostly as non-coms," wrote the American volunteer Voros during the Ebro campaign in 1938. The Brigades were rounding up every available man and putting them into the decimated combat units. They were "a pitiful lot ... men ruthlessly evicted from the hospitals, half-healed ... unfit for battle; the sweepings of the military offices in the rear, soft and flabby." And, he continued, the few new recruits still trickling in from the United States and elsewhere were handed rifles and sent to the front with a week or two, if that, of training—"lambs offered up for the slaughter."[16]

From the Brunete campaign to the end of the war, the main field of action shifted from the central (Madrid) area to the eastern (Aragon) area. There the Loyalists launched three major offensives: the Aragon or Belchite-Quinto campaign of August-September 1937, the Teruel campaign of December 1937-January 1938, and the Ebro offensive of July 1938. Each followed a similar pattern: initial breakthrough, stall, Nationalist counterattack, Loyalist retreat. None proved successful in the long run. While the International Brigades fought in all these campaigns, their military significance, in an army of 500,000 men, was strictly limited.[17]

7 Comintern Politics

While the purely military role of the International Brigades became of progressively less consequence after the spring and summer of 1937, the political significance of the Brigades as an element in the Comintern's overall operation in Spain (and in the wider Popular Front strategy) continued to be seen as of the greatest importance. Thus the Communists sought to maintain the Brigades as a viable and reliable Comintern-controlled force within the framework of the Loyalist political-military structure.

To succeed in this objective over the long run presented a greater challenge than it had during the earlier period when the Brigades had consisted almost entirely of disciplined and highly motivated party cadres, when most internal problems could easily be brushed aside in the first flush of enthusiasm, and when the Loyalist regime itself had little cohesion or authority. But to the Communists the effort was worthwhile, for from their perspective the Brigades offered a number of political assets and advantages which they would not willingly relinquish.

For one thing, so long as the Brigades continued to exist as Comintern controlled units, they remained a source of prestige, political leverage, and reliable military strength for the Communists within the Loyalist camp. The Communists made no secret of the pride they took in the military prowess of the Brigades and stressed from the beginning the key role performed by the Brigades in setting an example of military organization, discipline, and efficiency for the Spaniards. That example, they held, had been largely responsible for the successful creation of the Loyalist People's Army.[1] "The International Brigades by their high technical qualifications and their discipline, have been one of the bases of this new Army," wrote André Marty. "This has been one of the essential services that the International Brigades have rendered the Spanish Republic.... The International Brigades ... have been a living example of what must be done to win the war."[2] Franz Dahlem, leading German member of the Brigade commissariat, wrote: "The International Brigades exerted quite a considerable influence over the growth of the military and moral strength of the Spanish People's army.... They have maintained their character as the basic brigades of the People's army, its core."[3] The Brigade press emphasized this point repeatedly. The "immense prestige" and the "discipline on which they [the Brigades] were founded did much to help the remodeling of the army," claimed the *Volunteer for Liberty*. The *Boletín de Información* pointed out how the Internationals had aided the Spaniards by their example of "discipline and the maximum acquisition of military technique."[4]

Comintern spokesmen continued to insist on the significance of the Brigades in the military sphere throughout their existence in Spain. Addressing himself to this question, Longo told a conference of political commissars in August 1937, "The International Brigades have had a great role in the resistance. Now we must be the animators of the decisive victory."[5] Similarly the Brigades' school for political commissars, as late as 1938, continued to instruct its charges that the Brigades yet had a crucial role to play: "To build the People's Army, to conquer all weaknesses, to aid the Spanish Popular Front."[6] In this context, too, the possibility always existed that the Communists would see fit to take over the Loyalist regime completely by some type of coup d' etat. Two of the most knowledgeable students of the Spanish war have concluded that they could have done so at most any time.[7] Although never put to the test, had the Communists ever decided to do so, their control of the Brigades would have been a key element in their chances of success.

The Communists saw the Brigades as much more than simply a reliable military and political force within the framework of Loyalist Spain, as important as that undoubtedly was. For the Brigades could and did serve a number of political purposes for the Comintern on a larger stage than Spain itself. One of the most important of these focused on the Brigades as representing the most outstanding example, the embodiment in action, of that international and proletarian solidarity of which there had long been much talk but little visible evidence. The International Brigades, commented the *Communist International*, "represent the highest expression of international solidarity, of the anti-fascist united front and of proletarian honor, devotion and courage."[8] The Brigades were, according to the Communists, "the pride of the working class, the *avant garde* of combat ... a symbol of antifascist unity ... the greatest and most active force of international solidarity ... the burning point of international politics."[9] They represented the "highest expression, the most living witness of the solidarity of the labouring masses." They constituted "the highest testimony to international solidarity."[10] The Spanish Communists were equally unstinting in their praise of the Brigades, calling them a "living expression of international solidarity of the popular masses throughout the world." "The Comintern was proud," said

Mundo Obrero, "on counting many of its best militants on the battlefields of Spain."[11]

The Communists recognized too the significant prestige and leverage that the Brigades brought to them not only in Spain but elsewhere. Numerous statements by leading Communist spokesmen attested to this attitude. "One of the greatest achievements that our party has ever made is the building of the Lincoln and Washington battalions of the International Brigades," declared Earl Browder.[12] The central committee of the United States party assured the American members of the Brigades, "Your heroic deeds . . . have brought glory and honor to the working class. . . . Your name has become a symbol of heroism and inspiration to all of us at home." Maurice Thorez, leader of the French party, in referring to the overall Communist role in the Spanish war, stressed particularly the contribution of the party in having had "many of its best men" fight in the International Brigades.[13] Calling the Brigades an "International of steeled and disciplined revolutionary fighters," British Communist chief Harry Pollitt said, "The comrades of the International Brigades, now covering itself with glory in Spain, are a real People's Army." Later, he declared, "The Spirit of the Anglo-American volunteers is an inspiration to the movement at home."[14] The German party hierarch Franz Dahlem wrote: "The Communist International, the Communist Parties of Germany and Austria, as the Communist Parties of other countries, can justly be proud of their fighters in Spain. They have borne aloft the Party banner." "The International Brigades show in practice the high value of the International solidarity of the defenders of democracy and, thus, in all capitalist countries assist the growth of the anti-fascist People's Front,"[15] claimed the Comintern's official publication. The Brigade *Boletín de Información* agreed: "The International Brigades are a powerful lever for the creation of united international action, for the creation of the international People's Front. The unity between all anti-fascists is an accomplished fact in the International Brigades. The Brigades are a school for internationalism." The *Communist International,* once more stated: "The experience of the International Brigade is above all of tremendous positive significance on the wide field of the anti-Fascist struggle in all countries. The example of the . . . Brigade must be an important step toward the unification of all anti-Fascist forces for a similar struggle in other countries."[16]

The Comintern also saw the Brigades as an instrument through which new members could be brought into the Communist parties. That would be accomplished directly through proselytization of non-party men within the Brigades and indirectly through the enhanced attraction of the party to a broad spectrum of persons because of its identification with the Brigades and the Loyalist cause in Spain. "I make the categoric statement," said Robert Minor, a leading United States party hierarch, "that the heroic fighting of the American boys in Spain, and the consequent interest and sympathy and pride awakening among the American people are a major factor in the political life of this country."[17] That the Communists made a continuous effort to proselytise nonparty men within the Brigades was clear from both the content of the Brigade press and from the policies followed by the political commissars. They approached this task for the most part, as befitted the general Popular Front orientation of the time, by constantly emphasizing the correctness of Communist policy in Spain and elsewhere, by consistently representing the Comintern as the guiding light (and only trustworthy component) of antifascism and by repeated and unstinted praise and glorification of the Soviet Union. On this theme the United States party representative John Little, who had just returned from a visit to Spain, reported to a New York party convention on the American members of the Brigade: "Their fighting spirit, love for our Party, love for the Soviet Union have increased a hundredfold.... They want above everything else to continue to build our party."[18]

Another important view of the Brigades as seen from within the structure of the Comintern focused on their value as a forge from which would come "steeled and disciplined revolutionary fighters,"[19] cadres who would lead the party's troops in future battles throughout the world. On the battlefields of Spain, Longo told the men of the Brigades, "we have learned lessons that will serve us and our own peoples in the struggles in our own countries. We have been able to learn important political lessons."[20] That these lessons were to be applied in other times and places was clear from the pledge taken by graduates of the XV Brigade officer training school. "We pledge an eternal fight against fascism wherever it may be found and in whatever guise it may hide; we pledge to the international working class that we will fulfill the trust they have placed in us."[21]

Men who served in the Brigades were looked upon, said Marty, as "worthy members of the World Party of Bolsheviks. They are worthy sons of that Party which, formed and led by the greatest minds of our time, Lenin and Stalin, has overthrown the Old World ... All are worthy of that great Antifascist and Communist, Georgi Dimitroff." The *Communist International* opined, "The working class must understand what a treasure and what experience the fighters for freedom now returned from Spain bring with them, into what worthy cadres of the movement these fighters have grown." The American party spokesman and sometimes political commissar in Spain Bill Lawrence wrote: "Our Party, though making terrific sacrifices [in Spain], is at the same time developing marvelous cadres."[22]

In line with that attitude the Comintern hierarchy treated those party cadres who served in the International Brigades with special favor and granted them special recognition and opportunities for advancement within the party ranks. At a meeting of the politburo of the Communist party of the United States in November 1937, party chief Earl Browder introduced four men recently back from Spain: "The presence of these leading comrades is of special signficance for us," he said, "because they represent ... one of the greatest assets that our Party has.... The fact that these comrades are back with us now gives us an opportunity to show how much the Party appreciates such sterling, fundamental contributions." Browder then proposed that Steve Nelson, one of the four comrades present, be recommended for "co-option into the Central Committee of our Party."[23]

Given the value of the Brigades in the eyes of the Communists it followed that they would make every effort to maintain the Brigades as an autonomous Comintern-controlled force. The effort to do so became a central theme for the Brigade political hierarchy throughout their sojourn in Spain.

The nexus through which the Comintern exercised control over the internal affairs of the International Brigades was the Brigade general political commissariat. The formation and functioning of the political commissariat itself assured that its policies and operations meshed perfectly into the overall Comintern apparatus and policy in Spain. Just as the party controls the state apparatus in Communist countries by filling all key state posts with disciplined party members whose loyalty and duty remain first and last to the party, the Comintern ensured the political reliability of the Brigades by filling all key political (and most military) posts with disciplined party members. Thus the Brigade political commissariat, composed entirely of Communist stalwarts, operated at all times under the discipline and authority of the Comintern. Indeed, it was for all practical purposes simply a direct extension of the Comintern itself.[24]

The Soviet-Comintern apparatus further ensured the reliability of the International Brigades by assigning numerous individuals of non-Russian origin who had been living in the Soviet Union prior to the outbreak of war in Spain to military and political commands throughout the Brigade structure.[25] Some of those so assigned were Soviet army officers while others were trained intelligence and espionage operatives who were or had been used by Soviet military or Comintern intelligence apparatus in various parts of the world. For example, Wilhelm Bahnick, a German Communist, a graduate of the Moscow military-political school, and a member of one of the Comintern's *apparats* in Germany was assigned to the International Brigades. Victor Sukulov, a Latvian by birth, a Red army officer who worked in a Comintern espionage apparatus in Belgium and France in the 1930s, served as captain in the International Brigades.[26]

The Italian Communist Guido Picelli likewise arrived in Spain directly from the Soviet Union. Picelli was apparently something of a hero among Italian Communists for his actions inside Italy during the early 1920s prior to the full consolidation of the Fascist dictatorship. The Italian Communists in the International Brigades evidently expected great things of him and were bitterly disappointed when he was killed in action after only a month or two in Spain.[27] Italian party stalwarts Barontini, Raimondi, and Mallozzi also came to Spain directly from the Soviet Union. Barontini had left Italy for exile in France in 1931 at the orders of the party. Then, in 1933, he had gone to Moscow where he worked for the Comintern. On his arrival in Spain he was appointed political commissar of the Garibaldi battalion and later of the entire XII Brigade. The American Robert Merriman also came to Spain from the Soviet Union and, within a brief time, was placed in command of the American battalion.[28]

Another indication of the complete fusion between the Comintern and the Brigades was the way in which the hierarchs of the Brigades continued to operate quite openly in their capacity as Comintern representatives, not only inside Spain but elsewhere. An outstanding example of that occurred at the meeting between representatives of the Second and Third Internationals in June 1937 in Switzerland. Conspicuous among the five-man Comintern delegation were Longo and Dahlem, both high-ranking commissars of the International Brigades.[29]

That the Comintern considered its functionaries in the Brigades as remaining completely at the disposal of that organization was further demonstrated by the frequent shifting of Communist personnel from the Brigades to other party posts. An example of that interchangeability was the high functionary who had played an important role in the formation and early development of the Brigades, Nicoletti. The party subsequently transferred Nicoletti from the International Brigades to Paris where he assumed the post of editor of the party publication *La Voce degli Italiani.*[30] Likewise, the American David McKelvey White was withdrawn from the Brigades at the volition of the party to be used in another capacity. After a brief tour in Spain the party ordered White out of the Brigades and back to New York where he set up a party front organization known as Friends of the Abraham Lincoln Brigade.[31] The American party also withdrew Bill Lawrence from the Brigades and assigned him to other duties in the United States.[32]

The experience of the American John Gates offers another example of the commissariat's control over Brigade personnel. In the summer of 1937 the political commissariat of the International Brigades offered Gates the choice of remaining with the International Brigades in Spain or returning to the United States where he would be used in propaganda and fund-raising campaigns. Gates chose to remain and the commissariat appointed him political commissar of the American section at Albacete. Similarly, Auguste Lecouer, originally assigned to the International Brigades by the French party, was later pulled out of the Brigades and reassigned to party propaganda work in France.[33] In fact, the commissariat completely controlled Brigade personnel and, in the case of Communist cadres, the commissariat and the various Communist parties moved them in and out of the Brigades at will.

Brigade members were also assigned to partisan, guerrilla, espionage, and sabotage units as well as the police apparatus operated by Soviet and Comintern personnel in Spain. They were recruited as Soviet espionage agents to operate in areas having no relation to the Spanish war. Alexander Foote, for example, a member of the British battalion, returned under orders to England in Semptember 1938, ostensibly for the purpose of attending the Communist party congress in Birmingham. At that time the party leadership assigned him the duty of acting as a courier between Communist party headquarters in London and the command in the British battalion in Spain. Suddenly, however, he received new instructions to go to Geneva, Switzerland. Foote proceeded as instructed and soon found himself working in a Soviet espionage *apparat* for the Red army.[34]

A number of American Brigade men served in one of these categories. Robert Minor, active in a variety of capacities in Spain, recruited Americans from the Brigades to work directly for the Soviet mission.[35] William Aalto, an American who served in one of the guerrilla units that were organized, trained, and controlled directly by the Soviet staff, later wrote an article in which he said, "In Spain, guerrilla warfare was organized under Soviet advice and according to Soviet principles. . . . Our Soviet military advisors in Spain brought us the principles of that science . . . in our guerrilla schools, lessons from the

Red Army's experience were taught us, verbally and through Spanish translations of Red Army manuals."³⁶

The controversy within the Loyalist camp over the use of guerrilla warfare tactics offered a striking example of the way the Comintern apparatus bypassed the Loyalist government, as well as how it controlled the International Brigades. In January 1937, while the XI Brigade was in rest quarters at Murcia, Renn received a visit from a representative of the Soviet military mission who spoke to him in strict confidence about the partisan work the Soviet experts wanted to organize. The object, according to the Russian, was to foster widespread guerrilla activity in Nationalist territory. But, he continued, Largo Caballero opposed it. "We cannot, therefore, do it officially," he explained, "so we must organize it unofficially."³⁷ The idea, then, was to enter the roughly one hundred and twenty men involved on the rolls of the XI Brigade so as to account for their presence in Spain. Renn, chief of staff of a military unit that claimed to be under the orders of the Spanish government, agreed to the request of a representative of a foreign power to contravene the policy of that government. The connection between Renn and the Soviet agent, a connection that completely short-circuited the Loyalist government, was the Comintern to which they both owed their first allegiance and the Soviet Union, which was the true fatherland of both.³⁸

Also indicative of the close ties between the Brigade commissariat and the Soviet mission in Spain was the establishment of a Brigade historical commission. The American base commissar at Albacete, Bill Lawrence, informed Voros that, at the request of the Soviet military authorities in Moscow, the Comintern had ordered the formation of such a historical commission in the Brigades and that Voros, on orders from the Comintern, was to be chief of the Anglo-American section. Voros was then transferred to the political commissariat of the Brigades where he began work on his new assignment.³⁹

A further illustration that the Comintern and not the Loyalist government or its military staff controlled the Brigades concerned the authority exercised over the Brigade and its personnel by individuals who had no connection with that organization except through their position within the Comintern hierarchy. For example, Togliatti, the top Comintern figure in Spain, often appeared at Albacete where he consulted with the Brigade's political chieftains. Despite the fact that he had no official position or authority either within the Loyalist government or the International Brigades, the Brigade hierarchs recognized his authority.⁴⁰ The role played by Prosper Moquet, a French Communist deputy, further illustrated the point. Moquet, who was merely on a temporary tour of Spain and had no juridical relationship with either the International Brigades or the Spanish government, could and did pledge his word, along with that of Auguste Lecouer, that certain actions would or would not be taken by the political directorate of the Brigades.[41] Likewise, Robert Minor, the representative of the United States party in Spain, with no official connection with the International Brigades nor the Loyalist government, exercised authority over American Brigade men solely on the basis of his position in the Communist party. Voros, for example, carried instructions to Minor from the American party regarding the return to the United States of certain American party members from Spain.[42]

Another factor in the Comintern's ability both to maintain control of the internal affairs of the Brigades and to maintain their autonomy within the larger Loyalist framework was the nature of the military chain of command. The original International Brigade generals were either Red army officers or old Comintern stalwarts who, with the single exception of "Gomez" had served in the Red army. Furthermore, the Brigades and their military commanders operated under the watchful eyes and close direction of the Soviet military staff in Spain. All International Brigade commanders had Soviet army advisers on their staffs who represented the direct authority of the Soviet military mission in Spain.[43] And, finally, many of those same foreign Communists who originally commanded the International Brigades later commanded the Loyalist People's Army divisions of which the International Brigades were component parts.[44] Thus, while the International Brigades were organizationally assimilated into the framework of the military structure of the People's Army, they continued to be under Communist military command, not only at the Brigade level but at the divisional level.

That the Comintern, and not the Loyalist government, controlled the personnel and internal authority structure within the International Brigades can also be seen in certain developments during the spring and summer of 1937 when the Brigades were experiencing serious internal problems. The XIV Brigade, for example, suffered a severe morale and disciplinary breakdown in the wake of the Jarama fighting. Despite everything the officers and commissars could do, dissension, desertion, and drunkenness continued to plague the Brigade until it came to resemble more "a band of savages" than an elite military unit. The Brigade newspaper, *Le Soldat de la République,* alluded to this state of affairs in an article condeming what it called the "malcontent." "An antifascist soldier," it declared, "cannot be a malcontent. The volunteers for liberty condemn absolutely the bad comrade who is never content."[45]

One reason for this state of affairs was that following the elevation of General Walter to a division command, Colonel Putz, a former batallion commander, became commander of the XIV Brigade. Putz, well thought of by his officers and men, had proved himself a competent and courageous combat commander. But, as a non-Communist, he did not wield the intrinsic political authority that, in the International Brigades, was the ultimate sanction behind the authority of the military commanders.

The Albacete directorate soon took steps to alter the situation by placing a staunch party stalwart in command and by reinforcing both military and commissar staffs with reliable Communists. On April 22 *Le Soldat de la République* announced the assumption of command by Colonel Jules Dumont. Putz was posted first to Walter's divisional staff and then to command of a Basque division in the northern zone, thus being completely removed from the International Brigade command structure.[46]

With Dumont's assumption of command of the Brigade, his French party colleague Marcel Sagnier took command of the Commune de Paris battalion. The French Communist Vittori, a longtime activist in the French Communist party, assumed the post of Brigade commissar.[47]

Dumont, a longtime Communist activist with strong roots in the French party, immediately instituted a severe disciplinary regime in the XIV Brigade. The troops were informed that a "pioneer company" was being formed and that all who continued to indulge in drunkenness and undisciplined behavior would be assigned to it. Its purpose was "reeducation" and when the first group selected for this discipline company were mustered, they were told that only after their reeducation was obvious would they be returned to their units. They were also reminded that a military prison existed for incorrigibles. But discipline companies and guardhouses were not the ultimate sanction for indiscipline. During this period the firing squad was introduced as an instrument for the punishment of serious cases.[48]

This draconian disciplinary regime was not limited to the XIV Brigade but was in line with the general policy laid down by the Albacete commissariat. The commissariat's demand for "ruthless action," including executions, against indiscipline in the International Brigades brought a political crisis in the British battalion where both battalion commander Copeman and political commissar Aitken opposed the implementation of such severe measures. Disturbed at hearing that death sentences were being carried out in other Brigade units, Copeman felt not only that such measures were unnecessary and wrong but that any such actions in the British battalion would likely provoke mutiny.[49] These disputes brought a thorough shakeup in the political hierarchy of the battalion in May 1937. Springhall, who had been British commissar on the Brigade staff, and Peter Kerrigan, battalion commissar, were both recalled to England. The British Communist party replaced them with three new party stalwarts, William Paynter, who became British base commissar at Albacete, Bert Williams, who assumed the post of battalion commissar, and Walter Tapsell, ex-circulation manager for the British *Daily Worker.* George Aitken, previously at battalion level, moved up to the Brigade political staff.[50]

These changes sufficed to bring the difficulties under control temporarily, but a new crisis developed from the battalion's experience in the Brunete offensive in July. When, after having been withdrawn due to heavy casualties and general exhaustion, the British were ordered back to the front, the battalion balked. Political commissar Aitken finally convinced Brigade headquarters that a return to the lines was impossible.[51] But bitterness and recrimination flared. Battalion commissar Tapsell was arrested for making disparaging comments about the Brigade command. On hearing of this, battalion commander Copeman went to Brigade headquarters determined to secure Tapsell's release, telling his machine-gun commander to bring his guns and rescue him if he did not return within two hours. On his arrival at Brigade headquarters Copeman found that not only had Tapsell been arrested but that Cunningham, now attached to the Brigade staff, was being blamed for the failure. The Albacete commissariat, supported by certain of the British political commissars,[52] was again demanding the death penalty be imposed for indiscipline and leaving the lines during the battle. Tapsell, whose release Copeman secured, decided that only the party hierarchy in England could straighten out the political chaos within the battalion. He told Copeman that he should return to England with Tapsell so as to be available for the "inevitable political fight" that he expected. Copeman agreed. "I saw no reason why indiscriminate shooting of volunteers should be permitted," he wrote. "The fight between us and the others would have to be settled."

Tapsell, Copeman, and Cunningham did shortly return to England and a fierce argument before the politburo of the party ensued. Cunningham became so alienated as a result of this affair that he never returned to Spain and soon left the party. The politburo's decision was that Copeman and Tapsell were to return to Spain while the leaders of the British political commissariat, with the exception of William Rust, would remain in England. Feeling that this decision "amounted to a sentence on us," Tapsell and Copeman demanded, and got, a letter from British party secretary Pollitt, "assuring our authority while in Spain."[53] This episode demonstrates clearly that such internal Brigade matters were seen as political issues within the Comintern and were dealt with and decided not by the Loyalist government but by the Communists themselves, acting through either the Albacete commissariat or the party hierarchies of the national contingents within the Brigades.

Developments in the American battalion also demonstrated the point. Bitterness over the Pingarron massacre led to a protest delegation going to Albacete and demanding that the contact be made with the American party at once. The battalion was in such bad shape that Brigade headquarters appointed a Belgian officer, Captain Van der Berghe, as temporary commander. In early March Martin Hourihan, an American of more or less undefined politics, became battalion commander by a sort of popular referendum on the part of the battalion. Battalion commissar Stember became so unpopular that he was replaced in mid-March by David Jones, like Stember a Communist party man. Stember returned to the United States where the party propagandists soon began using him as a living example of the heroes of the Lincoln battalion on fund-raising tours. At about this time Captain Alan Johnson, an American, arrived on the scene. He had been involved in the organization of the original American recruits in New York and apparently came to Spain with authority to make changes in the command structure of the Lincoln battalion, for shortly after his arrival he replaced Hourihan and Jones with Oliver Law and Fred Lutz, both Communist party members. Shortly after this, Johnson went to Tarrazona de la Mancha where he assumed command of the recently established American training base. He remained in that position until the fall of 1938. Neither Johnson nor those he appointed to command in the battalion solved the problems however.

The threat of an embarrassing scandal if word of the sad condition of the Americans leaked out spurred the party hierarchy in New York to dispatch a number of trusted cadres to Spain to fill the leadership vacuum.[54] One of them, Sandor Voros, an American of Hungarian descent who had long been active in the party, had volunteered to go to Spain earlier, but the party had refused to allow it. The policy was to keep the experienced cadres at home where they were needed rather than to send them to Spain and possibly lose them. But several months later, Saul Mills, a member of the central committee of the Communist party in the United States, told Voros that the party now wanted him to go to Spain. The party, Mills confided to Voros, was in trouble over the Spanish imbroglio. All that glorious hero business that the *Daily Worker* was putting out was so much propaganda. The American comrades in Spain were completely demoralized and wanted to get out. Desertion was a serious problem. If the truth got out, there would be a tremendous scandal. The party was now sending some seasoned leaders over to try to get the Americans into shape. For a party functionary such a request was an order and Voros soon left for Spain. At about this same time the American party also sent party activist Steve Nelson to Spain and the Brigades. Shortly after his arrival Nelson, without previous service in or connection with the International Brigades, assumed the position of political commissar of the Lincoln battalion. Another American who was sent to Spain by the United States party and who assumed a ranking commissar post upon arrival was Young Communist League functionary Dave Doran. He ultimately replaced Nelson as XV Brigade commissar.[55]

The methods and mechanics by which the Comintern controlled the Brigades were also indicated by an episode involving the French party, the Albacete commissariat, and the XIII Brigade. In February 1937 Auguste Lecouer, a French Communist activist, was approached by the French party about serving in the Brigades in Spain. The situation in the Brigades, the party spokesman informed Lecouer, was desperate. The high casualties of the preceding months and the subsequent demoralization was causing severe problems. Furthermore, the quality of those now being recruited left much to be desired. The Comintern had urgently ordered the French party to send more of its reliable cadres to the Brigades who would be capable of functioning as political commissars. Lecouer and some sixty others were chosen. They assembled in Paris where Maurice Thorez, chief of the French party, spoke to them, explaining the need and what was expected of them in Spain. They arrived at Albacete on February 25.[56]

Shortly after Lecouer's arrival Marty summoned him to his office. With Marty was a Pole, the political commissar of the XIII Brigade.[57] The XIII Brigade was experiencing severe morale and disciplinary problems, said Marty. Lecouer was to select two assistants from among the French cadres who had come with him and proceed immediately to assume the duties of political commissars in the XIII Brigade. As always Marty blamed the failings and shortcomings in the

Brigades on traitors, spies, and agents provocateur. Thus, he informed Lecouer, a key part of the task of the new commissars was to root out these elements.[58]

Albacete also assigned a party writer, Alfred Kantorowicz, to the XIII Brigade as information officer. His purpose was to help raise morale by giving this Brigade (which did not share in the glory of the Madrid battles) some publicity. This he did by writing a series of articles on the history and martial exploits of the XIII which appeared serially in the International Brigade's official publication, *Volunteer for Liberty*.[59] Although Lecouer was later reassigned to other political work by Marty, the commissariat continued to pick tested and reliable Communists to occupy the political commissar post in the XIII Brigade. In July 1937, for example, Blagoie Parovic, using the *nom de guerre* "Schmidt" in Spain, assumed that post. A member of the central committee of the Communist party of Yugoslavia since 1934 and a party functionary since 1924, Parovic had long been engaged in conspiratorial work. In Spain he had gained a reputation in the party as an extremely reliable political commissar who fought "with all energy and determination against counter-revolutionary Trotskyists . . . for the Bolshevik line of the party."[60] These developments involving three of the International Brigades, the XIII, XIV, and XV, illustrate the fact that the Comintern consistently and effectively used the agencies of the various national Communist parties and the Albacete commissariat to maintain its control over the internal structure and affairs of the Brigades.

The Communists' proprietory attitude toward the Brigades and their determination thoroughly to dominate and control them was also clearly shown in the case of Pacciardi and the XII Brigade. The issues between Pacciardi and Albacete stemmed, in part, from their different conceptions of the origin, nature, and role of the Italian volunteers in Spain. Pacciardi held that the Garibaldi unit was founded on the charter of the Italian antifascist committee in Paris, and his conception centered on the Italian nature of the Garibaldi military unit. The Communists, on the other hand, saw it differently. Longo took the position that the Garibaldi unit was, like all the International Brigades, an integral part of "a great political and military organization," which was able to do what it did, including solving the problems of rapport with the Spanish government, only because of its international character. The prevalence of Communists in the Brigades, their discipline and organization, and their international support, Longo held, were responsible for their success as compared to the other Italian efforts in Spain. Pacciardi, said Longo, was appointed commander of the Garibaldis by the Albacete commissariat on the same basis and by the same authority as all other Brigade commanders and commissars and was subject to the same authority and discipline.[61]

During the spring and summer of 1937 the differences between Pacciardi and the Albacete hierarchy became progressively more pronounced. Pacciardi's appointment of non-Communists to command positions and his generally independent attitude led to persistent criticism of him by the Communist politicos.[62] The Communists accused Pacciardi of being a chronic critic of the conditions under which the unit was committed to battle and one who saw things only from his own point of view instead of taking into consideration the big picture. Also, said the Communists, he wanted to be the sole authority over the internal affairs of the Garibaldi Brigade, accepting no interference from the political commissariat at Albacete. They complained that Pacciardi surrounded himself with those who admired him, shunned the higher authority of the commissariat, and made a point of appointing non-Communists to his staff, a situation, they said, that represented an error in a unit composed in the great majority of Communists. Pacciardi was quite aware of the attitude of the political commissariat toward him. He informed the non-Communist officer Penchienati, soon after the latter's appointment as battalion commander, of the political currents in the Brigade and told him that if he, Penchienati, had any trouble with the Communist politicos to come directly to him about it.[63]

The political tensions within the XII Brigade were exacerbated further by the outbreak of an internecine struggle within the ranks of the Loyalist camp and by repercussions of that on the Brigades. On May 3 the long-brewing enmity between the Anarchists and Communists flared into an open clash in Barcelona, and a state of hostilities, complete with machine guns clattering from rooftops, existed in the city until May 8. The real winners of the flareup in Barcelona were the Communists who exploited the situation to engineer the fall of the Largo Caballero government and to carry out a severe repression against their political enemies in the Popular Front camp. Neither the Communists' hatred of the Anarchists nor their antipathy to Largo Caballero was anything new. They simply took advantage of the outbreak of open fighting in Barcelona to force a showdown and settle old scores. The Communists had, in fact, been angling to oust Largo Caballero for some time. They had assiduously used the fall of Malaga in February to try to discredit him and his regime but were successful only in forcing the resignation of his undersecretary for war. Largo

Caballero had grown progressively more suspicious of the way the Communists were taking control and, as a result, had become more truculent toward them. So far as the Barcelona affair went, he was unwilling to allow the type of wholesale repression of "uncontrollables" demanded by the Communists. The Communist attitude toward the Barcelona clash was that "Anarchist adventurers and provocateurs, in accord with the Franquist espoinage agents, opened another war front at our backs." Using Largo Caballero's reluctance to crack down rigorously on the Anarchists as the reason for withdrawing their support, the party determined to force a cabinet crisis and oust him. As Jóse Díaz of the CPS put it, "Either the government must impose order or we will have a new government." In support of their campaign against Largo Caballero the Communists launched a virulent attack on him to the effect that he was an impediment to the war effort and, if not an outright traitor himself, was at least surrounded by and under the influence of traitorous elements.

The Albacete commissariat followed the party line to the letter. As Longo himself put it: "Agents of Franco had infiltrated into the ministry, the general staff.... Largo Caballero, was under the influence of traitorous officers.... The reason for all this [lack of stern suppression of "uncontrollables" by the Largo Caballero government] was that the head of government himself—with some of his ministers and many of his collaborators of the central general staff—were participating in the anti-Communist campaign of the Poumists and of the fifth column."[64]

While the Communists were forcing the cabinet crisis that ousted Largo Caballero and replaced him with the more pliable Juan Negrín, the Soviet-Comintern police apparatus, operating independently of Loyalist government authority, arrested and incarcerated thousands and shot an unknown number in their secret prisons.[65] They also either murdered or expelled from Spain a number of foreigners who had been associated with Anarchist or POUM military units, or about whom the Communists had some suspicion as to their "reliability."[66]

The Communist vendetta against what they more or less indiscriminately called Trotskyists, Franco or Gestapo agents, uncontrollables, or fifth columnists carried over, inevitably, into the International Brigades. In the period following the Barcelona rising the political commissars, following the direction of the Albacete commissariat, indoctrinated the troops in the Communist line that the affair represented an effort of traitors, fascists, and, above all, Trotskyists, to stab the Popular Front in the back and turn the country over to the enemy.[67]

The Brigade commissariat sent telegrams to the new premier, Negrín, pledging the Brigades' loyalty to the new government. The Brigade press editorialized that the change in leadership was a result of Largo Caballero's failures. The commissars stressed the necessity for the Brigades to remain calm, maintain strict discipline, and be vigilant against provocateurs and Trotskyists in their own ranks. An Albacete directive warned Brigade men who had cause to be in Barcelona to secure a special identification document due to the "vigorous cleaning up of all undesirable and uncontrollable elements by government authorities."[68]

The Brigade commissariat also took the occasion to attempt a thorough purge of uncontrollables from the ranks of the Brigades. The repercussions of that policy were felt primarily in the Garibaldi Brigade which was the only one with any substantial number of Anarchists (at least non-Spanish Anarchists) and the only one in which Anarchists were in any position to command. Pacciardi was determined that there should be no purge in the Garibaldi and also that the Garibaldi should take no part, on either side, in the Popular Front's internecine struggles. On May 5 Penchienati's battalion received orders to proceed to Valencia, ostensibly to participate in a parade. Instead of parading, however, the units remained in the vicinity of Valencia for several days and then moved to Tortosa, a coastal town about halfway between Valencia and Barcelona. A Spanish Communist officer who had come from Albacete then ordered the battalion to Barcelona. Concluding that his battalion was being ordered to Barcelona to be used in suppressing the Anarchists who were, as he put it, being persecuted because they disagreed with the Communists, Penchienati refused to move his battalion until he received personal orders from Pacciardi whom he contacted by phone. Pacciardi told Penchienati not to move until he got there. The Spanish officer in command threatened to arrest Penchienati and disarm his battalion. At that, Penchienati and his men returned to their quarters and set up machine guns, thus ending the threatened disarming of the battalion. Pacciardi soon arrived by automobile and had the officer in command arrested by order of General Lukacs. Penchienati and his battalion then rejoined the Brigade.[69]

Pacciardi's refusal to sanction the use of his troops in the suppression of "uncontrollables" or to modify his command structure and staff to "conform with recent events," as suggested by the International Brigade commissariat made the Communist politicos of the International Brigades more determined than ever to be rid of him. For them it was only a matter of waiting for the right moment.

Pacciardi on the other hand had by then become thoroughly disenchanted with the Communists and was determined that they should not completely usurp his authority in the Garibaldi Brigade. As he later put it, "I understood the political plots of the Communists, and I placed myself against them."[70]

While these political currents smoldered within the XII Brigade, the new Negrín regime sought to consolidate its position and establish its image as a government of victory by quickly launching two separate military offensives. One of these involved the XII Brigade in an attack on Huesca, a Nationalist bastion in Aragon. The decision of the Negrín government to engage in a military action in Aragon immediately after its accession to power and its use of International Brigade units in the operation seemed to many, including some International Brigade men themselves, to be motivated by internal political rather than military considerations.

The suspicion, distrust, and hostility of much of the population of Aragon and Catalonia toward the Loyalist regime was nothing new, and in much of the area the writ of the Valencia government ran more in theory than in practice. The Negrín regime, in which no Anarchist ministers participated and which came in the wake of the Barcelona affair, was even more suspect to the Anarchist-oriented population of Aragon than Largo Caballero's had been. Viewing the International Brigades as a Communist military force, much of the population of Aragon suspected the presence of the Brigades in their territory and feared that they were to be used as forces of public order.[71]

The attack on Huesca resulted in total failure and high casualties.[72] During the campaign Pacciardi wrote to his divisional commander protesting any further waste of men in continuing to attack a position without sufficient strength to hope seriously to take it. His protest was ignored and the offensive went on.[73]

The Albacete directorate took advantage of the vacancies created by the Huesca casualties to strengthen the Communist hand in the Brigade. Two party stalwarts, Raimondi and Mallozzi, both of whom came to Spain via Moscow, replaced the two battalion commanders who had fallen at Huesca. Felice Platone, the party functionary whom the Albacete commissariat had earlier forced on Pacciardi, remained Brigade chief of staff, and the equally reliable Barontini continued in the post of Brigade political commissar. The Brigade command structure now stood, except for Pacciardi and Penchienati, staunchly Communist.[74]

Within ten days of the mauling taken by the Brigade at Huesca it was reinforced by some 800 untrained, unarmed, and even ununiformed Spanish conscripts and on the following day orders arrived for the Brigade to proceed immediately to Madrid for further action (the upcoming Brunete offensive). This, said Pacciardi, was absurd. The battalions were disorganized and two of the three had lost their commanders. In addition, the task of assimilating, training, and equipping the large infusion of raw Spanish recruits into the ranks had not even begun. He therefore wrote to his division commander requesting a period for training and reorganization. But the answer was no: orders were orders.[75]

Pacciardi's open criticism of the Huesca operation and his subsequent questioning of the rapid commitment of his Brigade to more action further exacerbated the hostility toward him on the part of the Communist hierarchy. Open criticism was the most deadly of sins to the Communist politicos. Party discipline sealed tight the lips of the faithful. But for one who did not accept that discipline absolutely and who had the temerity to challenge openly the party's direction, the only answer was exorcism from the ranks of the International Brigades. For one of Pacciardi's stature, however, this presented something of a problem. The events of July and the Brunete campaign led to a solution to the problem favorable to the Communists.

During that offensive Pacciardi's long-smoldering dissatisfaction with both the Communist domination of the Brigade and the way in which the Brigade was being used flared into open confrontation. The Garibaldis, heavily laden with untrained Spanish recruits, suffered severely in the early phases of the Brunete campaign. Finally, faced with an order to launch one more attack which, he felt, would result in yet another senseless bloodbath, Pacciardi protested vehemently to General Kleber, and he followed that protest by a violent argument with the political commissar of the forty-fifth division during which he accused the commissar of trying to run the Brigade and of being a spy.

Informed of this crisis in command, Longo hastened to Garibaldi headquarters, where he addressed the highly ruffled troops and, in an attempt to soothe them, countermanded the order for the advance. A few hours later Pacciardi wrote a letter of resignation. That night he changed his mind but refused to go to divisional headquarters despite the repeated orders of the Brigade political commissar, Barontini, to do so.[76]

The XII Brigade became racked with dissension between those who supported Pacciardi and those who supported the commissariat. Pacciardi took the position that the Garibladi Brigade had become an Italian unit in name only, that the few Italians left were so submerged in the masses of Spanish troops composing the People's Army that militarily they were doing the Spaniards little good and that meanwhile the best cadres of Italian antifascism were being wantonly wasted. He proposed as a solution the retirement of the Italian volunteers for a period, the granting to them of leaves outside Spain if they so desired, and a new effort to recruit more men for a revitalized all Italian unit.[77]

The Albacete hierarchy by now was determined that Pacciardi must go, and the commissariat launched a concerted attack against him. The official organ of the XII Brigade, *Il Volontario della Libertá*, published a series of articles written by Longo himself which, without specifically naming Pacciardi, attacked his position regarding the role of the foreign fighters. One of the articles entitled "Discipline in the Army Is Necessary for Victory," concluded: "It is necessary that all the combatants have the maximum faith in the superior command and especially in the top command. Those who command must obey with the maximum discipline and promptness ... the password of our volunteers and of all combatants must be ... *discipline, discipline, discipline.*"[78] Pacciardi, in the face of this impossible situation, decided to present his case to the Italian exile committee in Paris.

Pacciardi's departure presented the Communist politicos with a golden opportunity to take full control of the XII Brigade, an opportunity they were quick to exploit. Brigade commissar Barontini told his subordinate commissars that he now really commanded and that Penchienati (who had been left in interim command) counted for little.[79] The commissariat activated its maneuvers for ousting Pacciardi permanently from command of the Garibaldis by informing the Spanish authorities that he would not be coming back to Spain and that a permanent replacement should be chosen. They planned to replace him with a reliable party stalwart, preferably Barontini. For once, however, the Communists failed to have their way. The Spanish authorities, led by war minister Prieto, refused to go along. This was all happening at a time when Prieto was taking a jaundiced view of the Communists' attempts to dominate the Loyalist Army and commisar system. As part of his efforts to curb the Communists, he sought to bring the International Brigades more fully under government control. Thus he refused to accept the appointment of a Communist politico as a commander of the XII Brigade. The immediate result was the continuation of Penchienati in the post, but now on a regular rather than an interim basis.

When an angry Pacciardi returned to Spain, the Communists urged him to accept a promotion to division staff. He refused at first, saying he had not come to Spain to make a military career but to lead an Italian unit. The Communists, knowing that Pacciardi had at his disposal a party organization and a newspaper in France through which he could greatly embarrass them and disrupt the always delicate facade of Popular Front unity, and aware of the deep cleavages within the XII Brigade, did not want him to leave Spain nursing a grudge against them. Having achieved their purpose in removing him from any effective role in the International Brigades, they now hoped he could be bought off by a powerless post at division level. Pacciardi, at the urging of both Penchienati and Nenni, finally agreed to accept the post of vice commander of the division for the duration of the imminent Aragon offensive as a gesture to buttress the badly shaken unity and morale of the Garibaldi Brigade.[80] In October, following the Aragon campaign, Pacciardi left Spain for good.[81] With his departure the Communists had successfully removed the only person within the International Brigades who could conceivably stand up to them or threaten their total control.

While the Brigade political commissariat served as a Comintern control mechanism in the internal affairs of the Brigades, it also acted as both buffer to and connecting link with the Loyalist regime. It was thus the key to maintaining the political autonomy of the Brigades within that larger political-military structure.

The Brigades' relationship to the Loyalist government in the beginning had been tenuous. In fact Longo, with the aid of the Spanish Communist and Comintern apparatus in Spain, established the base at Albacete, and the Internationals were already there in force, before the Loyalist government was ever officially notified.[82] Only then did Longo, accompanied by René Rebiere, a Frenchman, and Stephen Wisniewski, a Pole, officially pay their respects and offer the services of the Internationals to the president of the Republic, Azaña, and the prime minister, Largo Caballero, in Madrid. The conversation between Longo's delegation and the two Spaniards amounted to little more than formal and meaningless niceties. Both Azaña and Largo Caballero were cool toward the delegation and showed little enthusiasm for the entire project of the foreign volunteers.[83] Largo Caballero, who had earlier turned down suggestions for the organization of foreign units, now accepted the existence of the International Brigades, though without enthusiasm. The reason for his doing so was most likely that he was simply presented with a fait accompli and saw no way of avoiding it short of alienating the USSR and the Communists (both of whom he needed).

On October 17, 1936, Largo Caballero instructed Martínez Barrio, civil governor of the province of Albacete, to cooperate with the Comintern chiefs in the establishment of a base for the foreign troops. The political command of the Brigade, represented by the same three Comintern stalwarts, Longo, Rebiere, and Wisniewski, concluded a formal agreement with Martínez Barrio concerning their use of Albacete and on October 22 the base officially opened.[84] All these formalities thus amounted to nothing more than an ex post facto recognition of things already done.

All these public and official acts were done in the name of the international Popular Front in accordance with the policy of the Comintern that the specifically Communist role be muted as much as possible and that the Brigades appear as a spontaneous manifestation of antifascist solidarity. The Communists generally suffered from a logical dilemma on this point. They wanted credit for the Brigades as a Comintern-inspired and -directed unit but at the same time they needed to present the Brigades as an expression of a broad Popular Front antifascism. Their efforts to have it both ways produced some interesting mental gymnastics. For example, after arguing that the Brigades were not a Communist organization, Longo went on to insist that it was only the connection of the Brigades with the Comintern, the discipline, unity, and strength afforded by that connection, and the prevalence of Communist cadres in the Brigades which made the Brigades an effective organization and fighting force.[85]

The role of Pietro Nenni offers some insight into the nature of the relationship between the Brigade and the government. As leader of the Italian Socialist party, Nenni was an important figure in the overall Popular Front political picture. The fact that he and his party were affiliated with the Second International and at the same time firm supporters of the Popular Front program and of the Comintern policy in Spain made him uniquely valuable to the Communists. Nenni was perhaps the prime example of a well-recognized non-Communist proletarian leader being intimately involved with and committed to the Comintern's policies and program in Spain. Being a Second International man also made Nenni more trusted by the Socialist leadership of the Spanish Popular Front who, in the persons of both Largo Caballero and Prieto, were less than completely convinced of the trustworthiness of the Communists.

Nenni had been among the first foreigners to become actively engaged in the Spanish war and he apparently enjoyed close relations with the Spanish Socialists. He had, naturally, been involved in the negotiations of the Italian committee in Paris in creating the Italian legion, but he had no part in the origins or organization of the International Brigades. In fact, his first direct contact with the Brigades came only on November 25, 1936. On Nenni's first arrival at Albacete, Marty offered him the post of political commissar of the new XIII Brigade, but Nenni declined the honor. Unknown to Marty, Nenni already had in his pocket a letter from the Spanish authorities appointing him special commissar in charge of liaison between the International Brigades and the government. It was apparently in that capacity that he remained closely involved with, but not subject to the authority of, the Brigade political command.[86]

This arrangement seems to indicate several things: first, that the Loyalist government recognized that the Brigades were an essentially autonomous organization outside their direct control; second, that the Spanish leaders saw in Nenni a man who could, and did, work closely with the Communists and yet was not under Comintern discipline (and was thus more reliable from their point of view than anyone under that discipline could be); and third, that Nenni, despite his very close ties with the Comintern and his acceptance of their policies and direction, wanted to maintain the possibility of taking an independent stance and did not therefore want to place himself under Comintern authority by accepting a post in the hierarchy of the International Brigades.

In the early stage of the war, autonomous, party-controlled military units were characteristic of the Popular Front's fighting forces. But as the Loyalist regime developed more centralized control and built the People's Army, the situation gradually changed. This change eventually put the Brigade hierarchy in a difficult position. For while the Communists were the strongest proponents of centralized control and a unified army they, at the same time, strongly resisted all efforts on the part of the government to exercise any real control over the internal affairs of the International Brigades or to absorb the Brigades into the People's Army. Thus the Communists had to talk as if they favored control of the Brigades by the Loyalist ministry of war and general staff. But at the same time they consistently resented and thwarted any attempt on the part of the government actually to implement and make such control effective.

The ambiguity of their attitude toward this question can be seen in this statement by Longo: "The International Brigades were the expression of the world Popular Front, at the service and the orders of the Spanish Popular Front and nothing more. The safeguarding and defense of this position was the maximum preoccupation of all the

International volunteers, and was the essential mission, on the political plane and in the relations with the government and the various Spanish political movements, of the Commissariat General of the International Brigades."[87] Longo did not say that the Brigades were at the orders of the Loyalist government and military authorities. Using the standard Communist jargon of the day, Longo, in effect, said nothing more than that the Brigades were at the orders of the Comintern. For the Communists saw themselves and their policies as the only valid and reliable expression of the Popular Front, both international and Spanish. Indeed, Longo later harshly condemned the Loyalist authorities, both political and military, for their failure to implement fully the Communist program in general and the Brigade commissariat's proposals in particular. He believed that the reason for this failure was the anti-Communism of the authorities. "It was because of parties and groups, not the direct action of the enemy, that the difficulties to the normal and rational development of the International Brigades were artificially created," he insisted. "They [the Spaniards] feared their [the Brigades] force and their prestige, just as they feared the force and prestige of the Spanish Communist Party. They opposed and impeded a large mobilization of the masses, the creation of a strong popular army, because they feared that all these favored the development of the influence of the Communist Party." And, he continued, "they risked the war against fascism for fear of favoring the Party which was the most tenacious sustainer of the war and which had sacrificed to it the best of its cadres and its militants." Thus Longo's attitude, typical of the Communists in general, was that only those Spaniards who faithfully followed the Communists' lead were really the Spanish Popular Front. All others were consigned to the category of traitors. "Naturally," he said, referring to the Loyalist government and military authorities, "the Commissariat General and the command of the International Brigades could not close their eyes against the disgraceful actions of the fifth column and of Gestapo and Ovra agents. These people, in every way, in low and in high places tried to impede the fusion and the agreement between the Internationals and the Spaniards."[88]

In stating that the essential mission of the Brigade political commissariat was to ensure that the Brigades continued to represent the world and Spanish Popular Front vis-á-vis the Loyalist government, Longo was in effect underscoring the attitude of the Brigade directorate, and the Communists in general, that the Brigades were an autonomous political element and not simply a military unit within the regular framework of the Loyalist governmental or military structure.

The very fact that the International Brigades continued to maintain their own political commissariat, separate and distinct from the commissariat of war of the Loyalist government, or any other governmental organ, clearly indicated their autonomous political nature and status. Had the Brigade directorate been truly interested in a full assimilation of the Internationals into the Loyalist People's Army the disbandment of the Albacete political commissariat would have been an obvious move. No such thing was ever contemplated.

Both the determination of the Comintern to maintain its control over the Brigades and the relationship between the Brigade hierarchy and the Loyalist government were evident in the debate that arose over the question of the Brigades' role and status in the spring and summer of 1937. Following the heavy losses of the Jarama battle and the impossibility of replacing those losses with foreign recruits, Longo, speaking for the Brigade commissariat, proposed to the government that the Internationals be used more fully as cadres for the training of the large numbers of Spaniards being conscripted into the army. Significantly, the method for achieving this would not be the disbandment of the International Brigades as distinct units and the posting of the Internationals to regular units of the People's Army. Rather, the Brigade commissariat proposed that the number of International Brigades be doubled so that the experience and capacity of the International cadres could be used to train and command large numbers of new Spanish conscripts.

This approach had obvious advantages from the commissariat's point of view. It could be camouflaged as an effort to use more fully the talents of the International cadres and to assimilate the Brigades into the People's Army through the incorporation of Spaniards into the Brigades. In reality, it would be a method for increasing Communist influence within the Loyalist army while still retaining the essential political autonomy of the Brigades. The Spanish conscript troops who would fill these new Brigades would be trained, indoctrinated, and controlled by the Communist political and military hierarchy of the Brigades, and the Comintern would retain, and even expand, the benefits and advantages that accrued to it by having, in effect, its own army in Spain.

That the non-Communist Spaniards in the Loyalist government and army saw through this camouflage no doubt accounted for their failure to implement the Brigade commissariat's proposal to double the number of International units. The Spaniards could not, for obvious reasons, say what they thought. They, after all, needed the Communists. Longo reported having had many discussions with Loyalist political and military authorities about the best way to use the Internationals. He complained that while the Spaniards generally expressed agreement in principle, they never followed through in practice.[89] Thus the Brigade chiefs were thwarted in their desire to expand their role and influence much beyond the original five International Brigades. The Brigade commissariat did succeed, however, in maintaining the essential autonomy of the Brigades and in filling the steadily shrinking ranks of the Internationals with Spanish recruits. These recruits, commanded, trained, and politically indoctrinated by the International cadres, made possible the continued existence of the five International Brigades and thus of a Comintern-controlled army in Spain.

The commissariat's success in maintaining the International Brigades as a reliable Communist force as the number of foreigners dwindled was closely correlated with their success in training and indoctrinating the ever-increasing numbers of Spanish conscripts within their ranks. Marty, referring to this, called the Brigades "an immense anti-fascist school" in which the Spaniards would be turned into thoroughly indoctrinated antifascists. Dahlem called it "the most important question of the internal life of the Brigades."[90] In an article in the Brigade *Boletín de Información,* Commissar Inspector Longo set forth the problem and the solution. The new developments, he said, created several new problems for their military and political work. Admitting that some among the Internationals were beginning to doubt that the Brigades could any longer function in their old capacity as shock brigades due to the influx of Spanish recruits, he said this attitude was incorrect. To the contrary, "It must be the task of the veteran cadres, both military and political, to train, mold, discipline the new recruits." These new tasks clearly presented new problems. When the International Brigades were "mainly composed of comrades who had had a life of militancy behind them, the task of the military and political command was fairly easy.... Revolutionary consciousness, the spirit of sacrifice of our volunteers was largely sufficient to write glorious pages." Now the problems were more difficult. The most important task of the International cadres now must be "to transform these people [Spanish recruits] into advanced and heroic combatants." This, he concluded, was both a "problem of enlightenment and political propaganda" and "a problem of military organization and education." Finally, he said that these new tasks required "a much higher standard of discipline than before."[91] This became a permanent theme in the Brigade press. "The [new] troops must always be prepared for combat; they must always be prepared politically for the operation. This is the permanent task of the commissars, commanders and soldiers," insisted *Il Garibaldino*. *Le Soldat de la République* explained that the new Spanish recruits had little or no political understanding. Thus it was the duty of each veteran of the Brigade to instruct them "not only militarily but politically."[92]

In line with the commissariat's efforts in this direction, the Brigades established Spanish sections in all their training schools, both military and political, in which special attention was given to the problems of creating effective cadres from among the Spanish recruits. These efforts brought about what Longo referred to as "a profound transformation . . . in the work of our political commissars."[93] In this way the International Brigades remained in existence and continued to serve the Comintern's purposes both as a reliable military and political force in Spain and as a potent propaganda instrument in the overall Popular Front policy. By 1938, for example, the XII Brigade had only some 20 percent Italian effectives to 80 percent Spanish. Yet the Brigade was still called the Garibaldi, was still commonly viewed as the Italian Brigade, was still effectively commanded by Italians and politically controlled by the Albacete commissariat. The same situation existed to a greater or lesser extent in all the International Brigades.

In its efforts to maintain the Brigades as an autonomous Comintern army, the Albacete directorate faced its most determined opponent in the person of the Loyalist minister of war, Prieto. Since assuming the post of war minister in the Negrín cabinet, Prieto had become increasingly concerned at the ever-growing Communist predominance in both the army and the political commissar system. As a result he issued a number of orders designed to curb the Communists from further enhancing their position in these two highly critical organizations. As an integral part of his general efforts to decrease, or at least contain, Communist influence in the Popular Army, Prieto issued a decree in late September 1937 dealing in very specific terms with the International Brigades. The clear import of the decree was to begin the process of assimilating the Brigades into the People's Army and bringing them under full government control.

The Communists could not overtly oppose the decree's purpose. After all, the party had been saying that that was what they wanted from the beginning. They therefore took the public position that they favored the objectives of the decree. Longo spoke the official word for the Brigade commissariat on the decree by reaffirming that "a regular army and unified command" are essential. Therefore, "we receive with enthusiasm all those measures in the decree which tend to make our Brigades more and more intergral parts of the Spanish People's Army." Actually it fell like a bombshell among the Brigade politicos, for if energetically carried through it signaled the end of the Brigades as an autonomous Comintern army in Spain. The Communists pretended to be shocked and insulted by the decree's use of previous legislation which dealt with the old "Tercio de Extranjeros," or Spanish foreign legion, as the legal basis of the Brigades' existence. The Italian party stalwart Calandrone called the decree "a punch in the eye for us." But, he continued, "we are in Spain to fight fascism and we continue to fight in spite of any decree which offends our dignity as antifascist and as men."[94]

Still, a decree was one thing; putting it into effect, another. Only in the Garibaldi Brigade did it have any noticeable impact and even there the effect proved to be temporary. Prieto had intervened in the affairs of the Garibaldi Brigade following the replacement of Pacciardi as commander. Due to Prieto's stance the Brigade politicos had been forced to settle for Penchienati, another non-Communist in that post. Following the Aragon campaign in August 1937, Penchienati suffered an injury in an automobile accident, and the Brigade commissariat replaced him, on an interim basis, with Raimondi, a party stalwart. The commissariat now confidently expected to achieve its goal of a reliable commander of the Garibaldi Brigade.

Once more Prieto thwarted them. In October he appointed Arturo Zanoni as commander of the Garibaldis. The Italian Zanoni had served prior to this time in a Spanish unit and had no previous connection with the International Brigades. Unlike Penchienati, however, he had political connections (with Prieto and Nenni) which made him loom as a real threat to Communist control of the XII Brigade. Furthermore, he apparently had instructions from Prieto to put energetically into effect the spirit of the recent decree assimilating the Internationals into the regular Loyalist military and political framework.

The Communist chiefs who had maneuvered so ardously to oust Pacciardi were aghast. It was not the ends of the decree that they opposed, they said, but the speed with which Zanoni sought to implement them. Such drastic changes would disrupt the Brigade and lower its efficiency. Actually morale and efficiency in the Brigade could hardly have been lower than they already were. The Communists found fault with such inconsequential things as Zanoni's insistence on speaking Spanish to them instead of Italian and of his referring to the Brigade as the XII instead of the Garibaldi. All these faults were merely rationalizations for their opposition to the obvious import of Prieto's decree and his intervention in Brigade affairs. Zanoni's determination to put the new policy into effect and his refusal to be dominated by the Brigade commissariat made him the focus of the Communists' frustration. The attitude of the Brigade hierarchy showed clearly the falseness of their much-talked-of desire to make the Brigades a normal part of the People's Army.[95]

In the long run, the Brigade commissariat had its way. Prieto's effort to curb Communist influence in the Popular Army and the commissar system inevitably brought the mobilization of all sectors of the Communist apparatus in Spain against him and his ultimate fall from office.[96] Following his departure from the government in April 1938, the Communists once again held full sway in the military ministries. Premier Negrín himself assumed the title of minister of defense, but he had three Communist undersecretaries for army, navy, and air force. The "crypto Communist," Alvarez del Vayo, returned as chief of the revivified commissariat of war in control of the political commissar system throughout the entire army and it too was thoroughly Communist-dominated. With these changes at the top the Brigade commissariat regained complete control of the Garibaldi Brigade and appointed two party stalwarts, Martino Martini and Emilio Suardi, commander and commissar respectively.[97] Thus, despite the avowed Communist policy of establishing a regular army under centralized command and despite the attempts by Prieto to regularize the position of the International Brigades, which meant, in the final analysis, bringing them under the direct control of the government, the Brigades continued to be, in fact, a Comintern-controlled military force and an integral part of that interlocking directorate which was the Communist apparatus in Spain.

8 The Political Commissar

The International Brigade political commissariat maintained its absolute dominance over the internal affairs of the Brigades through a variety of means including control of the Brigade press, censorship, control of appointments to military and political posts, and, ultimately, the Brigade police apparatus, which carried with it the power to imprison and execute without recourse to or review by higher authority. But within the spectrum of the commissariat's control mechanisms, nothing was more important than the political commissar system.

A political commissar system functioned throughout the Loyalist People's Army from the date of its origins in late 1936 to the end of the war. The Communists had taken the lead and set the example in the use of political commissars in their own militia unit, the Fifth Regiment, from the beginning and were chiefly responsible for the adoption of the system by the Loyalist government.[1] The Loyalist government's political commissar system was, throughout the war, directed by the closest Communist collaborator in the Popular Front cabinet, Alvarez del Vayo, and the top echelons of the commissariat were always filled by Communist party cadres.[2] The Communists moreover took great pains to fill the ranks of the political commissars at all levels with reliable party members. So successful were they in doing so that both Largo Caballero and later Prieto attempted to reduce the virtual Communist monopoly on the commissar posts.[3] The Communists denounced as treasonous all such efforts to bring the political commissariat and the appointment of political commissars under the control of the ministry of war. Dahlem's statement that "Caballero's struggle against the political commissars . . . was a crime against the army and the country" epitomized the Communist attitude. He continued, "The more subtle, but nonetheless ruinous policy operated by Prieto, of introducing the spirit of 'no politics' in the army, was one of the reasons why there were times when the People's Army failed." Marty too took up the cudgels on this subject, denouncing Largo Caballero's attempts at "subjecting the political commissars' appointment to strict rules and subject to the Minister of War."[4]

The commissariat of war of the Loyalist government, while an element in the apparatus through which the Communists sought to control the People's Army, exercised no direct connection with or control over the political commissariat and the commissar system of the International Brigades. The two systems had, however, the same general purpose and philosophical-political foundation. From the Communist point of view, military organization, discipline, and strength were indissolubly linked to, were indeed essentially a function of, their political counterparts. The Communists frequently compared the Loyalist People's Army to the Soviet Red Army. Both were "essentially different from any imperialist army.... The special characteristics of the Red Army are due, not to the abstract thinking of military idealists, but to the nature of the political struggle out of which they were born."[5]

This view of the essentially political nature of Communist armies accounted for the Communists' prime emphasis on the role of the political commissar. "The International Brigades have never been nonpolitical," declared Marty. "Far from that. Not a unit has gone to the front without the political commissars being appointed.... It is here that the essential strength lies." Dahlem wrote: "Political work in the International Brigades was indissolubly connected with the military training and education of the men.... The fighting power... depended to a considerable extent on the political work."[6]

The Communists thus set the highest value on the work and effectiveness of the political commissars, both within the International Brigades and in the People's Army in general, and never tired of heralding the message of the political commissars' key role in the army. Dolores Ibarruri (La Pasionaria) summarized the Communists' glorification of the political commissars by calling them "the spirit and the heart of the army."[7] Another leading Spanish Communist and sometime subcommissar of war, Enrique Castro Delgado, wrote of the commissars: "They have been the permanent animators of our soldiers.... Their continued work in the development of the political content of our army is the firmest guarantee of its maintaining its popular and revolutionary character."[8] The leading Comintern figure, Vittorio Vidali, intimately associated with the commissar system, wrote: "The Commissar is the soul of a combat unit... is always the best, the most intelligent, the most capable."[9] Again, "The Commissar, the political essence of the most conscious strata of fighting antifascists, is the soul of this army. He has forged it into being."[10]

Indeed, the Communists placed far greater emphasis on the role of the political commissar than on that of the military officer, whom they saw primarily as a technical specialist. As Marty put it: "It is the military commander who places the sentries, the cannon and the machine guns and gives the command to fire at the right moment. But

The Political Commissar

it is ... the political commissars upon which the political and organizational work falls.... The Commissars constitute the veritable backbone, the heart and soul of the army." Again, "The Commissars were the unshakable rock on which the magnificent International Brigades were built." The work of the political commissars, agreed Dahlem, "must secure the fulfillment of the military task.... Commissars are the political soul of our Army; they inspire it with heroism, see to its ideological education.... Such an army as ours cannot function without Commissars."[11]

Given the Communists' attitude toward the political commissars, it was perhaps inevitable that friction between the commissars and the military command often presented a problem. The work and role of the political commissar was ostensibly separate from and complementary to the technical role of the military officer. The relationship between the political commissar and the military commander as the system was ideally supposed to work received much attention from those concerned with the commissar system. Generally the official formula could be summed up in the statement: "The political commissar was to be the first and best auxiliary of the Commander, to be his right hand ... without for a moment trying to decide military orders."[12] The commissar, however, subject to a separate chain of authority, was essentially independent of the military command. Thus the commissar was to be free to "complete his functions without interference from the command."[13]

Despite the effort to separate the roles and functions of the commissar and the military officer, there were many areas of potential conflict. The interpretation of what constituted strictly military decisions or what involved political considerations could vary greatly. Not only that, but the commissars' duties entailed large areas that were in fact of a military nature and clearly overlapped the duties of the military officer. For example, commissars were instructed that their duties included such matters as arranging and checking the transport of troops, loading of troop convoys, choosing and preparing campsites, cooking and mess facilities, and general control of troops during movements. When his unit relieved another at the front, the commissar was to check the state of the weapons and munitions and to ensure new supplies if needed. On taking an enemy position the commissar was to see that it was immediately fortified against possible counterattack, to see that his troops did not waste time stripping and looting the enemy dead, and to make sure sentries were posted and relieved.[14] The commissars also took the lead in such matters as sanitation and hygiene in their units. Lecturing the troops on the poor latrine facilities and generally poor sanitation situation in their unit, the commissars of the British battalion went so far as to hold up the British army as an example of the way such matters should be handled. "We must copy the good points of the Capitalist army," they concluded.[15] The commissars also carried on a continuous effort to promote general military efficiency by emphasizing the importance of care of weapons and equipment by the troops. This problem, and the commissars' attack on it, intensified with the introduction of Spanish conscript troops into the Brigades. For example, a front-page article, printed in *Il Garibaldino* in capital letters, exhorted the soldiers to take care of their weapons, to learn to be "military technicians." "We must dedicate ourselves to obtaining absolute dominance of the technique of war.... That every man in our Army shall be a true and efficient combatant!"[16]

The most serious area of ambiguity and potential conflict between the commissar and the military officer, however, lay at the very heart of the matter of command: where and with whom did final authority reside. The ambiguity of the situation was indicated in an article in the Brigade press on the role of the political commissars which concluded, "Only in special circumstances can the political commissar countermand the orders of the military commanders."[17]

This problem was never really solved. Indeed it could not be. From the Communist point of view the commissar represented the best, the most reliable, the most politically conscious element in the army as well as the most direct representative of the party.[18] Thus they could never consent to anything that would limit the scope of the commissar's role, nor could they accept the idea of his being placed under the authority of the military command. On the other hand, everyone recognized the necessity for a technically competent military command which must exercise authority in the area of technical military matters. In discussing the problem, Vidali wrote that the "relationship between commissar and officer should be 50–50." This, of course, answered nothing. He went on to emphasize the key role of the political commissar in the People's Army and to say that the commissar must participate fully in all phases of military operations, must indeed be "a good military chief himself."[19]

The problem also received considerable attention in the instructional material for the International Brigades' training school for political commissars. Here, perhaps more clearly than anywhere else and despite the effort to smooth over the problem, the crux of the matter of ultimate command authority was apparent. "The military commander is the chief of the unit," read these instructions. But, "once the plans of operation have been worked out and approved, if the command fails [to carry through or perform the orders] the commissar has the supreme duty ... to take into his own hands the direction of the unit in the attack."[20] The commissar, the instructions continued, must acquire at least a minimum understanding of the elements and weapons of war in order to perform his role in combat. This was necessary not only in the case where the commander fell during the operation, but to be able intelligently to check the work of the military commanders. "While the commissar does not place the machine guns it is clear that unless he has some military expertise he will not be able to suspect the faults committed in that area, that he will not be able to detect sabotage in cases where it happens." Commissars were "to check orders received by the military officers, verify that they are precisely transmitted and that the distribution of duties is fair." To the extent possible he should emphasize the lessons of previous battles and explain to the officers "the politico-strategic significance of the work at hand." The commissar was assured that his responsibility was not in the least dependent on circumstances or chance. Rather he was just as responsible as the military command for all aspects of the work of the unit. "The commissar is responsible, as much for political work as the military, as much for the morale of the troops as for their combat capacity and for the way in which the soldiers and the chiefs perform during the attack."[21]

Given the extensive overlapping of authority and areas of competence between the commissars and the military officers, conflict between the two was frequent within the People's Army, especially where the commissar was a Communist (and the large majority of them were) and the military commander was not. General Vicente Rojo, chief of staff of the People's Army, wrote of "the abrasive interpretation of their [the commissars] function of control which went so far at times as to act as censors of the orders and dispositions of the military command."[22]

In the Communist-dominated International Brigades the areas of conflict were reduced since the vast majority of the military commanders were also Communists and thus subject to the same political authority as the commissars themselves. In the Brigades, the political authority of the commissariat was clearly supreme and thus, in fact, the commissar was the dominant partner. In cases where the military commander was also a Communist party member of stature, the commissar might well hesitate to challenge him, due to the commander's political position rather than his military rank.[23]

The political commissar system within the International Brigades operated under the direct authority of, indeed was simply an arm of, the Comintern-controlled Brigade political commissariat. Subject to that authority each of the separate Brigades had its own commissariat directed by a Brigade-level commissar. Directly subject to the Brigade commissars were the battalion and company commissars.[24] At whatever level of command, the commissar, representing the central Brigade commissariat, carried the ultimate authority of the Comintern into the military units of the Brigades. As commissar inspector of the International Brigades, Longo made frequent tours of the various units of the Brigades at which time he gathered the commissars together for a report to him and for the purpose of informing them of any new policies or changes in old ones. He often appeared personally when serious trouble arose in any of the Brigades and also made it a point to be in evidence at the front when the Brigades were in combat. He used members of his own staff as troubleshooters on occasion and posted reliable men from the headquarters staff to focal positions, both political and military, when he felt the need for a firmer grip on a given unit. The work of the commissariats of the individual Brigades and battalions thus proceeded under the watchful eye and close supervision of the Comintern hierarchy of the Brigades.[25]

The two most fundamental roles and duties of the commissars were those of politically conditioning the troops and maintaining discipline. The Brigade commissariat attached the highest priority to the job of insuring the "correct political orientation of the soldiers," a function "indissolubly connected with the military training and education."[26] Men being trained to become commissars were taught that the most important of their duties would be the ideological preparation of the troops.[27] Commissar Inspector Longo credited the "education and political propaganda" work of the commissars with making the Brigades a "truly model unit," a "homogeneous bloc."[28] In performing this role when their units were at the front, the commissars were to carry out "the most intensive activity in political explanation and educational work," to impress upon the troops "the comprehension of the necessity of sacrifice," and thus to create "an atmosphere in which the soldiers submit voluntarily to military discipline and to orders received."[29] Commissars were to carry out the ideological preparation of the troops prior to combat by explaining the military, strategic, and political significance of the action to be undertaken, pointing out the problems to be overcome in carrying out the objective, and clarifying the importance of the action in the context of the overall political-military situation. In carrying out this task the commissar was to bring out the lessons of previous military actions and to warn of the activity of the fifth column and the Trotskyists. The techniques to be used in accomplishing this work of ideological preparation included use of the Brigade press, tracts, political meetings, and "the mobilization of the party activists."[30]

The Brigade commissariat also stressed the role of the commissar in directing propaganda toward the enemy. The most spectacular, or at least most widely publicized, effort of this sort occurred during the Guadalajara battle. The commissariat, knowing that Italian troops were on the other side of the lines and knowing from prisoners taken that the general level of morale among them was low, decided to launch a vigorous propaganda effort in the hope of encouraging mass surrender. Longo, his wife Estella, and his close aides, Camen, Calandrone, and Nicoletti all played a direct part in the effort. Rounding up all available typewriters, duplicating machines, and loudspeakers, they bombarded Mussolini's legions with both verbal and written propaganda, even dropping tons of leaflets behind the enemy lines. These messages urged surrender and promised good treatment and repatriation for those who took advantage of the offer.[31] They also attempted to appeal to them politically. "Italian brothers, the Spanish people are fighting for their freedom. Desert the ranks of their enemies! Come over to us! We will welcome you as comrades-in-arms."[32] The messages, both in leaflet and in spoken form, used the information gained from prisoners already taken and interrogated to touch the weak spots in the psychological armor of the enemy troops. Prisoners who were willing were used to speak to their comrades over the loudspeakers telling them of the friendly reception they could expect if they came over.

The initiators of the propaganda effort claimed that it brought about significant results in weakening the enemy's will to fight and in spurring surrenders.[33] Whether or not it did in fact produce noticeable results could not be proved. There were no mass surrenders and those surrenders that did occur, as well as the generally poor performance of the Italian units, were quite likely due to their poor organization and morale and the failure of their mechanized units to stand up under the weather and other difficulties encountered. The one positive effect the propaganda effort had on inducing surrenders was probably in its assuring the enemy troops that they would not be shot if they did so.

But while Guadalajara offered a unique opportunity for the Italians of the Brigades to use these techniques, the commissariat stressed the role of propaganda directed toward the enemy as a regular function of the political commissars of all units. An article signed by Gallo (Longo) in the *Volunteer for Liberty* laid down the commissariat's guidelines on this subject. An outline of topics to be covered in this propaganda included the reading of war bulletins, why we fight, what happens within our lines as compared with theirs, why Hitler and Mussolini send troops to Spain, the inevitability of Loyalist victory, crimes committed by invading troops, and how we treat our prisoners. Calling for "loudspeakers at every front," the article stressed that this work should be carried on systematically and continuously.[34]

The instructions to candidates at the Brigade school for political commissars also stressed this function. Candidates learned that their duties would include finding out the type of troops their units were facing, their condition and morale, and then pitching the propaganda effort accordingly. The future commissars also learned that both loudspeakers and written tracts were to be used in carrying out this duty and that they should use enemy deserters and prisoners, where possible, to talk to their comrades as a method of influencing them to surrender. The Brigade commissariat, calling this the "new artillery," showed the importance it attached to this whole operation by assigning top politicos to develop it, including even, in 1938, Vittorio Vidali.[35]

The commissar's role as political propagandist included much more than just the psychological preparation of his troops for battle and the direction of propaganda toward the enemy. At the very core of his ideological-political role was the duty to propagate the Communist point of view on all subjects. The Communists had in Spain, as elsewhere, a unitary line which explained all things and which was, for the true believer, the only correct explanation. It was the absolute duty of every party member not only to accept the party line but to be "ardent defenders and propagandists of the correct policy of our Party." All communist party members and especially all political commissars were expected to strive continuously to put across the "Bolshevik line of the Party" and to oppose all "faction mongers," a term elastic enough to include anyone who opposed that line. In the words of a top Brigade politico: "The concise line of the Communist Party . . . was the guiding star in the political training of our International Brigades cadres and in improving the political morale of the battalions."[36]

The process of indoctrinating the troops began with the indoctrination of the commissars themselves. The interpretation of each military and political development in Spain was worked out by the top echelons of the Albacete commissariat along with the best method of integrating the party line into the overall context of the war and of presenting it to the rank-and-file troops. An American Brigade member later recalled being present at a meeting of the American commissars where the leading United States party representative, Robert Minor, explained to the assembled commissars the party line on the fall of Santander. In the same vein, *Le Soldat de la République* carried a report on a meeting of all Brigade commissars at which they discussed the topic of the new Negrín government.[37]

Once the correct explanation had been decided upon, the commissars at all levels of command had the duty of presenting it in a convincing way to the troops. They used the Brigade press and periodic political meetings to do so. These political sessions were a regular feature of life in the Brigades and were considered highly important by the commissariat. As British Commissar Rust put it: "Morale and discipline was maintained and strengthened by organized political work." The American commissar Voros said that attendance at these meetings was compulsory. The commissars often used excerpts from official Comintern or Spanish Communist sources as the vehicle for conveying, through the Brigade press, the party's explanation of events to the troops. On the fall of Malaga, for example, the Brigade press printed the promulgation of the central committee of the Spanish party on the subject.[38] The Spanish party itself served chiefly as a convenient conduit for Comintern decisions and policies.

The other side of the commissariat's control of the press and propaganda output of the Brigades as a vehicle of political thought control was its strict censorship of all reading material not officially sanctioned by the party. Few nonparty newspapers and periodicals, either Spanish or foreign, could be obtained by the men of the Brigades, and those that were allowed were strictly censored for news or interpretations that conflicted with the party line. An American attached to the staff of the *Volunteer for Liberty* had as one of his duties the censoring of all American publications prior to their distribution to the troops. His orders were to remove any material which indicated that a Loyalist victory was not inevitable and any unfavorable references to the Soviet Union, the Comintern, or any Communist party.[39]

The actual effectiveness of the commissars as ideological mentors varied depending both on the quality and skill of the individual commissar and on the receptiveness of the people with whom he had to deal. Political interest among most of the Internationals was high to begin with. A large majority were Communist party members who, for the most part, accepted the party line as propounded by the commissars without qualm or doubt. As André Marty put it: "The Commissars have relied on the workers who form the majority in the units, and among them on the mass of Socialists and Communists who now in reality form one united body."[40] Even those in the Brigades who were not party members were not likely to find much to oppose in the line as propounded in Spain since it was, on the surface at least, oriented chiefly toward the general theme of the Popular Front and antifascist unity.

When the commissar won the respect of the men by courage in action, hard work, and sincerity of purpose, and when he carried out his job of explanation skillfully, the troops largely accepted and even appreciated his efforts as performing a necessary function. Wintringham wrote of the commissars: "For discipline they were more useful than any number of guard rooms," and through their meetings and talks and through their example they "strengthened and organized the morale, the political understanding, and determination that was the basis of discipline." He called theirs "the most valuable work in Spain." Gustav Regler, himself a commissar in the XII Brigade, saw the commissar's role as "a maid of all work, a democratic priest, an army doctor with his fingers always on the pulse of the Brigade." "The political commissar," wrote Dahlem, "is the guide, philosopher and friend of the men. He is always in the front line, and there are many cases when the command of units has been undertaken by the commissar." John Gates, the American Communist who became the chief commissar of the XV Brigade said: "The commissar was entrusted with the job of education.... While a military officer in combat, the commissar was a combination morale officer, chaplain, information and education officer in the rear."[41] Interestingly, however, Gates later referred to "the troops under my command," showing, perhaps unconsciously, the ambiguity of the role of the commissar, even to the commissar himself.[42]

Many commissars, however, became filled with self-importance and, determined to use the authority granted them by the commissariat, exhibited a haughtiness and arrogance toward both the troops and the military commanders which made them resented and, therefore, ineffective. Inevitably such arbitrary and unlimited power went to the heads of some. A commissar who gained a reputation as one who made use of his power to bully or threaten or who abused his authority to arrest, jail, or shoot men for breaches of discipline or criticism quickly became the object of bitter hatred. Reflecting on his own experiences as XV Brigade commissar, the American John Gates admitted, "I used my... authority to denounce and even jail men who dared to dispute my word." Another American, Sandor Voros, wrote of the death sentences imposed on Brigade men by the American commissar, Dave Doran. The most notorious case of a Brigade commissar's having men shot for "political dissidence" was André Marty himself, a proclivity that gained him a dreaded reputation in Spain.[43]

Other commissars warranted not hatred but merely contempt. They approached their job of political indoctrination or education in a pedantic way, gave "long, boring... political lectures... a schoolboy rehash of the propaganda poured out by the ton by the Communist Party."[44] Such an approach quickly bored the rank and file of the troops. Showing awareness of this problem, the Albacete commissariat warned that the commissars must guard against becoming bureaucrats. If the commissar was to be successful in getting through to the men, he must "bear in mind the peculiarities of each battalion, each company, the characteristics of their members.... The work must be done from different angles, adopted to the mentality and the general political education of the soldiers."[45] Some commissars, too, took a narrowly puritanical approach to conduct and discipline, frowning on such soldierly activities as hard drinking, free and easy use of four-letter words, and occasional visits to the local bordello. These, too, were looked upon with dismay and ridicule by the large number of men in the Brigades who made no remote claim to being "clean-cut kids" and could scarcely tolerate the lecturing of what they scorned as a "prissy clique of Y.C.L.ers."[46] Commissars who spent too much time in Albacete, especially when their units were at the front, met with that particular contempt that front-line troops reserve for rear-echelon officers and soldiers with cushy office jobs. They were tagged by the men with the ironical sobriquets "comic-czars," and "rearguard commandos"[47] and inevitably became the butt of doggerel poems and songs such as *The Albacete Generals:*

> On the front of Albacete
> Meet the generals of the rear,
> Oh! They fight the grandest battles
> Though the shells they never hear.
> For the wind is in their makeup.
> You can hear the generals say:
> "Yes, we're going to Jarama
> Mañana or next day."...

> See them strolling in the evening
> To the grogshops for their wine
> For they are the brave defenders
> Of the Albacete line.[48]

The second most important duty of the commissar, and one that related closely to his role as political mentor of the troops, was the maintenance of discipline. From the very beginning of the Spanish conflict, the necessity for discipline stood near the top on the Communist's list of matters of importance. As early as July 22, 1936, the party press was demanding "Discipline, Hierarchy, Organization." A manifesto of the central committee of the Spanish party stressed the point that "in all organization discipline is the fundamental base of power and strength.... Only in the measure to which this discipline exists will it be possible to conquer an organized and disciplined enemy." In this spirit commanders and commissars of the Fifth Regiment demanded a "discipline of steel" and at times exercised draconian measures to maintain it. Dolores Ibarruri (La Pasionaria) stated the Communist view when she said, "The Commissar's duty is especially the creation in the new army of a new discipline, a higher discipline than the old." Longo wrote that the commissar had to be above all things "an apostle of the necessity of a firm, rigorous, iron discipline." Thus the Communists stressed both the absolute necessity of discipline and the central role of the political commissar in achieving and maintaining it.[49]

In the matter of military discipline in the International Brigades, however, the Communists faced a rather special problem. The Communist line, at least in the western "bourgeois democracies," had long been "antimilitary." Many of the young men from countries such as France, Great Britain, and the United States who joined the International Brigades arrived in Spain with naive illusions of becoming part of a "democratic army," where liberty, equality, and fraternity were the guiding principles and where soldiers, officers, and commissars shared the good and the bad as comrades in a spirit of "proletarian brotherhood." As the British Communist party spokesman and sometime political commissar in Spain William Rust put it: "Some of the volunteers had rather extreme ideas as to what constituted democracy within an armed force, and thought that the International Brigade could be run by committees and elected officers like a trade union or political party. Some would have liked to elect a committee to examine the 'class content' of every order."[50]

The Political Commissar

In the earliest days of the Brigades, political commissars were sometimes elected by the men themselves,[51] a phenomenon often pointed to as indicative of a "democratic army." But this took place during the hectic period of organization as a matter of expediency rather than choice. The Brigade commissariat had not yet had time to organize itself sufficiently to undertake systematic appointments. Even so, commissar posts at Brigade and battalion level inevitably went to Communists of known reputation and reliability.[52] Once the Brigade commissariat had time to organize itself, all appointments to political commissar posts came under its authority and they were, almost without exception, filled by reliable Communist cadres. Writing of the problems of establishing discipline in the early days of the Brigades, Longo recalled that it was only with a certain amount of difficulty that the Brigade directorate imposed the concept that officers and commissars were appointed from above and that they were responsible only to their superiors and not the rank and file. This was accomplished primarily, he said, through the work of "the most qualified Communists." Marty also gave credit to the Communist cadres who filled the commissar posts. They were, he declared, "the unshakable rock on which the magnificent International Brigades were built." Dahlem concurred: "The establishment of this type of political commissar is the great merit of the central political commissariat of the International Brigades."[53]

Actually the problem of military discipline presented relatively few problems so long as the Brigades were composed overwhelmingly of seasoned and dedicated party activists. These men were accustomed to strict party discipline and the political commissars derived their authority among them on the basis of being the spokesmen of the party. Thus it was political discipline and authority deriving from the party and not military discipline deriving from the International Brigades as a military unit which held the Brigades together in the earliest period.

Recognizing the strength and value of party discipline as a method of enhancing and ensuring their firm control of the Brigades, the Communists maintained a regular party cell structure within each military unit. This assured them of a solid core of reliable party cadres, a disciplined and unified group that could be counted on to carry through the party position on any given question. This party structure offered a tighter and, for the party member, more rigid control mechanism than could possibly be exercised through any other form. Within the party cell unit the rank-and-file party member could be told in a straightforward and authoritative way just what party policy was and what the party expected of him. The extra baggage of the Popular Front line could be dispensed with and problems could be dealt with frankly on their merits as seen by the party hierarchy. As Dahlem put it, "Many difficulties that arose out of the specific character of the International Brigades and of the influence of the inner political struggle for the life of the battalions were only able to be solved with the aid of the Party organizations which existed in the battalions from the very outset and the decisions of which were always carried through by the Communists."[54]

While many of the more naive of the rank-and-file Internationals, especially those from the western democracies, continued to suffer under the delusion that blind obedience was unbefitting a "democratic, proletarian and revolutionary army," no such dewy-eyed nonsense influenced the professional Communists who carried out Comintern policy in Spain and in the International Brigades. While Communist propaganda continued to speak of their "revolutionary" discipline as opposed to "bourgeois," "class," "medieval," or "capitalist" discipline,[55] the practical difference, so far as the individuals concerned, was impossible to discern. Indeed, the disciplinary techniques used in the International Brigades proved a good deal harsher than in most "bourgeois" armies, and the period of romantic illusions about the International Brigades being something new and essentially different in the way of a military organization faded quickly. Many Brigade men became embittered by the contrast between the democratic, revolutionary fraternity of equals which they had expected an army run by Communists to be and what the International Brigades were in fact. Instead of comradely equality they found as great or greater rank differentiation as existed in "bourgeois" armies, including not only higher pay for officers and commissars than for the rank and file, but officers' clubs from which the troops were strictly excluded, an officer's mess, and officer's uniforms which sharply differentiated them from the common soldier. Instead of comradely discussion of matters and a fraternal equalitarianism throughout all ranks and stations they found a stern discipline imposed from the top and often brutally enforced.[56]

Even in the International Brigade hospitals commissars worked zealously at their roles of ideological preparation and the maintenance of discipline. "The life of the hospital," wrote a volunteer nurse, "was carried out in an atmosphere of preparation for the front." Activities of the hospital commissars included the production of a "wall newspaper," the distribution of *L'Humanité*, the organization of political and "self-criticism" meetings, and song fests at which antifascist songs were sung in various languages. The political commissar of the hospital, she continued, was "a very sectarian German comrade" who insisted on rigid discipline, even though many of the comrades, "especially the French, did not like it."[57]

The problem of maintaining a high level of discipline within the Brigades became progressively more difficult as the war dragged on, bringing the inevitable boredom, frustration, and disillusionment to many of the foreign volunteers as well as a decline in the numbers of hard-core party activists among them. Also, the ever-increasing numbers of Spanish recruits assigned to the Brigades, most of them nonpolitical conscripts, presented new disciplinary problems. On the problem of the Spanish conscripts, Commissar Inspector Longo wrote: "The veteran cadres, both military and political, must go all out to train, mold and discipline [the new recruits]. The task is not only a problem of enlightenment and political propaganda, but also a problem of military organization and a much higher standard of discipline than before." On the same problem, and indicative of the Communist view of the essentially political nature of military discipline, Franz Dahlem wrote of the "considerable amount of political education required to impose military discipline on these [Spanish] troops."[58]

An interesting approach to the problems of inculcating discipline, motivation, and military technique to the ever-increasing numbers of Spanish conscripts who, by 1938, far outnumbered foreign combatants in all the International Brigades was the "Activist" program. This was an effort to foster the soldierly virtues by creating a special category, the Activist, which would attract the more highly motivated troops. They would then, as Activists, serve as examples and exhorters to their less highly motivated comrades. In an article entitled "Soldados Activistas," Commissar Inspector Longo answered the question "What is an Activist," by saying, "The activist is the first and the best." He must be a "model combatant ... and ... an example for all his comrades. ... He must be the most loyal collaborator of the officers and commissars." The organ of the XIV Brigade defined the role of the Activist this way: "The Activist must be in the forefront at all times in accomplishing whatever work there is, especially in fortification, vigilance and discipline. They must be also the leaders in combat, animating all their *compañeros* of their unit. If there are comrades who are ignorant of what we fight for, it is the duty of the Activist to explain clearly. ... To gain victory, we must all be Activists."[59]

In the face of all difficulties the commissars hammered away zealously at the task of inculcating and maintaining discipline. As early as February 1937, *Le Soldat de la République* was demanding that "all acts of indiscipline . . . be dealt with in an exemplary fashion. We must have an army with discipline of iron . . . both in the front and in the rear." In March 1937 *Our Fight* was strongly condemning indiscipline and insisting that "measures must be taken to punish the culprits and to eliminate bad elements. . . . We are confident that the political commissars will do their utmost to irradicate all tendencies to indiscipline and so carry on the political education of our comrades so as to make our battalion worthy fighters."[60]

The Brigade press enthusiastically endorsed the decree on military discipline issued in June 1937 by the Loyalist government. "The necessity of assuring discipline within the army calls for a penal code of adequate sanctions against indiscipline," editorialized the organ of the XV Brigade when publishing the new code. Few would argue that "adequate sanctions" were not included in this one. Among the stipulations of the code were: Any soldier who left his post, twenty years or death; anyone who fled in the face of the enemy, immediate execution; any soldier who struck an officer, twelve years or death; any soldier who disobeyed an order or failed to execute an order, twenty years or death; any of the above perpetrated at the front or in combat could be punished by death immediately by either military or political officers without recourse to higher authority.[61]

Along with this the commissars conducted a vigorous and continuous campaign in the Brigade press designed to convince the troops that military discipline was not "unproletarian." One point in this effort involved the question of saluting officers. "A salute is not undemocratic," the men were informed. "A salute is a sign that a comrade who has been an egocentric individual in private life has adjusted himself to a collective way of getting things done." In a eulogy to the American commissar, Dave Doran, John Gates, new XV Brigade commissar, wrote: "We vets remember when it was thought bourgeois to salute an officer." Now, thanks to the work of such exemplary commissars as Doran, concluded Gates, we have learned better.[62]

Meanwhile the Brigade press campaign emphasizing discipline continued unabated, the commissariat insisting in the most unequivocal language that an army could not function without "iron discipline, absolute and blind obedience." The Brigade *Boletín de Información* summarized the commissariat's attitude succinctly when it ran the slogan, boxed and in bold type, "Discipline is to the army what blood is to the body."[63]

Another important disciplinary function of the commissar was to act as a political police agent within his unit, to ferret out "fifth columnists," "Trotskyists," and "defeatists," terms broad enough to include anyone who proved recalcitrant, critical, undisciplined, or merely unenthusiastic. The official formula for this function was that "the political commissar must be always vigilant against and liquidate energetically all tendencies of treason in our ranks." The political commissars were to exercise "political vigilance against provocation" and to "maintain constant vigilance toward defeatist elements, Trotskyists and deserters."[64]

That Trotskyism and desertion were lumped together illustrated the ambiguity in Communist thinking regarding discipline. They tended to make little or no distinction between political discipline and military discipline. This resulted in the tendency to see political dissidence, "enemy agents," or Trotskyism behind all disciplinary problems and to react to all indiscipline as if it were politically inspired and treasonous.

Typically, both Marty and Longo took the attitude that all signs of indiscipline within the Brigades were inspired by Trotskyists and fifth columnists. Marty saw Trotskyists lurking everywhere and was convinced they were doing everything possible to "split and demoralize the International Brigades." That the work of these "provocateurs" did not succeed was due, claimed Longo, to the "quick and firm reaction by the political commissars." It was the political commissars, he continued, who overcame the disruptive attempts of "enemy agents" within the Brigades.[65]

9 Comintern Propaganda Instrument

Among the most important roles played by the International Brigades within the Comintern's Popular Front strategy during the Spanish war was that of an extremely potent propaganda instrument: both as source and as symbol. As source, the voluminous propaganda output of the Brigades themselves consistently adhered to and reinforced Comintern policy in its specifically Spanish and in its larger international aspects. As symbol, the very existence of the Internationals in Spain made them a tremendously attractive propaganda vehicle that could be, and was, exploited to appeal to a number of different audiences.

Within the Brigades themselves the commissariat's control of all press and propaganda activities was a vital element in carrying out its political and ideological function. Commissar Inspector Longo exercised direct authority over that most potent instrument of control throughout the entire International Brigades. As early as December 1936 the XII Brigade commissars were turning out mimeographed news sheets, *Noi Passeremo* for the Italians, *Vers la Liberté* for the French, and the *Dombrowski* for the Poles. On January 10, 1937, Longo ordered Alfred Kantorowicz, a German Communist writer, to set up and edit a newspaper for the German-speaking volunteers of the XI Brigade and to recruit someone to translate it into French. During the four months thereafter Kantorowicz organized and edited the German and French editions of the *Volontaire de la Liberté* from Valencia. On April 27 the operation was moved to Madrid at which time Kantorowicz was assigned to the XIII Brigade for the purpose of producing some publicity for that theretofore largely ignored unit. He subsequently produced a series of articles on the XIII Brigade which appeared in the *Volunteer for Liberty*.[1]

At a conference of political commissars held on the night of February 14, 1937, during the heat of the Jarama battle, Longo promulgated a new policy on press and propaganda operations within the Brigades. From that time forward every Brigade and battalion was to publish brief and frequent news bulletins that would reflect the immediate experiences and concerns of the troops. These bulletins would be, as Longo put it, "the instrument of military and political direction of the Commissariat."[2]

The various Brigade and battalion commissariats quickly acquired the equipment and personnel necessary to begin immediate publication of their "bulletins of information and orientation." The XV Brigade, for example, set up, during the long trench vigil following the Jarama battle, a mobile office in a large, camouflaged truck. On one side it carried its wall newspaper called *L'Internationale*. These wall newspapers were common throughout the Brigades and were apparently highly thought of by those in charge of press operations. The XIV Brigade journal, *Vers la Liberté*, for example, ran a front-page article in which "le journal mural" was said to have "immense utility" and to be "a necessity."[3] Inside the truck a duplicating machine and three typewriters provided the hardware with which the staff turned out the Brigade's bulletin, a task which at that time in the XV Brigade had to be accomplished each day in three editions: the French *Notre Combat*, the English *Our Fight*, and the Spanish *Nos Combats*. It was also translated into Croat and Czech for the Slavic units of the Dimitroff battalion.[4]

The overall press and propaganda apparatus of the Brigades underwent further systemization and elaboration at a conference of political commissars held shortly after the Jarama fighting. In addition to the bulletins of the various units there was now to be a centrally edited and published newspaper which would serve as the official organ of the commissariat. That publication, to be called the *Volunteer for Liberty*, would be published simultaneously in French, German, English, Italian, Polish, and Spanish.[5]

The *Volunteer for Liberty*, as the official organ of the Brigade commissariat, was carefully edited to ensure the correct application of the party line to all subjects. The editorial staff met regularly to discuss the treatment to be given various topics to ensure the proper integration of the party line into them. They were guided in this by a careful study of the positions taken and the interpretations given by various official party publications and statements.[6]

In addition to the *Volunteer for Liberty* and the various individual unit publications, the commissariat published a centrally edited news bulletin, the *Boletín de Información de las Brigadas Internacionales*, which appeared daily beginning in March 1937 in Spanish, French, Italian, German, Polish, Hungarian, Czechoslovakian, and English. The news bulletin normally consisted of from four to six mimeographed pages. The standard format featured news flashes from the fronts, Spanish news, international news, articles, and reproductions of commissariat orders or notices of changes in the Brigade commissariat's personnel. The news flashes from the front were almost invariably optimistic and meaningless, and the Spanish and international news and articles always reflected the general party line, much of it being excerpts from *Mundo Obrero, Izvestia, Pravda,* and the British *Daily Worker.* In line with the heavily Spanish composition of the Brigades, the publication of the *Boletín de Información* in non-Spanish languages ceased in December 1937. From that time each unit produced a similar bulletin in the Spanish language for which the commissariat continued to furnish news, information, and direction.[7]

The Brigade commissariat maintained a Madrid headquarters in a large building on the Calle Velasquez. From there emanated the large and varied press and propaganda output of the commissariat as well as political direction and editorial support for the agitation and propaganda activities of the various sub units. A staff of some thirty-five in the Madrid headquarters published approximately 2,500 bulletins in eight languages each day.[8] Under Longo's overall supervision the editorial staff in Madrid was headed by his trusted lieutenants of the Italian Communist party, including Edoardo D'Onofrio and Giacomo Calandrone and Longo's wife, Teresa Noce ("Estella"). Representatives of the various nationalities in the Brigades were regularly assigned to the editorial staff. For example, the English Communist and sometime Brigade political commissar Ralph Bates served as the editor of the English edition of the *Volunteer for Liberty* when it began publication in May 1937. The American Edwin Rolfe, late of the United States *Daily Worker* staff, took over that position in July 1937 and was later succeeded by his assistant, the American Communist John Tisa. The last to occupy the editorship was the American party functionary Sandor Voros.[9]

The Brigade commissariat also demonstrated the high value it placed on propaganda by the publication of expensive productions designed for various audiences. One example, issued in magazine format, using high-priced glossy paper, a multicolored cover, several types of print, and many photographs, was entitled *Nuestros Españoles.* Aimed chiefly at the Spanish population, it glorified the role of the Yugoslav element in the International Brigade. The introduction reiterated the usual Popular Front propaganda line and used the International Brigades, and in particular the Yugoslav element, as the great example of the Popular Front in action. The strictly Communist nature of the message was quite overt. The cover displayed the hammer and sickle emblem prominently. The publication was dedicated to Blagoye Parovic, whom it described as a member of the central committee of the Communist party of Yugoslavia, and contained a full-page photograph of Georgi Dimitroff. Another page was devoted to glorification of Dimitroff and made the statement that "the Yugoslavs fight in Spain in the name of and under the banner of Comrade Dimitroff."[10]

The Brigade commissariat's press and propaganda section also edited a number of yearbook or souvenir book publications which were highly propagandistic in nature. Longo, his wife Estella, and Calandrone collaborated on the production of one such publication for the XII Brigade called *Garibaldini in Spagna*. Following the battle of Brunete, Alfred Kantorowicz devoted himself, at the direction of Longo, to editing a book on the XIII Brigade which he called *Tschapaiev: Das Batallion Der 21 Nationen.*[11] Theodor Balk performed the same task for the XIV Brigade in his *La Quatorzième*, and the XV Brigade produced *Nos Combats: Livre de la 15eme Brigade* which also came out in an English version.

The voluminous propaganda output of the Brigade commissariat unfailingly echoed the Comintern position in all respects. The Popular Front strategy required the Communists to pitch their propaganda toward "antifascist solidarity," the "defense of peace and democracy," and "defense of the Republic" in Spain, and to avoid an overt or exclusive emphasis on Communism or "revolution." Thus, as was intended, Communist propaganda during that era, including that emanating from the International Brigades, seemed on the surface to be concerned only with democracy and antifascism. To the Communists, however, antifascism, for all practical purposes, meant pro-Soviet Union, and democracy meant Communism. That this was indeed their underlying premise came through clearly, if perhaps unconsciously, in much of their propaganda output. For example, this statement from the Brigade *Boletín de Información:* "The defense of the USSR is a fundamental duty of all anti-fascists.... The enemies of the USSR are the mortal enemies of all humanity.... The USSR is the invincible lever of peace, of real democracy, of progress and humanity throughout the entire world."[12]

Thus, despite the broad antifascist and Popular Front facade of the Brigade press output, it meshed smoothly in all respects with the larger Comintern propaganda effort. While this was so of its overall tone, it was especially clear in a number of specific areas in which the party line was consistently followed. Among these were a virulent and vociferous anti-Trotskyism; a consistent condemnation of all proletarian or labor organizations that failed to follow the Comintern's lead; a 100 percent pro-Soviet Union and Comintern orientation (including an inordinate amount of coverage of the USSR for a press supposedly directed to and concerned with Spain); consistent adherence to the Soviet-Comintern line that the Sino-Japanese conflict was an integral part of an international fascist conspiracy; and a never-failing acceptance of the Communist position on all internal Spanish affairs. This orientation was further shown (and reinforced) by the almost exclusive use of Soviet and Comintern sources, the most prevalent of which were *Pravda, Izvestia, Communist International, Imprecor, Mundo Obrero, Frente Rojo, L'Humanité,* and the *Daily Worker.*

Perhaps the most conclusive of these specific areas was the Brigade's treatment of Trotskyism. The Trotskyist hysteria, which was at that time running its grotesque and bloody course in the purges in the Soviet Union, cast its spell over the Comintern leadership and apparatus. It became one of the main preoccupations of the Communists in Spain to liquidate Trotskyism. "One of the necessary conditions for the victory of our people must be the destruction, with an iron hand, of the Trotskyite traitors.... The Trotskyites are just as dangerous as the armies of fascism," declared a leading Communist spokesman in Spain.[13]

As interpreted by orthodox Stalinists of the time the term *Trotskyism* came to include virtually anyone whose political persuasions were to the left of the party line. In Loyalist Spain that created something of a problem for the Communists because a substantial part of the population, especially the Anarchists and their large labor organization, the CNT, were in fact more revolutionary than the Communists. The Communists worked around the problem by concentrating their anti-Trotskyist fire on a small left-deviationist Marxist party, the Partido Obrero Unificación Marxista (POUM). They then invented a special denomination, the "uncontrollables," to cover those Anarchists and left-wing Socialists who opposed Communist policies. "Who are the enemies of the people?" asked José Díaz, chief of the Communist party of Spain. His answer: "Fascists, Trotskyists and uncontrollables."[14]

The International Brigade leadership marched in lockstep with the Comintern on this. The Brigade press zealously took up the chorus and, like the Communist press in general, raged mightily against the Trotskyists. An article by the German Communist writer and political commissar in the XII Brigade Gustav Regler began by admitting that the purge trials in Russia were causing some differences of opinion between the leaders of the Second International and the Comintern. It then proceeded to defend the trials by saying, in effect, that since the USSR represented the socialist revolution it could not be wrong. "Every comrade must understand that the trial that is developing in Moscow is part of the international fight against world fascism, the same fight as the International Brigades themselves are in. To disturb the unity of the Soviet state is to disturb the Popular Front of all Europe.... The people accused of being enemies of the Soviet Union are also enemies of our Brigades."[15] In another rationalization of the purges in Russia the Brigade press declared that the "unmasking of the Trotskyist center in the USSR has shown that Trotskyism is an agent of German-Japanese fascism." The Trotskyists, it warned, are "employing against the heroic fighters of Spain the same methods of combat which served the saboteurs, spies, and terrorists condemned by the Moscow trials."[16]

A feature article entitled "Fascismo y Trotzkismo" in the official organ of the XIV Brigade offered an outstanding illustration not only of the anti-Trotskyist line but of a number of other basic Communist assumptions which regularly, if less blatantly, found expression in the Brigade press. The first of these was that "Capitalism, caught in its contradictions, developed a new phase, fascism." Fascism was defined as "the rule of finance capital." Then, by an extremely convoluted logical jump, the reader was told that one of the methods by which this finance capital rule called fascism achieved its ends was— Trotskyism! Thus, the principal allies of fascism were the Trotskyists: "the bloodiest enemy of the working class" and the "chief support of fascism." Finally, the real reason for the necessity for proletarian unity and no talk of revolution in Spain until the war was won was "in order to take the succession of the capitalist regime which is in decomposition."[17]

The strange logic by which the Trotskyists became, in Communist terminology, fascists, showed the basic attitude that anyone who opposed the Communits was, by definition, a fascist. This was apparent in a speech by José Díaz: "In their hate against the Soviet Union, against the Great Party of the Bolsheviks and against the Communist International they [the Trotskyists] show the hand of fascism."[18]

The Communist nature of the Brigade press and propaganda was also clear in the inordinate amount of space devoted to, and the absolute adulation of, the Soviet Union, Soviet leaders, and Soviet policies. Articles appeared regularly on topics concerning the Soviet Union. Typical of these was one entitled "Twenty Years Ago the People Took Power," which appeared in a special edition of the *Boletín de Información* celebrating the anniversary of the Bolshevik revolution. The cover page featured a picture of a Soviet worker with hammer and sickle held high and a Red army soldier behind him. Others included "A Recent Stalin Speech," "Soviet Agriculture,"

"Twenty Years Ago in the USSR," "Capitalist Maneuvers on the Eve of the Russian Revolution," and an essay on Lenin in which he is quoted with approval as saying, "The only criterion by which human conduct must guide itself is to discern if it aids or if it hinders the cause of Socialism."[19] Soviet military specialists discussed the campaigns in Spain, the statements of Litvinov, Molotov, and Voroshilov were quoted on various topics, and Stalin received the virtual deification which had become de rigueur among Communists.[20]

This sustained attention to the Soviet Union in the Brigade press continued in this sequence from the *Boletín de Información* in December 1937: on the fourth of the month, an article on Sergei Kirov, "Hero of the Soviet People"; the fifth, John Strachey defending the Soviet purges; the seventh, "Soviet Socialism Comes of Age," by Sidney Webb; the eighth, portraits of the candidates in the Soviet elections; the ninth, another full-page coverage of the elections in Russia; and on the twelfth, a special edition devoted entirely to the Soviet elections and the "Stalin Constitution."

The Brigade propaganda machine went into raptures over the Soviet elections. The theme was that these were the "only truly democratic elections ever held anywhere," and no opportunity was lost to compare them with the "sham elections" of the bourgeois democracies. "The elections will be the demonstration of the fact that only Socialism, only the dictatorship of the proletariat can realize the real democracy for the workers," declared the Brigade press. Again, "The USSR is the most liberal and democratic country in the world."[21] The Red army was consistently depicted as "the best guarantee for peace among peoples" and as a shining example for the Spanish People's Army.[22] In a full-page spread on the Red army by Marcel Cachin, in which he glorified its strength and military virtues, he was able to discuss its origins without so much as mentioning Trotsky. "The Red Army was constituted," he declared, "by Lenin and Stalin with other old soldiers."[23]

The same heavy emphasis was devoted to the Comintern and its leading figures and policies. The basic theme here was that the Comintern and its leadership were the true originators and only staunch defenders of the Popular Front which in turn made them the only true and trustworthy leaders of antifascism. Georgi Dimitroff, chief of the Comintern, was regularly praised as the leading light of the world antifascist crusade and the moving spirit in the creation of the International Brigades. There were also frequent articles dealing with other well-known Comintern leaders, their activities and statements. The German and French editions of the *Boletín de Información* ran stories on Ernst Thaelmann, leader of the KPD; the English-language editions often featured Earl Browder and Harry Pollitt, leaders of the American and British Communist parties. Frequently featured also was Maurice Thorez, chief French Communist. "It would be ungrateful not to recognize and underline the forces represented by Maurice Thorez," declared the Brigade press. "He is the spiritual leader of the French people." The first several issues of the Brigade journal, *Vers la Liberté*, included the articles "Trois anniversaries—Lenin, Rosa Luxembourg and Karl Liebknecht," a "Message from La Pasionaria," a reprint from *L'Humanité* of an article by Maurice Thorez entitled "Huit mois de government de Front Populaire," and the article "Le 5 Regiment passe dans l'armee populaire," which included passages from speeches by Commandante Carlos (Vidali), José Díaz, La Pasionaria, and XII Brigade commissar Gustav Regler.[24]

In the area of Spanish politics the Brigade press emphasized almost exclusively the writings and statements of leading Communists who, naturally, adhered strictly to the policy and position of the Comintern. For example, every article in the July 25, 1937, issue of the *Boletín de Información* came directly from leading Communist functionaries and spokesmen.

In many ways the Brigade press seemed almost a Comintern house organ. News, notes, and messages regularly appeared which dealt with strictly Comintern affairs and personalities that had nothing directly to do with Spain or the International Brigades. For example, when Paul Vaillant-Couturier died he was eulogized in the Brigade press, being identified as a "leading French Communist writer." A message of condolence to the French Communist party from Dimitroff, speaking for the executive committee of the Comintern, was carried in the *Boletín de Información*. Another example of this appeared in an article to the effect that "we fighters of the International Brigades thank the vanguard of the proletariat, the Comintern, for having expelled from its ranks such traitors as Doriot, Mastow, and Ruth Fischer."[25] The Brigade press also frequently carried messages to the Brigades from the Communist parties of various countries and reported on the activities of the Communist parties at home. The English-language edition of the *Volunteer for Liberty*, for example, carried full coverage of the Congress of the British Communist party, in June 1937 at which D.F. Springhall, former political commissar of the British battalion, offered several resolutions condemning the British government and the British Labour party for their policy toward Spain and paid a glowing tribute to the British battalion, which, he declared, "has saved the honor of the British working class." The

Congress ended by sending greetings to the British, Irish, and American comrades in the Brigades. Similarly the *Boletín de Información* carried a "Greeting to the International Brigades from the Young Communist League of France at their 9th Congress." It read, in part: "We greet all you young antifascists [in the Brigades]. We greet the Young Communists among you at the head of which are found members of our Central Committee: Richard, Guguet, Escure, Lafout, Hacke, and Clonet."[26]

The Brigade press consistently took the Comintern position regarding the relations between the Comintern and the various European proletarian and labor organizations. This position was unfailingly hostile to the British Labour party leadership which was characteristically referred to as "reactionary." Labour party policy was described as "a shameful betrayal of the Spanish workers... a stab in the back." The British should "take the line of the Soviet Union and the Popular Front."[27]

The same echo of Comintern policy was apparent regarding the Second International and the International Federation of Trade Unions. The Communists wanted very much to get those two important "proletarian" organizations to follow their lead and worked hard to achieve proletarian solidarity. "Unity between antifascists all over the world is the only force that can and must put an end to the vast fascist conspiracy. Comrade Dimitroff has said that this unity is well on the way to becoming a fact.... The working class of the capitalist countries has almost liquidated the split provoked in the world movement by social-democracy.... The existence of the great Socialist country [the USSR], powerful bulwark in the struggle by the world proletariat, bulwark for peace, liberty and progress, is the greatest factor for liquidating the split in the world movement."[28] Not only did the Brigade press report extensively on the Comintern's efforts in this direction, but two of the Comintern representatives in its negotiations with the Second International were the top Brigade politicos, Luigi Longo and Franz Dahlem.[29]

In April 1937 a significant delegation of European Socialist and Syndicalist leaders visited Spain and the International Brigades. Among them were Fritz Adler of the Second International and Louis Schevenels of the Federation of International Syndicalists. Later that year another important figure, Louis de Brouckere, chief of the Second International, visited the Brigades. All these dignitaries received the full VIP treatment.[30] As a follow-up to these visits the Brigade commissariat dispatched the following messages that were published in the journal of the XIV Brigade:

We have been fighting as anti-fascists in Spain for six months in the columns of the International Brigades.... We ask you to hear our appeal for your help.

Your authority ... in the II International means your voice will be heard, and we, anti-fascists, hope that those forces which could be realized in this moment of unity of international action will be utilized to aid Republican Spain.[31]

The same issue carried a similar message to Adler and Schevenels:

We have fond memories of your visit to our XIV Brigade in April... We, who are giving our lives and our blood in the fight against fascism were proud to see you in the company of responsible Communist comrades. It is for us the assurance that the union of all the workers in favor of Republican Spain is in the process of being realized.

How good we felt to hear you, Adler, exalt our work of international solidarity in the name of your organization. How good we felt, Comrade Schevenels, to hear your assurance of the complete solidarity of the International Syndicalist Federation. But speed is essential in realizing common action of the Communist, Socialist and Syndicalist Internationals.... Resolutions in favor of Republican Spain are fine but we need action....

We are certain, Comrades Adler and Schevenels, that our appeal will be understood.[32]

The reluctance of the leadership of the non-Communist proletarian and labor organizations to "adhere to the unity line called for by Dimitroff" led to frequent and often bitter condemnation by the Comintern, a position fully reflected in the Brigade press.[33] Some of these recriminations went so far as to imply that Trotskyism lurked behind any failure to toe the Comintern line. In an article significantly entitled "Franco's Trotskyist Allies against International Solidarity," this implication was quite clear: "After the eloquent example of the Communist International's demand for the common action of all workers organizations in favor of the Spanish people, when already it had done everything humanly possible, such as the sending of volunteers for the International Brigades ... and the creating of enthusiastic popular demonstrations in favor of Spain, none can deny that international solidarity does not exist." The article then goes on to condemn groups of Trotskyists in various countries as being "splitters of the workers" and "disguised agents of fascism."[34] The reader was left to draw the obvious conclusion.

The Brigade's propaganda line on the Chinese-Japanese conflict, in complete conformity with the Comintern's, followed the rather strained interpretation that Japanese aggression in Asia, like fascist aggression in Spain, was an integral part of a worldwide fascist conspiracy.[35] "Faced with the monolithic block of totalitarian states plotting with imperialist gold, faced with the bloody campaign of all warmongers, faced with fascist audacity, only a rigid union of all workers of the world ... can preserve liberty.... Pitting against that block the union of all the proletariat our victory ... is secure."[36] Also emphasized were the key role of the Chinese Communist party and their Popular Front with the Chinese Nationalists and the international working class's interest in the Asian conflict.[37] "In spite of the resistance of a series of leaders of the Second International and the reformist leaders of the trades unions, enormous masses have been mobilized in favor of Spain.... The Chinese people will find the same support." As to the International Brigade's own role toward the Chinese, the theme went: "We are aiding the Chinese People by direct action.... With our Spanish Comrades of the Popular Republican Army, we shall register further blows against Hitler and Mussolini. Each defeat for Hitler, Mussolini and Franco in Spain is, at the same time, a defeat for the Japanese bandits in China."[38]

The Brigade press regularly took a vocal and partisan view of internal political affairs within Loyalist Spain, a view that always conformed perfectly with the Comintern line. This was true in the position on Trotskyism and the general implication that those elements within the Loyalist ranks who did not conform to Communist policies were "uncontrollables" and, in fact, traitors.[39] It was also true in the attitude taken on the necessity for unity, a unified army and command, military and civilian discipline, and "no revolution."[40] The Brigade leaders and press did not hesitate openly to condemn or support Spanish government leaders and their policies. The Communist vendetta against Largo Caballero, and later against Indalecio Prieto, was faithfully reflected in the Brigade press and propaganda. André Marty set the tone by saying that while Largo Caballero served a useful purpose for a while he "did not grow with the situation." The *Volunteer for Liberty* handled the replacement of Largo Caballero by Juan Negrín in what appeared on the surface to be a straight news story. The "objective facts" were arranged to justify the change in government as being a result of Largo Caballero's failures. The same issue carried the text of telegrams sent, in the name of the International Brigades, by Luigi Longo to Negrín, Prieto, and Alvarez del Vayo, members of the new cabinet, pledging the enthusiastic support of the Brigades to the new government. Also, interestingly, the same issue carried a message from the "coordinating committee of the Socialist and Communist parties" ordering all their militants to remain calm and to follow the orders received directly from their respective national committees during "any difficulties which the solution of the present crisis might provoke."[41]

The undiluted Communist nature of Brigade propaganda was crystal clear too in the training of political commissars. The study guide provided for instructional use in the Brigade school for commissars devoted itself, in large part, toward the political-ideological indoctrination of the students. This indoctrination followed, in all respects, the Communist position. The first theme, for example, purported to cover the history of Spain. The emphasis, however, was on the fascist nature of the military *pronunciamiento* of July 1936 and in placing that event in the context of the "world fascist conspiracy." Fascism was defined as "the reaction of the most reactionary elements of finance capital." These elements were "preparing to conduct the imperialist war for a new partition of the world." Fascist methods for conquest were described as "collaboration with fascist forces and the bourgeoisie" in the country to be attacked. Trotskyism acted as an "agent of fascism" in this preparation by dividing the working class, and the POUM acted as the main Trotskyist element (and therefore fascist collaborator) in Popular Front Spain. To complete the picture of the war in Spain as an integral part of the fight against the "world fascist conspiracy," a connection was drawn between the war in Spain, the Sino-Japanese war, and the "fascist war against the USSR." Required readings for this theme included two articles by the secretary of the Comintern, Georgi Dimitroff, excerpted from the *Communist International,* and one by Brigade chief André Marty. Thus the war in Spain was placed in the correct perspective for the student commissars.

The second theme dealt with "The character of the Spanish revolution" and the policies of the Spanish Popular Front government. It condemned what it called "the policy of division of the fight against the Spanish Communist Party of the Caballero group," and Largo Caballero's policy "against the Commissars of War." It accused that group of trying to form a block with "the agents of Trotskyism and the extremist elements of the Anarchists." It then praised the Negrín government which, it said, "was opposed by the UGT, CNT and FAI but was supported by the masses." Thus, in a strange way the largest mass organizations of Popular Front Spain were cast into the ranks of the opponents of the masses. This left only the Communists as the true representatives of the masses. Assigned readings included an analysis of the Spanish revolution by Togliatti (Ercoli) and a speech before the Plenum of the Communist party of Spain by José Díaz.

Theme Eight dealt entirely with the subject of Trotskyism. Here the Trotskyists were, as usual, identified as "the agents of fascism in all countries." The reasons given for their being such were: they opposed the Bolshevization of the party; they opposed the Popular Front policy; they opposed the policy of the Soviet Union; they opposed the Comintern. They were "the direct agents of the Gestapo" and the "chief enemies of the people."

The opportunity was used to smear a number of other groups that were anathema to the Communists with the broad brush of Trotskyism. For example, the German Social Democratic party was labeled "the principle channel for the activity of the Trotskyists." Trotskyists had "infiltrated the Anarchist leadership" and the "left wing of the Spanish Socialist Party." In other words, all political elements that opposed Communist policy were tarred with Trotskyism and thus cast into the outer darkness as "agents of fascism." The clear duty of the party and of all antifascists was the liquidation of Trotskyism and the "purifying of antifascist organizations." Readings for this theme included the "Resolution of the Executive Committee of the Comintern of September, 1937, Concerning the Fight against Trotskyism," and a speech by José Díaz to the Plenum of the CPS entitled "The Enemies of the People." In this speech Díaz asked the rhetorical question, "Who are the enemies of the people?" His answer: "fascists, Trotskyists and uncontrollables." Given the broad definition of these terms by the Communists, that meant, in effect, anyone who opposed the party line. Thus the would-be commissars were indoctrinated into the specifically Communist attitude toward Trotskyism which was so broadly defined that it included virtually all political forces in Popular Front Spain (and in the world proletarian movement) which did not sympathize with and support Communist policy.

Theme Seventeen entitled "Twenty Years of Soviet Power: The Victory of Socialism and Democracy in the Soviet Union," devoted itself entirely to praise of the USSR and Communism. The "result of the Communist line," the theme ran, "has been the victory of Socialism over one-sixth of the globe." The result of "the line of the capitalists and reformists is the victory of fascism." The power of the Soviets reinforces a policy of peace against the policy of war of the bourgeoisie and "the Social-Democratic leaders." The theme concluded by stating that "the defense of the Soviet Union is the duty of men of the entire world." Readings listed included the *Report of Comrade Stalin to the VII Congress of Soviets on the New Soviet Constitution, the Resolutions of the VII World Congress of the Comintern,* various selections from *Imprecor,* and Stalin's *Problems of Leninism.*[42]

In addition to serving as a direct source of propaganda, the Brigades were a potent symbol for dramatizing and publicizing "proletarian solidarity," the Popular Front, the Loyalist cause in Spain, and the Comintern itself. "The Brigades," declared the *Communist International,* "represent the highest expression of international solidarity, of the anti-fascist united front and of proletarian honor, devotion and courage."[43] Here was a theme that the Spanish Communist press and the Brigades' own press never tired of repeating. The Brigades were the "living expression of international solidarity of the popular masses throughout the world," declared *Frente Rojo* in October 1937.[44] The organ of the XII International Brigade, *Il Garibaldino,* said: "These glorious columns are the bearers of international solidarity in the people's fight against international fascism." The *Boletín de Información* opined, "In the history of the working class, the action of the glorious International Brigades will always be engraved in letters of blood. They are the best sons of the International working class."[45]

That the Brigade directorate saw the Internationals as a major force among the world proletariat was crystal clear in this passage from the organ of the XV Brigade in commemoration of May Day 1937: "In every part of the world when the workers gather together today to demonstrate their solidarity with one another, we will be in their thoughts. They will think of all the comrades in the International Brigades with love and pride.... And as they listen to the story of the heroic deeds of our Brigades they will pledge themselves to increased support of us volunteers and of the heroic Spanish people." In a similar vein *Le Soldat de la République* reminded its readers: "We don't forget that we constitute the first International Popular Army known to history and that the entire world is watching us.... Therefore, we must be an example of proletarian unity." This view of the Brigades was also clearly in mind when the Brigade political commissariat ordered the creation of a historical unit for the Brigades: "The popular anti-fascist movement will have to know the history of the International Brigades, so as to be furnished with the ideological weapons to carry on the struggle against fascism."[46]

The Comintern also saw the Brigades as an especially good instrument for appealing to a much wider public than the specifically proletarian. In this respect the Brigades served especially well the Popular

Front policy. The American journalist and supporter of Loyalist Spain Louis Fischer reported an interview with Georgi Dimitroff, then secretary of the Comintern, in which Dimitroff voiced the hope that an American Popular Front could be forged from the Americans in the International Brigades.[47] Since there were only a few thousand Americans in the Brigades, Dimitroff could only have had in mind that the propaganda appeal of the Brigades would be the catalyst for the formation of a Popular Front in the United States.

Evidence that Dimitroff's optimism about the effects of the Internationals was fully shared by the American party's hierarchy was reflected in this Christmas Greeting message to the Americans in the Brigades.

> Your heroic deeds ... have brought glory and honor to the working class of America, have encouraged and inspired hundreds of thousands and millions to fight against the disgraceful policy of isolation and false neutrality.
>
> Your great deed is having a profound and enduring effect upon every section of progressive America. Your deeds and heroism are today the proud boast of all that is best in America from coast to coast. Your name has become a symbol of heroism and inspiration to all of us at home.[48]

Somewhat later Robert Minor, a leading hierarch in the Communist party in the United States, said: "I make the categorical statement that the heroic fighting of the American boys in Spain, and the consequent interest and sympathy and pride awakening among the American people are a major factor in the political life of this country." The perspective from within the Brigades themselves was much the same. "The heroic struggle of the Americans in Spain has, to a great extent, been responsible for winning the sympathy of the American people to the support of Republican Spain. This support is expressed in pressure on the American Government to speak out against the agressors in Spain and China, in contributions of large sums of money and supplies ... and in the increasing numbers of Americans and Canadians arriving in Spain to join the struggle against International Fascism," editorialized the Brigade press.[49]

This optimistic view of the propaganda value of the Brigades was not limited to America. "The International Brigades show in practice the high value of International Solidarity and, thus, in all capitalist countries assist the growth of the anti-fascist people's front," declared the *Communist International*. Again, "The experience of the International Brigade is above all of tremendous positive significance on the wide field of the anti-Fascist struggle in all countries. . . . The example of the . . . Brigade must be an important step toward the unification of all anti-Fascist forces for a similar struggle in other countries." The Brigade press echoed this sentiment: "The International Brigades are a powerful lever for the creation of united international action, for the creation of the International People's Front."[50]

The central committees of the Communist parties of Germany and Italy assured their colleagues in the Brigades that by fighting in Spain they were "a symbol of resistance" to the regimes in their respective countries.[51] From England, Communist party chief Harry Pollitt declared: "The spirit of the Anglo-American volunteers is an inspiration to the movement at home."[52] The Brigade press assured the troops: "At home in England, the presence in Spain of so many brave comrades has produced profound impressions, and has led to many actions in support of Republican Spain. Important contributions of money and materials are being made every day and the significance of the struggle in Spain has led to a strengthening of the home fight against reaction, fascism and war."[53]

The Brigade press dramatized this point through an interview with an American lawyer, Levinson, who, apparently, had defended Dimitroff in the famous Reichstag fire trials in Germany. In answer to his interviewer's questions as to his view on the influence of the International Brigades on international politics, Levinson replied: "The influence of the International Brigades is felt immediately by the people and has its reflection on the politics of the nation and the world."[54]

Among the most valuable of the Brigades' propaganda roles in the overall Communist effort in Spain was that of maintaining the interest of large sections of the public in the various western nations in the Spanish conflict. The constantly reiterated fact that Americans, or Englishmen or Frenchmen, as the case might be, were fighting and dying in Spain exercised an undoubted effect in their respective countries in keeping alive the identification of at least segments of the population with that war. In that respect the Communists could count on the help of much of the bourgeois press of the various nations, many of whose correspondents in Spain were strongly sympathetic to the Loyalist cause in general and the International Brigades in particular. The group of newsmen and writers who were more or less permanently domiciled in Spain during the war, men such as Herbert Matthews, Vincent Sheean, Ernest Hemingway, Henry Buckley, Louis Fischer, Sefton Delmer, Louis Delapree, and George Seldes, mingled freely and continuously with the men of the International

Brigades, especially with their more appealing and articulate members such as Gustav Regler, Ludwig Renn, Hans Kahle, and General Lukacs.

Typical of the good press afforded the Brigades by bourgeois writers and correspondents was this by the American Louis Fischer: "The International Brigade is a daily reminder of the importance of events in Spain to the cause of democracy.... The Spaniards greatly appreciate the lofty idealism that moved each foreign volunteer to leave his peaceful home." Martha Gellhorn wrote in the mass circulation magazine *Collier's:* "The men who came all this distance, neither for glory nor for money and perhaps to die, knew why they came.... But it is nothing you can ask them about.... It belongs to them.... But you can think about it at night, with the windows open, listening to the thud of trench mortars.... You can think of it with respect."[55]

New York Times correspondent Herbert Matthews summed up his view of the Lincoln battalion this way: "You cannot dismiss these youngsters with the contemptuous label of 'Reds.' They are not fighting for Moscow, but for their ideals." Vincent Sheean wrote: "In the darkest moments of the whole dark year of 1938... I could think of the International Brigades in Spain and be sure that courage and generosity still existed somewhere on this planet.... In the long epic of the war [the International Brigades]... suffused the total effort with a moral value more precious than their lives."[56]

The Brigade commissariat was keenly aware of this sympathy and cultivated it carefully. The commissariat's instructions for commissars specifically mentioned that the American "bourgeois press" was very friendly to "the workers."[57] The close relations between the Brigades and the foreign correspondents as well as the exploitation of this relationship by the Brigade commissariat was apparent to those in a position to know. For example, Arturo Barea, a Spaniard who was a close observer of the foreign press through his position in the Loyalist censorship bureau in Madrid, wrote of the "foreign writers and journalists [who] revolved in a circle of their own... with a fringe of men from the International Brigades." He also mentioned that the Brigade political commissars "visited us as a matter of course and gave us information which we could pass on to the journalists."[58]

Similarly, numerous books on the Brigades were written by Communist party members and published by bourgeois publishers. These normally made no mention of the party affiliation of the author and thus were read by the uninitiated public as objective accounts. Typical of these were Edwin Rolfe's *The Lincoln Battalion,* Alvah Bessie's *Men in the Ranks,* William Rust's *Britons in Spain,* Tom Wintringham's *English Captain,* Geoffrey Cox's *Defense of Madrid,* and Gustav Regler's *Great Crusade,* which had a foreword by Ernest Hemingway.

The Brigades also served an important propaganda function in providing a focal point for the activities and interests of numerous foreigners coming and going in Spain. A great many of these people visited one of the Brigades. Many others communicated with the Brigades in writing. This type of activity served not only to focus attention on the Brigades themselves but to develop and maintain foreign interest and sympathy toward the Loyalist cause. Among those who visited the International Brigades frequently was Maurice Thorez, chief of the French Communist party. His visits were the occasion for reviews, festivities, speeches, and exchanges of fraternal greetings. The organ of the XII Brigade, *Vers la Liberté,* carried a description of a visit by Thorez as its lead article under the heading: "Maurice Thorez brings the salute of the Popular Front of France to the XII Brigade." The next edition again gave major space to Thorez's speech to the Brigade.[59] Other French visitors reported on in the Brigade press included a Comrade Zyromski who assured the troops that "the International Brigades represent that which is most influential in the International workers movement. The XIV Brigade is a symbol for us."[60]

Numerous Americans also visited the Brigades. In reporting on the festivities in honor of the first anniversary of the International Brigades, the English-language edition of the Brigade press noted that along with "La Pasionaria," "Gallo," and other Communist stalwarts visiting the Brigade were "Congressmen Bernard and O'Connell from the U.S.A.... Bernard applauded as vociferously as any and clenched his fist in the Popular Front salute many times. He stated that he had seen President Roosevelt before leaving the U. S. and the President had requested that he bring back a personal report on the Spanish situation and about the Americans in Spain."[61]

Another American admirer of the Brigades was the writer Anna Louise Strong. The *Volunteer for Liberty* reported a visit by her to the American battalion and a speech she made to the United States over the Loyalist government radio. The speech was a panegyric of the Americans in the International Brigade stressing the often expressed Popular Front interpretation that they were showing their patriotism by fighting in Spain. This was followed by a message from her to "the boys of the Lincoln, Washington, and Mackenzie-Papineau battalions" which assured them that they were indeed great heroes.[62]

In May 1937 *Notre Combat* carried an article, with photographs, of United States party representative Robert Minor and "Comrade Ford," the vice-presidential candidate on the Communist party ticket in the elections of 1936, who were visiting the XV Brigade. "Comrade Minor," the article stated, "will remain in Spain indefinitely as the representative of the *Daily Worker,* among other duties." In July these two again visited the Internationals, this time conversing with XV Brigade commander Vladimir Copic. With them also was the British Communist Ralph Bates, shown "lecturing the boys of the *regiment de train.*" That edition also carried a greeting from Francis Gorman, president of the United Textile Workers of America, and a member of the North American Committee to Aid Spanish Democracy. Paul Robeson also made a much-publicized visit to the Brigades. Robeson had the advantages, from the Communist's point of view, of being an American black who was both a well-known singer and a devout admirer of Communism and the Soviet Union. He thus combined the useful qualities of representing one of the earth's downtrodden people, of being an artist-intellectual, and also a firm adherent of the Popular Front and its chief protagonist. British party leader Harry Pollitt selected the active Charlotte Haldane to accompany Robeson as guide and interpreter on his Spanish tour.[63]

From England, too, came numerous visitors to the Brigades, among whom was Harry Pollitt.[64] "The English comrades are feeling inches taller today in consequence of the surprise visit of Comrade H. Pollitt," declared *Our Fight.* A greeting from Pollitt to the British battalion went, "We are proud of your glorious achievements and pledge ourselves to ever greater support from Britain."*Our Fight* announced in May 1937 a visit to the British battalion of Communist party members Will Paynter and Ted Bramley. Paynter, the readers were informed, was going to remain in Spain, taking over a post as political commissar at Albacete. One of the more important non-Communist British visitors to the Brigades, and one whom the political commissars tried particularly hard to exploit for Popular Front propaganda purposes, was the well-known Labour party Member of Parliament Clement Attlee. The Brigade press gave his visit extensive coverage and the First company of the British battalion took the name "Major Attlee Company."[65]

The International Brigade also proved a valuable propaganda instrument in its role as a focal point for various organizations outside Spain in professing their solidarity with the Loyalist cause. For example, the Brigade press carried a notice that the North American students who were fighting in the Brigades presented a flag to the

Federal Union of Spanish Students. The flag bore the words "American Students Union" and was presented by George Watt who was recovering from wounds received at Fuentes de Ebro. "The greatest proof of the solidarity of American students in Spain," the article continued, is that "American students have been fighting in Spain side by side with their international comrades." All this was seen as "proof of the friendship between students in American and Spain and antifascist students throughout the entire world."[66]

Another example of this friendship was the report of a message received from the World Youth Congress which had recently convened at Vassar College. The message, addressed to John Gates and all the American boys in Spain, told of the wild cheers that had greeted the reading of a message from the title page of a book about the XV Brigade signed by John Gates, George Watt, and Milton Wolff, members of the Abraham Lincoln battalion. This was "certainly the proudest moment that Americans at the Congress had," the message continued. "In fact it was the only moment at which American young people could say that the international cooperation we all talked so much about was actually being put into practice by American students."[67]

Other organizations were created by the Comintern specifically as auxiliaries to the International Brigades. Among these were the Friends of the Abraham Lincoln Brigade in the United States and the Dependents Aid Committee in England. Organized by the Communist party and staffed by party functionaries who had spent at least a brief period with the Brigades in Spain, the Friends served as the most direct open link between the United States and the Americans in the Brigades. The United States party used the Friends as a propaganda agency, sponsoring meetings and fund-raising campaigns, recruiting, publishing propaganda material, and supervising the statements of returned American veterans to the press. An example of the latter of these functions was the experience of Lincoln veteran William Herrick. Upon his return to the United States, *Life* magazine interviewed Herrick. When asked why he had gone to Spain he answered that he had gone as a member of the Communist party. At that point the representative of the Friends told Herrick to change his statement and say that he had volunteered because he was Jewish and wanted to join the fight against fascism."[68]

In Britain the Dependents Aid Committee served the same function as the FALB in the United States. Party worker Charlotte Haldane acted as chief spokesman for the DAC at the request of Harry Pollitt. Her staff consisted of paid party functionaries but, in good Popular

Front style, numerous prominent persons were solicited to become patrons of the organization. The *Daily Worker* ran a daily ad for contributions. Later, in the fall of 1937, Pollitt replaced Haldane with Fred Copeman, ex-commander of the British battalion, now returned to England after being seriously wounded in action.[69]

Given the Comintern's attitude toward the Brigades as the best example of proletarian solidarity and the Popular Front in action, the Communists naturally viewed propaganda emanating directly from the Brigades or from those closely identified with them as especially valuable. As the Brigade commissariat itself put it: "Every people, of every nation, must know who are their best sons, what heroic things they have done, how they have fought, how they have died and in what manner they have finally won. All of you must communicate this to your people, from your lips they must know the truth about the fight and the heroism of your comrades."[70] With this in mind, the Brigade leadership regularly used selected Internationals for broadcasting to their various homelands over Radio Madrid, an especially valuable method of getting propaganda into those countries where other methods could not be used. The Brigade press informed its readers of these activities on occasion and sometimes included excerpts from the texts of the broadcasts.[71]

Another technique for using the Brigades as an instrument to influence opinion outside Spain involved a continuous stream of written messages sent in the name of the Brigades to persons or groups in various countries. The German and Czech sections of the Brigade's officer training school, for example, sent a message to the president of Czechoslovakia expressing sympathy on the death of Jan Masaryk.[72] An example of how the Brigades were used as a symbol of and a vehicle for the Popular Front was this telegram sent to the United States in the name of the Lincoln battalion in commemoration of Independence Day 1937:

> We, Americans in Spain fighting for the preservation of world democracy, are proud to celebrate today the national festival of our American ideals on Spanish Soil. . . .
> As Lafayette, citizen of France, urged by impulses which all American democrats will honor today, sailed from his own land . . . so we have offered ourselves to the Spanish government. . . .
> Let us unite in our efforts to preserve democracy in Spain, in America, and throughout the world.[73]

This passage typified the approach taken by the Brigade commissariat when trying to appeal to the broadest possible audience, and especially in the identification of the Brigades with "democracy," the "Spanish government," and "American ideals." Typical also was the total absence of any mention of Communism or that the party had any remote connection with the Brigades, the war, or the message itself.

From the other end, widely publicized messages sent to the Brigades from various sources could serve much the same purpose. For example, this one to the Lincoln battalion from the American Leo Gallagher, identified as a "liberal lawyer":

> The progressive forces, [in America] ... know that the victory of democracy in Spain will immediately strengthen the United front, democratic forces throughout the world, and specifically in the United States....
>
> The role of the members of the Washington–Lincoln Battalion can be understood when one realizes that the fight in Spain is likely to shape the future of society....
>
> For this reason, we in America scan each day's paper for news about the Washington–Lincoln Battalion. We have read with pride the record of your struggles—volunteers who on foreign fields are defending American democracy.[74]

The commissariat also demonstrated its interest in propaganda and the Brigades' image by ordering writers in the Brigades, Alfred Kantorowicz, Ludwig Renn, Jef Last, Ralph Bates, and Bodo Uhse, to attend the International Writers' Conference in Madrid in July 1937 and by assigning a number of the Brigades' intellectuals to the duty of making foreign propaganda tours. In the summer of 1937 Renn went on the propaganda circuit in the United States, Canada, and Cuba. In the fall Gustav Regler performed the same role in the United States. Pietro Nenni made a propaganda tour of Europe in September of 1937, as did Jef Last. Many of the lesser lights of the Brigades were also used on propaganda tours in their own countries.[75]

The commissars also exhorted the men of the Brigades to make every effort to influence opinion back home. The commissar of the British battalion, for example, after telling his readers that "we are playing our part here but [Aneurin] Bevin and Company [the British Labour party] are stabbing us in the back," reiterated the point that the men of the British battalion must "use all influence to change the course in Britain and force unity [of the Labour party with the Communist position of Spain]. One interesting method of getting Brigade-oriented propaganda out of Spain was the printing of postal cards with propaganda posters and slogans on them and the label "Comisariado de las Brigadas Internacionales." Another technique was by encouraging the men to mail their issues of the various Brigade publications home. For example, the *Boletín de Informacíon* asked its readers: "Are you still sending the bulletins to your organizations in Britain and America? It is a powerful weapon for combatting press lies."[76]

The *Volunteer for Liberty* ran letters from home which, no doubt, encouraged this practice. For example, a letter from the Friends of the Mackenzie-Papineau Battalion, the Canadian version of the FALB, sent a letter thanking the men of the battalion for sending them copies of the Brigade journals which were "very helpful in gaining support for the common cause." The Communists also used letters from Brigade men to people back home for propaganda purposes by sponsoring their publication in printed collections. Numerous such letters also appeared in sympathetic periodicals. Those selected for such publication naturally conformed to the accepted Popular Front view. "What impresses one immediately," ran one letter published by the *Nation*, "is the complete and unbroken solidarity of all the workers and peasants in wanting the war won." Then the writer, identified as a twenty-year-old volunteer with the Lincoln battalion, exhorted his readers to "mobilize every possible group to give aid to Spain." He concluded by pointing out that "the fight in Spain is extremely important for the future of the world."[77]

10 Dissidence, Desertion, and the Terror

The mentality of political suspicion, hatred, terror, and murder that was then running its grotesque and bloody course in the Soviet Union and that cast its spell throughout the Comintern spilled over into Spain and the International Brigades. An NKVD contingent arrived with the Soviet diplomatic and military missions in September 1936, under the control of the veteran NKVD officer known as Alexander Orlov. The NKVD, or "Cheka" as it was commonly called, became notorious in Spain due to its widespread campaign of terror which included the jailing, torture, and physical liquidation of numerous elements of the political left, most of whom were lumped together under the elastic and inclusive term *Trotskyists*. This included numerous groups within the Spanish Popular Front who were too revolutionary as well as a large number of foreigners in Loyalist Spain, many of whom had been attracted to that country for the very reason that it was in the throes of a revolutionary situation. Of the operations of the Cheka in Spain the Soviet Intelligence officer General Krivitsky wrote: "Thousands were arrested, including many foreign volunteers.... Any criticism of methods and unflattering opinion of the Stalin dictatorship in Russia, or association with men of heretical political beliefs became treason. [The Cheka] employed all the methods familiar in Moscow of extorting confessions and of summary executions."[1]

Franz Borkenau, a man of the left and Loyalist sympathizer, was, like hundreds of other foreigners in Spain, arrested by the Cheka and accused of Trotskyism. Referring to what he called "Trotskyist paranoia," he wrote: "The Communists have gotten in the habit of denouncing as a Trotskyist everyone who disagrees with them about anything.... In the Communist mentality, every disagreement in political matters is a major crime, and every political criminal a Trotskyist. A Trotskyist, in the Communist vocabulary, is one who deserves to be killed."[2] "Trotskyist" referred to "left" disagreements. "Right" disagreement as surely labeled one a "fascist," although the circle closed as the "Trotskyists" were also labeled a "fascist fifth column" and the "direct agents of Franco."[3]

George Orwell, too, found himself caught up in the Cheka reign of terror which reached a peak in the wake of the Barcelona crisis of May 1937. He wrote of the many foreigners with "doubtful political records" from the Communist point of view who were "on the run with the police on the track" and of the "horrible atmosphere produced by fear, suspicion, hatred ... crammed jails ... and prowling gangs of armed men."[4]

The NKVD carried out its operations in Spain independent of the authority or control of the Loyalist government although it also rapidly infiltrated the ranks of the official Loyalist police organizations.[5] Virtually all the firsthand accounts of arrest and imprisonment for political reasons in Loyalist Spain make very plain the fact that the police apparatus was full of foreign Communists acting essentially as Cheka agents under the guise of government police. Indeed Loyalist cabinet ministers Prieto, Zugazogoita, and Irujo affirmed that the Loyalist police were heavily infiltrated with Communists, that the police carried out mass arrests without government authority, and that the Communists operated, in addition to all this, their own independent police apparatus.[6]

An example of the techniques of the Cheka was the case of Peter Elstob. Elstob, a young Englishman of twenty volunteered to go to Spain as a pilot. Somehow he ended up with a contingent of men destined for the International Brigades and, despite his efforts to explain that he was a pilot, he was retained with this contingent at Figueras, the entrepôt for the Brigade volunteers in Spain. Finally, for no apparent reason, he was placed under arrest and held incommunicado for several weeks. Among the people who arrested, imprisoned, and interrogated him were foreigners of various nationalities. Many of his fellow prisoners were also foreigners. While in prison he witnessed the summary execution of numerous men who were stood against a wall and shot. At one point during his detention the London Communist party representative in Barcelona appeared at the prison for the purpose of inquiring about Elstob's case. No more was heard from this individual, however, and Elstob was finally freed and expelled from Spain thanks to the efforts of the British counsul.[7]

A similar experience was that of Olaf DeWet. An Englishman flying for the Loyalists, he had volunteered not through political conviction but for adventure and money. Suddenly, and without apparent cause, he was arrested and imprisoned. Those who arrested, incarcerated, and interrogated him were foreigners. He mentioned particularly various Germans among his interrogators. He also witnessed the execution of a number of his fellow prisoners who were taken from their cells at night and dispatched with a revolver.[8]

An even more pointed example of Cheka terror was that of the Englishman Robert Smillie. Smillie, a member of the British Independent Labour Party (a "left deviationist" Marxist party), was associated with the POUM in Spain (and was thus a "Trotskyist" in the eyes of the Communists). He was arrested, incarcerated, held incommunicado by the Communists, and eventually died in one of their secret prisons.[9]

This atmosphere of political terror carried over, perhaps inevitably, into the International Brigades. The Brigade hierarchs—staunch, dedicated, and disciplined party members all—naturally adhered fully to the pervading Communist attitudes and were determined to maintain the political purity of the Brigades. The search for political dissidence, its unmasking and punishment, became one of the primary concerns of the Brigade commissariat. As Brigade man Jef Last put it: "One of the principal activities of the GPU [NKVD] in Spain was to imprison, torture and often kill volunteers of the opposition parties with the intention of ferreting out their relations with the so-called Trotskyists abroad who could then be handed to the Gestapo."[10]

While the regular Brigade political commissar system served in part as a political police, the main instrument by which the search for political dissidence was carried on within the Brigade was the so-called Servicio Investigación Militar (SIM). One of the Loyalist government's secret police units had the same initials, but the Brigade SIM was an autonomous organization; there was no connection between the Brigade organization and the government. In reality the Brigade SIM was simply a special unit of the Comintern designed to perform the role of a political police apparatus within the Brigades.[11] It was staffed by Comintern functionaries and party cadres of diverse nationalities, many of whom had performed similar services for the Comintern prior to the Spanish war.[12]

The Brigade Cheka, as the SIM was commonly called, operated from headquarters in Albacete and at the direct disposition of the political commissariat of the International Brigades. The Brigades maintained their own prison at Albacete until Brigade headquarters moved to Horto, near Barcelona, in 1938, at which time the Brigade established its prison at Castel de Fells in the same area. Commandant of the prison at Castel de Fells was a Lieutenant Copic, younger brother of the Colonel Copic who commanded the XV International Brigade.[13]

The Brigade Cheka was a microcosm of the police state in action. Once a man fell into its clutches he was completely at its mercy. No judicial review of any kind existed within the Brigade structure and no review of the internal matters of the Brigades was seriously attempted by the Loyalist government or military authorities.[14] Among the examples of this were the experiences of Brigade men Gillain and Honeycomb. Gillain, an officer with the XIV Brigade, fell afoul of the Brigade leadership and was arrested and imprisoned. Knowing that no hope existed of any intervention into Brigade affairs by the Loyalist authorities, he sought the help of Longo, General Walter, and, finally, de Brouckere of the Second International. None of these, however, proved willing to interfere in the workings of the Cheka. Honeycomb, an American, sought the intervention of the Loyalist authorities in his efforts to leave the Brigades and Spain. He was informed by the Spanish ministry of war that the matter was not within their authority, that the International Brigades had "complete autonomy." Honeycomb was subsequently arrested, along with several other Brigade men rounded up in Barcelona, and taken to the front.[15]

The Cheka placed undercover agents in all units of the Brigades to report any words or actions that might be construed as "dissidence," a term that very definitely included criticism of the Communist party or Communist policy. Any individual reported to Cheka headquarters, either by Cheka agents, who in some cases were also the official political commissars, or by others, faced arrest, imprisonment, or death. If the arrested person was a Communist party member, he was likely to be charged as a Trotskyist and "traitor to the party." For non-Communist Spaniards, the usual charge was "fifth columnist." German and Italian volunteers, whether party members or not, were likely to be labeled Gestapo or OVRA agents respectively. In the Brigade prison the Cheka attempted to force confessions from the suspects through the use of the same techniques then being used by the Gestapo and their own parent organization, the Soviet NKVD; solitary confinement in windowless cells too small for a man to move about in, the withholding of food, water, and sleep, all-night interrogations, beatings, and various other refinements. The final technique of the Brigade Cheka was the firing squad in the courtyard or a walk into the cellar and a pistol bullet in the back of the neck.[16]

If prisoners died under torture, the case was usually written off as a suicide. "Suicide à la Beckman" was the ironical term coined to cover this contingency in the International Brigades. It stemmed from the case of a German Brigade captain who was arrested by the Cheka in May 1937 because it learned that Beckman had written a letter to the Loyalist authorities criticizing the activities of certain of the Brigades' Communist chieftains including Marty, who, Beckman affirmed, had ordered the execution of four soldiers and a captain from Beckman's battalion. He was subsequently arrested by the Brigade Cheka and incarcerated in the prison at Albacete where he was tortured to death during the attempt to force him to confess that he had written to the Loyalist authorities because of a personal quarrel with Marty. Meanwhile, advised of Beckman's arrest and incarceration by a friend of his, the Spanish authorities sent officials to Albacete to investigate. When they arrived, Beckman was dead, a so-called suicide. The affair provoked a small scandal within government circles and a few demands for investigation. But at the demand of Marty and Longo, backed up by the Comintern and the Spanish Communist members of the cabinet, the matter was not pursued.[17]

The Brigade Cheka was controlled directly by the Comintern hierarchy of the International Brigades. According to Penchienati, Vittorio Vidali, the ubiquitous Comintern stalwart of Fifth Regiment fame, acted as the first chief of the Brigade Cheka. Both Marty and Longo, as the political chieftains of the Brigades, were, no doubt, intimately involved. The well-known German Comintern figure Walter Ulbricht played a role in this activity too. According to Ruth Fischer, Ulbricht, operating from Brigade headquarters in Albacete, organized the Cheka unit dealing with the German-speaking elements in the Brigades, personally directed the search for Trotskyists among his fellow Germans, and ordered the death of many of them.[18] Another highly placed German Communist and ex-chief of a GPU apparatus in Germany, Heinz Neumann, operated with the International Brigade Cheka, sometimes using the name "Enrique Fischer."[19] An American assigned to the Brigade commissariat where part of his duty was to read outgoing mail for signs of dissidence, especially any criticism of the party or its operation of the Brigades, worked under the direct supervision of Neumann who told him on numerous occasions that he, Neumann, had recently caught and killed "Trotskyite Fascists."[20]

The Cheka recruited agents from among party cadres of all nationalities. As the British Labour Member of Parliament John McGovern (who visited Spain and participated in an investigation of the terror there) put it, there were two International Brigades in Spain, the military unit of that name and a horde of Comintern gangsters and gunmen—the Cheka.[21] One of the better documented examples of the type of person who carried out this work was the American George Mink. Mink, a long-time Communist, had been involved in party work in the seaman's unions in the United States as early as 1930 and had worked for the Soviet secret police in various capacities, including that of assassin, for years prior to the Spanish war. Supplied with a false passport under the name "Alfred Hertz" by the NKVD, he entered Spain in early 1937 and took up his work as a Cheka agent.[22] Mink bore striking similarities to the stereotype of the gangland "torpedo." "I met him in a hotel in Barcelona in April, 1937," said an American who had previously been a party member himself. "He [Mink] got drunk and boasted about his NKVD work.... He showed me a roll of bills and he was wearing a London tailored suit which cost him $150.00 and he had very expensive leather luggage and said that that was the way to get a good reception in a hotel."[23] He apparently worked directly for the Soviet NKVD in Spain and was involved in their activities against various elements of the left. Mink "operated in the safe hinterland," wrote Jan Valtin. "His apartment in the Hotel Continental [in Barcelona] became the breeding place of many of the murderous GPU night raids on the homes of anti-Stalinists in Barcelona." Liston Oak reported that Mink talked to him about the Communist plan to provoke the POUM into a violent encounter and implied that Mink had some part in the murder of POUM leader Andrés Nin.[24]

Mink was also deeply involved in the Cheka operations in the International Brigades. He was, in this sense, an example of the close interconnection between the Soviet NKVD and the Brigade Cheka activities. He offered Liston Oak an assignment "to put the finger on 'untrustworthy' volunteers [in the International Brigades] ... such as members of the British Independent Labor party and the American Socialist party." Another American member of the International Brigades who had known Mink personally through their party work prior to coming to Spain, testified that he had been present when Mink and another Cheka agent shot and killed two American Brigade men. As to the reason for this execution, the witness did not know whether the men had tried to desert the Brigade and leave Spain or whether it was for some kind of political deviation. Yet another former Communist also testified regarding Mink's role toward the Americans in the Brigades, "I know that plenty of American Loyalists [Brigade men] would like to get their hands on George Mink. He was responsible for shooting many Americans in the back over there."[25]

The American party functionary Steve Nelson was also a good example of the interlocking nature of the various components of the Communist apparatus as it operated in Spain. Nelson had attended the Lenin Institute in Moscow where he received training in espionage and organizational work. Later he worked as a Comintern agent in China and was sent to Spain in 1937 where he apparently worked closely with the NKVD. "I heard much of his courage and ruthlessness in stamping out Trotskyists for the secret police," said Louis Budenz, then editor of the *Daily Worker*. In early May 1937 the party sent Nelson to Spain where, without previous service in the International Brigades, he assumed the post of political commissar of the Lincoln battalion and subsequently that of commissar of the entire XV Brigade. As a result of his work in Spain the central committee of the Communist party in the United States "co-opted" Nelson in 1938, an unusual procedure to distinguish a man who had performed exceedingly valuable work for the party. At that time United States party chief Earl Browder spoke "in glowing terms of Nelson's great services . . . in uprooting anti-party elements," recalled Budenz. But Nelson later told Budenz that Browder and the American party hierarchy had no choice in the matter. They had been ordered to do it by "the people he [Nelson] was working with in Spain," that is, the Russians.[26]

In February and March of 1937, when the Brigades were threatening to fall apart under the combined impact of the heavy casualties incurred in the Jarama battles and the widespread disillusionment and poor morale, the Comintern ordered even more of its reliable cadres into the Brigades to strengthen the party's control. Most of these men were assigned either to political commissar posts or to specifically police work.[27] This approach reflected the essence of the Communist attitude that military discipline was essentially a product of political discipline. This attitude accounted for the tendency of the Brigade directorate to see political dissidence, treason, and Trotskyism behind any and all disciplinary problems from desertion to such common soldierly foibles as drunkenness, apathy, frustration, and general griping. It also accounted for their proclivity to treat all disciplinary problems as extremely serious and deserving of the most rigid countermeasures. The problems of low morale, indiscipline, and desertion led the Albacete commissariat to demand "ruthless action" by political and military authorities in the Brigades and the use of the death penalty to maintain discipline. Lecouer referred to this period as one in which summary executions and "promenades" (a euphemism for shooting political enemies) became common in the Brigades.[28]

From at least as early in the war as March 1937, men were deserting or attempting to desert in large enough numbers to make it a major issue in the Brigades. As early as February 1937 reports from United States consular officials in Spain began to ask instructions for dealing with American deserters from the Brigades who turned themselves in to United States consuls for protection and repatriation.²⁹

The Brigade press also began to attack the problem of desertion during the spring of 1937. In an article entitled "The Battalion Gets Cleaned up of Cowards," British political commissar George Aitkin said that as a result of the recent combat and tours in the lines there were some grumblers and some attempted desertion. The deserters, he added, were caught and sentenced to disciplinary labor battalions for work in the front lines. *Le Soldat de la République* warned its readers against believing a document recently put out by the Nationalists telling Frenchmen in the Brigades that they would be given safe passage to France if they came over to the Nationalist lines. The document also told French Brigade members that if they turned themselves in at any of the French consulates in Spain they would be repatriated. Do not believe this, cautioned the Brigade press. It represents the work of fascist agents and will only get you in serious trouble.³⁰

The problem of those in the International Brigades who, for one reason or another, wished to bid a personal farewell to arms was complicated by a number of factors. One was that the volunteers never signed any definite contract as to their length of service in the Brigades, nor did they take any formal oath of allegiance to the Spanish government. Many assumed that since they volunteered for no particular period of time that they had the prerogative of leaving when they so desired. Indeed many of the volunteers had been told very specifically that their term of service would be three or six months, after which time they would be free to go or stay as they saw fit.³¹

Numerous French and Belgian volunteers, arrested on charges of desertion, claimed that they had been assured by the Communist functionaries at the recruitment centers that they would be allowed to return to their own countries after three-months service in Spain. When they applied for repatriation, however, they were told that no such verbal agreement was binding and that they were in for the duration.³² So also did various American and British men. On November 22, 1937, the United States consul in Valencia reported that a number of Americans from the International Brigades had presented themselves at the consulate asking for help in getting out of Spain. They said their contracts with the Brigade had terminated but that they could not obtain discharges. These men said they had just come from Albacete where they had witnessed the arrest of some twenty-five Americans who had left the front and reported to headquarters for discharges because their contracts had expired. After a fake court-martial the twenty-five had been taken back to the front under guard and executed.[33]

Numerous men also claimed that they had been lured to Spain with the promise of high-paying jobs. Once in Spanish territory the Brigade authorities took their passports and informed them that they were in the army. When the men complained, the answer given was that since they had no passports they were strictly subject to the Spanish authorities and that if they attempted to "desert," they would be shot. An experience of this type was recounted to the American newspaper correspondent Edward Knoblaugh by Lawrence Mullers, a Canadian, and Tim Kennan of Dublin when he met them on board a British naval vessel. They had succeeded in reaching the British consulate in Valencia and had been put aboard the ship by the consul.[34] That men were sometimes recruited under false pretenses was also corroborated by a twenty-six-year-old American bricklayer from Minneapolis to a *New York Times* correspondent in France:

> I was born in Coleridge, Neb., where I joined the Communist party.... Last month I saw an ad in a Minneapolis morning newspaper for skilled workers for Spain to take the place of men who had gone to the front. The ad was signed by the Society for Technical Aid to Spanish Democracy.
>
> "I applied and soon received a ticket to New York. Only when I reached New York did I begin to suspect that the tools of my 'trade' were to be a rifle and bayonet."[35]

The problem of desertion grew in intensity as time went on because of the widespread disillusionment with the Brigades and the war. The disillusionment stemmed from various causes that were, in some cases, of a diametrically opposed nature. Some, the type whom party orthodoxy labeled "left deviationists," became dissatisfied because they came to feel that the party line in Spain was not "revolutionary" or "socialist" according to their understanding of the terms. An example of this was the case of Henry Scott Beattie who, in a letter to the editor of the *Canadian Forum*, voiced the sentiment that the party's "Spanish policy was nothing less than a betrayal.... To crush the mass parties of the Spanish workers and farmers in order that the war ... might be made respectable and Spanish capitalism preserved. Anyone inside or outside our [Communist] Party who was openly against the protection of private capital was in danger of arrest by our own secret police."[36] Others became embittered by the contrast between the democratic revolutionary fraternity of equals which they had expected an army run by Communists to be and what the International Brigades were in fact. Indicative of this was an article by a deserter from the British battalion in which he recounted how the recruiter at Communist party headquarters in Glasgow, where he had joined, had presented a picture of an army of brothers who shared all things equally. This, said the disillusioned Brigade man, was far from being the case. Rather the difference in living standards between the Brigade officers and the rank-and-file soldier was immense. It was not "communistic."[37]

On the other side of the coin were those who became alienated due to the too blatantly Communist nature of the Brigades. The English writer and Loyalist supporter Stephen Spender told of the disillusionment of some of the British volunteers who had originally joined the Brigades because they identified the Republic with liberalism. Once in the Brigades they had become embittered by the overbearing Communist control.[38]

That there was a widespread desire on the part of many of the Internationals to depart from Spain, either permanently or, as it was more usually put in official circles, on leave, was too obvious for the Brigade directorate to deny. Yet the Communist hierarchy of the International Brigades, quite logically from their point of view, opposed any policy that would have allowed the Internationals to leave the Brigades or Spain. A situation in which troops could simply quit and go home any time they wanted would be disastrous for discipline and morale in any military organization. The difficulty of the position of the Brigade chiefs in the face of a situation in which a goodly percentage of the troops would have left had they been able was epitomized by the comment of British political commissar Kerrigan, when asked to send to a rear echelon post a young British volunteer who was clearly unfit for combat duty: "It is difficult to withdraw one man without discouraging the rest," he said.[39]

The obvious impracticality of a policy of allowing men simply to leave whenever it suited them could certainly have been replaced by a policy of specified enlistment periods. The Communists, however, had reasons for opposing any policy of allowing men to leave the Brigades and Spain on any conditions, except in those cases where the party itself and for its own purposes reassigned men from the Brigades to party functions elsewhere. One reason was the impossibility of replacing the men who would leave if given the opportunity. Indeed, it was impossible even to replace casualties except with Spanish recruits.[40] The Communists wanted the Brigades to retain their international character to the greatest extent possible; only in that way would the Brigades remain a stronghold of Comintern military and political power in Spain and would the propaganda value of the Brigades as the most vivid example of the international and Popular Front nature of the Spanish war be maintained. Alvah Bessie, a devout Communist himself and a late volunteer to the Brigades, said as much in his book on his experiences in Spain, *Men in Battle*. Writing of the disastrous demoralization of the American battalion and the small number of Americans who were still among its effectives after the Aragon retreat in 1938, he said: "But for the benefit of the folks back home the Lincoln Battalion was always intact, and the constant figure of thirty-two hundred Americans were fighting in Spain. We understood why this was necessary, but it did not prevent us from becoming cynical."[41] Another reason why the Brigade directorate objected to the repatriation of men was the fear, quite justifiable under the circumstances, that a certain number of them would make public some of the more unsavory aspects of Communist operations in Spain. That would have further curtailed the value of the Brigades as a propaganda vehicle and would also have damaged the image of respectability that the Communists were trying to maintain in the western nations.[42]

On the question of granting leaves outside Spain, the Brigade directorate saw the same objections. Quite realistically they recognized that once safely out of Spain, few men would ever return. Longo claimed that the Brigade commissariat wanted to allow Brigade men to go on leaves outside Spain in the period after the Jarama battle but that the Spanish government refused.[43] That was extremely doubtful for several reasons, the most obvious being that men were moved in and out of Spain freely whenever it suited the Communists to do so. Second, it was highly unlikely that Largo Caballero, Prieto, or the Spanish military staff, none of whom had any great love of the Internationals anyway, would have stood in the way of allowing them to leave. Third, even if the Spaniards had objected, the Comintern certainly had sufficient political leverage to accomplish it had they so desired.

The facts were quite the opposite. As numerous statements and examples showed, it was the Brigade commissariat which adamantly opposed allowing men to leave and which, through the Communist apparatus in Spain, made certain no such policy would be adopted.[44] The attitude of the Brigade directorate toward this matter was clearly shown by their position on the contention of Pacciardi and numerous of the Italian volunteers who were affected by the original contract drawn up by the Italian committee in Paris. That document specifically mentioned six months service. The Communist chiefs took the attitude, however, that the contract was no longer pertinent to the case; that when the Italian unit became part of the International Brigades it became subject solely to Brigade authority. Thus, they held, the contractual document had no further validity.

That it was the Brigade directorate and not the Loyalist government which insisted on service for the duration was specifically stated to an American volunteer who had been told that he was signing up for six months. When he was not allowed to leave at the end of that period he went directly to the Spanish Ministry of Defense. In answer to his question as to whether it was true that the Loyalist government required the Internationals to remain in Spain, the answer was: "No, that is entirely up to the Brigade command." He, along with a number of other Americans who were attempting to leave Spain, was subsequently arrested in Barcelona and taken to the front under armed guard. The XIV Brigade officer Gillain claimed that following the battle of Brunete the Spanish authorities proposed to allow a certain percentage of the troops in the Brigades to go on leave outside Spain but that the Brigade directorate at Albacete successfully foiled the move. The anger of the troops, who heard of the government's plan, was responsible for even more numerous attempts at desertions.[45]

The actual attitude of the Spanish authorities on this question seemed to be ambiguous and vacillating. In March 1937 the United States consul in Valencia reported to the State Department that six American Brigade men were at the consulate asking for protection and repatriation. He said that one of these men had been turned in by the Spanish authorities themselves. He also reported that the French consul had told him that he, the French consul, had evacuated 400 French deserters aboard a French naval vessel with the acquiescence of the Spanish authorities. He added, however, that the Spanish government had since changed its attitude. The United States secretary of state directed the consul to inquire officially as to the attitude of the Spanish authorities toward evacuating American deserters on United States warships. On March 19 the consul at Valencia informed the State Department that the attitude of the Spanish authorities had been to allow foreigners, who so desired, to leave the country; but, as of March 3, that had changed, and since that date the policy was to treat them as deserters. According to the French consul, he continued, many arrests were being made among Frenchmen who were attempting to leave the International Brigades and Spain. The United States consul reported on March 16, however, that if he had authorization to put American deserters on United States warships he could probably obtain approval from the Spanish authorities. Later, in July 1937, the United States consul at Barcelona reported that a group of American deserters from the International Brigades had been arrested while trying to make their way to the frontier. Most of them said their passports had been taken from them at Albacete. The Spanish authorities, he continued, were willing to turn the men over to the United States consulate for evacuation before formal charges were brought against them.[46]

If the attitude of the Spanish government was ambiguous, that of the Brigade commissariat was clear enough. In June 1937 Auguste Lecouer, at that time political commissar in the XIII Brigade, received orders to report to Marty at Albacete. Marty told Lecouer that he had a particularly delicate job for him. There was a veritable underground railway in operation for smuggling French deserters from the Brigade out of Spain. The focal point of the network was the French consulate in Valencia where the deserters could secure food and protection before leaving the country. Marty ordered Lecouer to uncover the channels through which the men got to the consulate by posing as a deserter himself. Once inside he was to index the names of all whom he saw. Lecouer succeeded in doing this and, once inside, attempted to talk the deserters into returning to the Brigades. They said that if they returned they would be put in prison or shot. Lecouer promised them that if they would return they would not be punished but that if they did not their names would be sent to the leftist political organizations in France and they would be labeled deserters there. His promise of no punishment was backed up by the word of Prosper Moquet, a Communist member of the French Chamber of Deputies who happened to be in Valencia at the time. Most of the deserters decided to accept the opportunity to return to duty rather than face ostracism at home. The French consulate in Valencia continued to offer protection and repatriation to those Brigade men (at least the French and Belgian ones) who turned themselves in. The Belgian officer Gillain, fearing for his life, found refuge there and was eventually gotten out of Spain on a French naval vessel in 1938.[47]

Even those men who made good their escape from the Brigades and Spain were not free from the wrath of the Communists. Frenchmen who deserted were the object of slanderous stories spread among the leftist element of the population in their homeland. The mere threat of that had been enough to dissuade one group of Frenchmen, who were as good as free, from proceeding to France. If anyone had the nerve to denounce publicly the Communist role in Spain or the Brigade leadership once out of Spain, he was subjected to public humiliation by the posting of leaflets in his home area on which his name was prominently displayed along with the most violent denunciations and accusations.⁴⁸ Some were hounded by party thugs and beaten up.⁴⁹ The party also persecuted men it considered deserters by using its influence in various labor unions to pressure employers into refusing to hire them. The party did that not only with men who had actually deserted from the Brigades in Spain but to some who deserted from the party upon their return home.⁵⁰

Most of the victims of the harsh disciplinary and political police regime of the Brigades simply vanished with no record of their fate. There were, after all, numerous ways of getting rid of dissident elements and troublemakers. One of the easiest and least provable was to send men who had been arrested or otherwise designated to the front lines and keep them there. For especially difficult cases there was always the possibility of a bullet in the back and a "killed in action" explanation. Haldane had reason to suspect that such a fate had befallen the British commissar Wally Tapsall, who had constant disagreements with the Brigade commissariat's policies. He was, said she, "killed in obscure circumstances." She gathered also that this same method of doing away with troublesome elements in the Brigades befell an American Communist who had originally been assigned to recruitment work in France. After being sent to Spain he apparently had difficulties with the Brigade leadership and was ordered to the front, not with the American battalion but with a Spanish unit. He was soon reported "killed in action." When Haldane tried to find out the facts of his death from British commissar Rust, he told her, "He was sold down the river by his own Party."⁵¹

While many men simply disappeared in mysterious and unrecorded ways in Spain there were some who, through the knowledge and testimony of others, were remembered. One of these was Hans Krause. The German Communist Jan Valtin received word that Krause, an old friend and Communist party colleague, had been arrested by the Cheka in Spain. Krause, a veteran of the Profintern, had conducted arms shipments from Marseilles to Valencia and then volunteered for the International Brigades. While he was in the hospital recuperating from wounds received in action Cheka agents seized him and put him in prison. The accusation was the usual one of Trotskyism and espionage. The charge, said Valtin, was absurd. Krause's wife, in Antwerp, showed Valtin a letter from Krause which had been smuggled out of jail, "a bitter heart-breaking letter."⁵²

Another case of a German International Brigade man's being killed by the Communists in Spain was that of Mark Rein. Rein's disappearance from a Barcelona hotel room was inquired into by his friend and fellow Socialist Willy Brandt, who, a political exile himself, was in Spain as a correspondent for a Scandinavian newspaper. Brandt pursued his investigation of Rein's fate into the very top echelons of the German Communist party in Spain but was unable to get any satisfactory explanation of what had happened to his friend. Brandt found out later that Rein had been arrested, imprisoned, and eventually liquidated by the Cheka. Typical also of the type of politically motivated terror that permeated the Communist apparatus in Spain concerned the German Socialist Kurt Landau. While not specifically a Brigade affair, the individuals involved in Landau's murder were intimately associated with the Brigades and the techniques and rationalizations for his liquidation were essentially the same as those dealing with the Brigade men. Landau was arrested and murdered by German Cheka operatives in Barcelona. This was done at the orders of Walter Ulbricht and André Marty.[53]

While the political terror in the Brigades undoubtedly bore down most heavily on the Germans and East Europeans, there were a number of Americans, English, and French among its victims. One of them was Paul White. White, a Communist party member, was shot "presumably for political dissidence" since he "had not committed any offense ... that deserved punishment by death on military grounds." Another case was that of Albert Wallach. Arrested and put in the International Brigade prison at Castel de Fells, Wallach was later summarily shot on suspicion of being a spy.[54] A fellow American volunteer, while himself imprisoned at Castel de Fells, shared a cell with Wallach. He said that Wallach was taken out one night and was never seen again. While in Barcelona, he had left the International Brigade and taken a commission in a CNT unit. While at the CNT offices in Barcelona he was arrested by Cheka agents. Wallach's chief accuser and interrogator was Tony DeMaio, an American who operated as a Cheka agent in the International Brigades.[55] Marvin Stern, a party member who made the mistake of expressing open criticism of the Brigade leadership also fell victim to the fatal charge of political dissidence. He was arrested, assigned to a penal battalion, and subsequently disappeared. Later, when an American party delegation was touring Spain, an American Brigade man, a friend of Stern's, asked one of the party delegation about what had become of Stern. The answer he received was: "Party discipline is higher than all friendship, and if I were you, I would not discuss this matter any further."[56]

A similar occurrence took place in regard to the disappearance of the American volunteer Harry Perchuk. When a friend inquired about Perchuk from the political commissar of the XV Brigade John

Gates, he was told that Perchuk had been executed for criticizing the party. Asked how he could have been involved in such a thing when he knew him well, Gates replied: "You have to be a Bolshevik, and a Bolshevik would take care of his own mother. You have to introduce discipline."[57]

The use of terror as an instrument of discipline became even more pronounced as the war continued with disasters and defeats for Loyalist forces. Gillain referred to the mass executions of Brigade men during the fighting at Cuesta de la Reina in the fall of 1937 and, of the retreat in Aragon in 1938, Sandor Voros wrote: "The Kremlin leaders ... base their main reliance on terror. Officers and men are ruthlessly executed on their orders. The toll is particularly high among the Poles, Slavs, Germans and Hungarians, especially those who came to Spain from Moscow. These are summary executions, carried out in most cases secretly by the S.I.M."[58]

André Marty was himself a particularly virulent example of the general paranoia that afflicted the Comintern hierarchy in those years. "To Marty," wrote one of the French party men who worked directly for him on occasion in Spain, "the enemy was more inside the International Brigades and Loyalist territory than on the other side of the lines." Gustav Regler, appointed political commissar in the XII Brigade in November 1936 by Marty, wrote that Marty emphasized pointedly to him that Regler had full powers to deal with any difficulties. Later, in the aftermath of the bloody battle of Jarama, the remnants of the Franco-Belgian battalion of the XII Brigade were overindulging themselves on the wine found in a deserted cellar. Hearing of it through his spies, Marty ordered Regler to tie the men to trees to sweat it out in the sun and to "shoot a few in the presence of the others" if he had any trouble. Regler's final experience with Marty took place near the end of the war as the remnants of the International Brigades were crossing the French frontier just ahead of the advancing Nationalist forces. Marty and a number of his hardcore followers were attempting to liquidate a group of German Internationals before they could leave Spain and possibly reveal the things they knew of him and his activities in Spain to the bourgeois press. International Brigade men who were caught attempting, or openly threatening, to communicate any of the unsavory facts, especially of Cheka operations and the killing of Brigade men by the Cheka, were invariably shot.[59]

Marty's obsession with spies, Trotskyists, and a wide assortment of other dissident elements whose offenses ranged from criticism of the party or the Brigade directorate to desertion from the Brigades or merely routine breaches of discipline and his penchant for dealing with all problems by simply having the offenders shot became a scandal even among many Communists. In fact, his reputation as "Le Boucher d' Albacete" became so well known that the French party recalled Marty from Spain to explain his actions. In his report to the party, Marty freely admitted to the execution of some 500 from the ranks of the International Brigades. "These bandits," he said, "have committed all sorts of crimes: rape, robberies, murders, kidnappings of persons, and not satisfied with this, they have rebelled against the authorities of Valencia and undertaken espionage in favor of Franco ... they even killed the guards of the concentration camps where it became necessary to imprison them."[60] The Comintern, and thus all "good" Communists, however, continued to support Marty as a proletarian hero. He remained not only in high esteem and position in the French party but continued to be looked upon as the grand master of the veterans of the International Brigades organization.[61]

An interesting sequel to the "Boucher d'Albacete" affair was the furor raised in Communist circles by the unkind treatment dealt out to Marty by Ernest Hemingway in his *For Whom the Bell Tolls*. Hemingway was completely pro-Loyalist in sympathy and had been practically an honorary member of the Brigades among whose members he had many friends. He had allowed himself to be used, willingly, by the Communists to further their own causes and to add lustre to their image. They were totally chagrined, however, at Hemingway's brutally truthful account of some of the more unsavory aspects of the Spanish imbroglio and, most especially, at his stinging characterization of Marty. Calling Marty by name and identifying him as the "chief commissar of the International Brigades," Hemingway discussed Marty at length. "He is crazy as a bedbug. He has a mania for shooting people ... that old one kills more than the bubonic plague ... but he doesn't kill fascists as we do ... not in a joke ... he kills rare things, Trotskyites, Divagationers [sic]. Any rare type of beasts. ... He purifies more than Solvarson."[62]

As a result of that characterization, which was all quite accurate, Alvah Bessie, an American Communist who joined the Brigade in 1938 and who was on the editorial board of the party publication *New Masses* in 1939, wrote a review in that journal attacking Hemingway and the book. The Veterans of the Abraham Lincoln Brigade organization then adopted a resolution condemning Hemingway's book, and the Communist party in the United States and its affiliated organizations launched a concerted attack on Hemingway and his novel.[63]

The final act of the farce was played out in 1952 when the Veterans of the Abraham Lincoln Brigade published an anthology called *The Heart of Spain,* which included the works of a large number of people who had written from a pro-Loyalist point of view about the war. The editors scheduled several selections from Hemingway's works to be included. News of that intention raised a furor from the French Communist party and the French Brigade veterans organization. A number of letters passed back and forth between the American and French groups, and the veterans organizations in other countries entered the fray on the side of Marty. As a result, *The Heart of Spain* included no Hemingway selections.[64] The work of several other authors who had subsequently either left the party or adopted an openly anti-Communist position were also excluded. Among them were André Malreaux, Gustav Regler, Arthur Koestler, and Tom Wintringham.

Marty, however, was but the instrument, though indeed a particularly crude one, of the policy of his masters in the Comintern hierarchy and in Moscow. The hypersuspiciousness, narrow sectarianism, and totalitarian mentality that he epitomized only reflected the system of which he was a part.

Conclusion

On September 21, 1938, Prime Minister Negrín announced in a speech to the League of Nations that his government had decided upon the complete withdrawal of all non-Spanish combatants from its armed forces. He asked that the League create a commission to oversee the demobilization and repatriation process.

The League complied with Negrín's request and its commission arrived in Spain on October 14. This signaled the official demise of the International Brigades as participants in the Spanish Civil War and their passing into history. But their historical image has been a particularly fuzzy one. This has been true, in part, because of the nature of the sources and, in part, because of the continuing emotional and ideological associations of the Spanish Civil War.

The greatly oversimplified view of that war as a clear-cut struggle between "democracy" and "fascism" has exhibited amazing staying power despite the work of many historians pointing out the complexities of that struggle. The widespread sympathy for the Loyalist side and the identification of that side with "democracy" have made it difficult for many to accept or acknowledge the key role played by the Comintern in the Loyalist regime. These same emotional attachments have made it difficult for many to accept a sharp focus on the International Brigades as a Comintern-controlled military and political entity. And yet that is what the record shows.

Certainly there were non-Communists in the Brigades. Certainly there were many who joined the Brigades to fight for "democracy" or against "fascism." Neither of these truisms alters the fact that the Brigades were, from beginning to end, a Comintern army.

The Brigades would never have existed but for the Soviet-Comintern decision to call them into being. That this was done resulted from both the general Popular Front strategy of the period and the specific Soviet decision to sponsor, through the apparatus of the Comintern, an international army for use in Spain. Some non-Spanish volunteers did fight with Spanish militia units before the organization of the International Brigades, but they never numbered more than a few hundred. Only with the decision of the Comintern to raise an army to fight in Spain did the number of foreigners become significant. And only through the use of the existing Comintern organization and the strenuous efforts of its various branches were these men recruited and transported into Spain.

While the Comintern apparatus provided the machinery through which the Brigades were recruited and transported into Spain, Comintern functionaries provided direction and control. Working in conjunction with the Soviet-Comintern apparatus in Spain, including the Spanish Communist party, they obtained the necessary cooperation from the Loyalist government authorities to quarter, equip, and train the incoming recruits. And, in conjunction with the same elements, the Brigades entered the battles for Madrid.

Militarily the Brigades were considered to be crack units and were often referred to as "shock troops." Certainly they deserved such esteem, at least by the standards of the Spanish Civil War. The Brigades played a crucial role in all the battles for Madrid in the winter of 1936–1937. While unprovable, it seems clear that the Internationals made the difference between survival and defeat for the Loyalist side during the defense of the capital from November 1936 through January 1937 and, perhaps even more decisively, during the Jarama fighting in February 1937.

The military efficiency of the Internationals resulted from several factors. A great many of the men in the Brigades had had previous military training and even combat experience. Also, the Brigades were strictly disciplined units. The Communist military and political hierarchy of the Brigades emphasized, in conformance with general party policy, the absolute necessity of firm and unquestioning discipline. Military discipline was heavily reinforced by the strict political discipline demanded of all Communist party members.

The Brigades' efficiency could also be accounted for, in part, by the nature of their military command. They had the advantage of being commanded, for the most part, by professional officers rather than amateurs. Kleber, Walter, Gall, and Lukacs were Red army officers with long training and experience. Kahle, Renn, and Pacciardi also had significant military experience as did numerous other Brigade officers. Further, the Internationals operated from the beginning under the tutelage of professional Soviet advisers attached to each Brigade. Finally, the Brigades received the best of the weapons and equipment available within Loyalist Spain.

But far more important than the stress on military discipline was the political discipline imposed on the Brigades by the Comintern stalwarts who dominated them. While the Brigades operated militarily within the organizational structure of the People's Army (once that army had been created), they remained throughout their

Conclusion

sojourn in Spain an essentially autonomous organization so far as their internal affairs were concerned. Military and political commissar appointments were filled at the discretion of the Brigades' Political Commissariat and all matters of internal discipline and control came under that same authority. Party cadres from various countries were moved in and out of the Brigades freely at the volition of the Commissariat (which was itself staffed entirely by individuals sent by and representing the various Communist parties). Thus, from beginning to end, the Brigades' command structure, both military and political, was overwhelmingly Communist and the Political Commissariat, the highest authority within the Brigades, was made up completely of seasoned and disciplined party cadres.

The Political Commissariat maintained its control over the Brigades chiefly through a political commissar system. The political commissar structure existed at all levels of command throughout the Brigades. It was staffed almost exclusively with seasoned and reliable party cadres and exercised ultimate authority (in the name of the Commissariat) within the Brigades. The political commissars were chiefly responsible for the maintainence of both military and political discipline within the Brigades as well as morale and political indoctrination of the troops. The Brigade Commissariat also controlled the press, the police, the hospitals, the prisons, and the officer and commissar training schools of the Brigades. Thus the Brigades were, for all practical purposes, an autonomous Comintern army.

After the Jarama and Guadalajara campaign in February-March 1937, the military significance of the Brigades began to wane as the Loyalists built a mass People's Army. But despite their relative decline in military significance, the Brigades continued to be a highly important component in the Comintern's overall operations regarding the Spanish Civil War and the Popular Front strategy in general. This was true especially in the propaganda sphere. The Brigades were held up as the most concrete and heroic example of the Popular Front and antifascism in action. Nothing served better than the Brigades in keeping alive the interest and sympathy of large segments of the population in many countries of the world. The Brigades were also seen by the Comintern as a highly significant school for party cadres, a school in which important lessons for future struggles would be learned and from which steel-hardened party leaders would be created.

The Comintern proved determined to maintain the Brigades as an essentially autonomous organization (and thereby to maintain them as a Comintern-controlled force) even after the growth of the People's

Army had reduced the military significance of the Brigades. They did so in the face of attempts on the part of the Loyalist authorities to incorporate and assimilate the Brigades into their army in a meaningful way. The Comintern's success in this meant that the International Brigades remained to the end what they had been from the beginning, an integral part of the Comintern's interlocking directorate in Spain.

Notes

CHAPTER 1

1. The junta in command of the *pronunciamiento* included the generals Sanjuro, Mola, Cabanellas, Goded, and Franco.

2. The dilemma and the weakness of the left republicans are summarized succinctly by R.A.H. Robinson, *The Origins of Franco's Spain* (Pittsburgh, 1970), 264-65, thus: "lacking masses, they were doomed to be prisoners either of the Socialists or of the Right." The weakness of the left republicans in mass support was clear from the electoral results of February 1936. The final count showed a very close split between the left (Popular Front) coalition and the right. If we take into account both the fact that the real mass base of the left was the Socialist party and that the left also received votes from other proletarian sources, it is clear that the left republican parties, as such, were lacking in mass voter appeal. The ex-Communist Enrique Castro Delgado, *Hombres Made en Moscú* (Barcelona, 1964), 148-49, says the weakness of the Spanish Republic was the lack of republicans in Spain. But Salvador de Madariaga, *Spain: A Modern History* (New York, 1958), has it more nearly right in saying that the Spaniards destroyed the Republic by being unable to agree on what kind it should be. If all factions from Azaña's Republican Left to Gil Robles's CEDA had been able to work within the same framework, the Republic would have been safe. But the republicans split, polarizing Spanish politics into irreconcilable opposites and opening the way for the antirepublicans on both ends of the spectrum to move in and destroy the Republic.

3. Speech by Largo Caballero printed in *El Socialista,* January 1936, as quoted in Robinson, *Franco's Spain,* 246.

4. Alvarez del Vayo in the Madrid daily, *ABC,* January 1936, as quoted in Robinson, *Franco's Spain,* 246; Araquistain quoted in Stanley G. Payne, *The Spanish Revolution* (New York, 1970), 193-94.

5. Robinson, *Franco's Spain,* 261.

6. This was a notorious fact that was freely admitted by both left and right (although each blamed the other). The only source I can locate which emphatically denies this was the United States ambassador to Spain, Claude Bowers, *My Mission to Spain* (New York, 1954). He was an ardent devotee of the Republic. For details on the breakdown of public order, see Payne, *Revolution,* 206-17; Robinson, *Franco's Spain,* 258-60.

7. *El Socialista,* May 2, 1936, as quoted in Robinson, *Franco's Spain,* 260.

8. Ibid., 273.

9. Julio Alvarez del Vayo, *Freedom's Battle* (New York, 1940), 261. The army and police actually divided fairly evenly between the two sides at the beginning of the conflict, but the Loyalist regime, caught up in revolution on the left, proved incapable of effectively using this potential source of strength. Payne, *Revolution,* 316.

10. Pietro Nenni, *La Guerre d'Espagne* (Paris, 1960), 43-48.

11. Payne, *Revolution,* 218-21.

12. Manuel Azaña, *La Velada en Benicarlo* (Buenos Aires, 1939), 96.

13. There were several reasons why the revolutionary parties saw it in their interest to maintain the fiction of the Republican regime. It lent a facade of legitimacy and respectability to their cause outside Spain. They could, and did, claim to be defending the legitimate, elected, and democratic government of the country. Thus the government was recognized diplomatically and would presumably be able to elicit support internationally. In an article in *Nuovo Avanti* of December 19, 1936, Pietro Nenni frankly explained to his followers that the real reason for the continuation of the "republican element" in the Popular Front government was as a sop to public opinion outside Spain. Also, it suited the policy of the Comintern at the time to play down the revolution in Spain and to cast the struggle there in terms of "defense of the Republic" and "antifascism." The fiction of the Republic was maintained by the Popular Front throughout the war even though from September 1936 on the government was completely dominated by the proletarian parties.

14. "During the three months that I was director of propaganda for the United States and England under Alvarez del Vayo," wrote Liston Oak, "I was instructed not to send out one word about this revolution ... nor are any foreign correspondents permitted to write freely of the revolution that has taken place." As quoted in Burnett Bolloten, *The Grand Camouflage* (New York, 1961), 121.

15. Franz Borkenau, *The Spanish Cockpit* (London, 1937), 69; George Orwell, *Homage to Catalonia* (New York, 1952), 4–6.

16. Peter Stansky and William Abrahams, *Journey to the Frontier* (New York, 1966), 316.

17. Louis Fischer, *Men and Politics* (New York, 1941), 352–62; Arturo Barea, *The Forging of a Rebel* (New York, 1946), 536–37.

18. Georgi Dimitroff, "The Peoples Front of Struggle against Fascism and War," *Communist International* 13, no. 11 (December 1936): 717–34

19. This was from a Litvinov speech to the League of Nations. It was reprinted from *Pravda* and published in the *Boletín de Información de las Brigadas Internacionales*, no. 269 (October 3, 1937).

20. Arthur Koestler, *The God That Failed*, ed. Richard Crossman (New York, 1950), 29.

21. Castro Delgado, *Hombres*, 191–92

22. Koestler, *God That Failed*, 55; Douglas Hyde, *I Believed* (London, 1952), 59; Earl Browder, *Next Steps to Win the War in Spain* (New York, 1938), 3; Arthur Koestler, *Invisible Writing* (London, 1960), 257.

23. Stansky and Abrahams, *Journey*, 229.

24. Kermit McKenzie, *The Comintern and World Revolution* (New York, 1964); Castro Delgado, *Hombres*, 221; Hyde, *I Believed*.

25. Georgi Dimitroff, "The United Front of the Struggle for Peace," *Communist International* 13, no. 5 (May 1936): 290–93; Carola Stern, *Ulbricht: A Political Biography* (New York, 1964), 70.

26. José Díaz, *Communist International* 13, no. 6 (June 1936): 406 (from a speech made in February 1936); Stern, *Ulbricht*, 66–67.

27. Koestler, *God That Failed*, 56.

28. Ruth Fischer, *Stalin and German Communism* (Cambridge, Mass., 1948), 613–14.

29. John Gates, *The Story of an American Communist* (New York, 1958), 37-39; Louis Budenz, *Men without Faces: The Communist Conspiracy in the U.S.A.* (New York, 1948), 32-34; Hyde, *I Believed*, 61.

30. Harold Lavine, *Fifth Column in America* (New York, 1940), 235; Lewis Coser and Irving Howe, *The American Communist Party* (New York, 1962), 324.

31. Earl Browder, *Lenin and Spain* (New York, 1937), 7 (pamphlet containing a speech by Browder in Madison Square Garden in January 1937); Robert Coulondre, *De Staline à Hitler: Souvenirs de Deux Ambassades, 1936-1939* (Paris, 1950), 39-40, as quoted in Gordon A. Craig and Felix Gilbert, *The Diplomats* (New York, 1965), 2:559.

32. Concern over the loss of Soviet-Communist influence over the "world revolutionary movement" was expressed by a Soviet leader to the United States ambassador to Moscow in early August 1936. U.S. Department of State, *Foreign Relations of the United States, Diplomatic Papers, 1938* (Washington, D.C. 1955), 2:461.

33. This was done, for example, in the post Popular Front period after the Nazi-Soviet pact of 1939 when the European war was written off as an "imperialist war" in which the workers (i.e., the Soviet Union) had no interests. This changed with the German attack on the USSR, when the war suddenly became a struggle between "democracy" and "fascism."

34. Jef Last, *The Spanish Tragedy* (London, 1937), 25. Last, a Dutch Communist writer, was attending a conference in Moscow in July 1936. At the various official and social functions he "noted with much indignation a complete lack of interest in events in Spain. They were not discussed at any gathering and ... personal opinions seemed to be anxiously avoided." In late August, when the official blessing for Popular Front Spain was given by Stalin, widescale enthusiasm suddenly became noticeable.

35. The nonintervention agreement was an attempt by the British and French to isolate the Spanish war. The agreement was officially adhered to by most European governments but was systematically violated by Germany, Italy, and the Soviet Union. See David T. Cattell, *Soviet Diplomacy and the Spanish Civil War* (Berkeley, 1957), 30-45.

36. *International Press Correspondence* 16, no. 35 (August 1936): 927-30.

37. Hugh Thomas, *The Spanish Civil War* (New York, 1961), 214 n. 4. Thomas says the Prague meeting has been confirmed by Albert Vassar, a German who was then a Comintern representative with the French Communist party. At any rate it is not at all improbable that such meetings took place, based on the actions of the Comintern.

38. *International Press Correspondence* 16, no. 5 (August 1936): 929-31.

39. Franz Dahlem, *Communist International* 15, no. 5 (May 1938): 446; *International Press Correspondence* 16, no. 35 (August 1936): 930; Harry Gaines, *How the Soviet Union Helps Spain* (New York, 1936), 30-45.

40. *International Press Correspondence* 16, no. 37 (August 1936): 18-19.

41. Philip Toynbee, *Friends Apart* (London, 1954), 87. Toynbee, then a student at Oxford and a Communist, received party orders to "proliferate Spanish Defense Committees throughout the university."

42. As an indication of the number of organizations that sprang from the Spanish conflict, see U. S., Congress, House, *Guide to Subversive Organizations and Publications*, Document No. 398 (Washington, D.C., 1961). This publication lists some fifteen organizations devoted to the cause of Popular Front Spain. See also Cecil Eby, *Between the*

Bullet and the Lie (New York, 1969), 4 n. 3, for a list of sponsors to the North American Committee to Aid Spanish Democracy (a front organization).

43. Koestler, *Invisible Writing,* 209-10; Gustav Regler, *The Owl of Minerva* (New York, 1960), 162, 171, 173.

44. Even before the outbreak of the civil war numerous Comintern figures had been assigned to Spain. The most important of them was Vittorio Codovila, who went by the name "Medina" in Spain and spoke Spanish with a strong South American accent. He was the chief Comintern representative to the Spanish Communist party in 1935-1936 and, as such, exercised ultimate power within its ranks. He played a major role in accomplishing the party's Popular Front policy of fusion of the Socialist and Communist youth organizations in Spain prior to the outbreak of the war. Of Italian birth, Codovila had lived in Argentina since 1911 and was a high functionary in the Communist party of Argentina before being assigned to Spain by the Comintern. He was to remain a powerful figure behind the scenes throughout the Spanish war. Other important Comintern agents operating in Spain prior to the outbreak of the war were the Pole Stepanov, who served as Comintern adviser to the politburo of the Spanish Communist party during the war, and the Hungarian Erno Geroe who was the behind-the-scenes director of the newly unified Socialist-Communist party of Catalonia. See Castro Delgado, *Hombres,* 331; Enrique Lister, *Nuestra Guerra* (Paris, 1966), 24.

45. Marty Archives (Harvard University). Marty says that Togliatti and Geroe were the top Comintern representatives in Spain. M. Einaudi, *Communism in Western Europe* (Ithaca, N.Y., 1951).

46. Ilya Ehrenberg, *Eve of War, 1933-1941* (London, 1963), 146-47, 152; Louis Fischer, *Politics,* 361-62, 395, 398; Walter G. Krivitsky, *In Stalin's Secret Service* (New York, 1939), 114-18.

47. Ehrenberg, *Eve of War,* 124; Robert Colodny, *The Struggle for Madrid 1936-1937* (New York, 1958), states that during crucial periods of the battle of Madrid, Koltsov maintained direct telephone contact with Moscow. Regler, *Owl of Minerva,* 276, also indicates that Koltsov was much more than merely the *Pravda* correspondent in Spain.

48. Louis Fischer, *Politics,* 361; Krivitsky, *Secret Service,* 100-101; Alexander Orlov, *The Secret History of Stalin's Crimes* (New York, 1953). According to Orlov himself he was assigned to Spain by the politburo on August 26, 1936, and left the USSR en route to Spain on September 9, 1936. This is from Orlov's written reply to questions submitted to him by Stanley G. Payne in 1956 (hereafter cited as Orlov Memo).

49. Krivitsky, *Secret Service,* 99-108.

50. Payne, *Revolution,* 234-35.

51. *Communist International* 13, no. 10 (December 1936):632-38. "The Decision of the Presidium of the Executive Committee of the Communist International on the Communist Party of Spain," ibid., 14, no. 2 (February 1937): 865; and for a general exposition and defense of the Popular Front policy, Georgi Dimitroff, *Spain and the Peoples Front* (New York, 1937); and André Marty, *Heroic Spain* (New York, 1937).

52. For example, Bertram Wolfe, *Civil War in Spain* (New York, 1937); Liston Oak, "Alert," *New Leader* (March 15, 1937).

53. Louis Fischer, *Politics,* 361; Colodny, *Struggle,* 61. Most historians seem to agree that Thorez made this trip although there is apparently no hard documentry evidence.

54. Gustav Regler, *Owl of Minerva,* 176, states that Koltsov showed him a coded telegram from Moscow which stated that the decision had been made for the formation of an international military unit.

CHAPTER 2

1. Lister, *Guerra,* 22-27.
2. Payne, *Revolution,* 204-5 n. 16.
3. Robinson, *Franco's Spain,* 254.
4. Jesús Hernández, "The Development of the Democratic Revolution in Spain," *Communist International* 13, nos. 7-8 (August 1936): 437.
5. The United States consul in San Sebastian reported shortly after the outbreak of hostilities that the "proletariat has certainly obtained arms and barricades have been erected and bridges blown up." *Foreign Relations of the U.S., 1936,* 2:440-41.
6. Partido Obrero Unificación Marxista was a small but militant "left deviationist" Marxist party which was more revolutionary in outlook than the orthodox Communist line of the day.
7. José Martín Blasquez, *I Helped to Build an Army* (London, 1940), 189.
8. Louis Fischer, *Politics,* 357, reports being told this by Largo Caballero.
9. Orwell, *Catalonia,* 48-49.
10. Carlo Rosselli, *Oggi in Spagna, Domani in Italia* (Paris, 1938), 17-20.
11. Last, *Tragedy,* 63; Nenni, *Guerre,* 186-88.
12. As quoted in Payne, *Revolution,* 222-23.
13. Borkenau, *Cockpit,* 86-87.
14. As quoted in *Vers la Liberté (Journal du battalion André Marty: 12e Brigade Internationale),* no. 6 (January 30, 1937). On the hypocrisy of the Communist party of Spain posing as the defender of the Republic, see Castro Delgado, *Hombres.* Last, *Tragedy,* 15, says the Spanish militiamen in his Communist unit referred to the Republic as "la vieja puta."
15. Orwell, *Catalonia,* 19-20; Borkenau, *Cockpit,* 101-5; Stansky and Abrahams, *Journey,* 327.
16. Orwell, *Catalonia,* 3-18.
17. In Catalonia and Aragon the Anarchist militia columns, recruited and organized for the most part in Barcelona, were active in bringing the revolution to the countryside. In many villages where the local inhabitants had not disposed of the "fascists," the militia performed the operation for them. The usual procedure was to arrest all those suspected of reactionary activities, usually including the local priest, lawyer, landowners, and better-off peasants, assemble them in a group, and shoot them. Then the militia column, having proclaimed the Anarchist ideal of "comunismo libertario" to be in effect, moved on to the next village. See Borkenau, *Cockpit,* 98-99, 109-10.
18. E.M. López Muñiz, *La Batalla de Madrid* (Madrid, 1943), 6.
19. Stansky and Abrahams, *Journey,* 327.

20. José Manuel Martínez Bande, *La marcha sobre Madrid* (Madrid, 1968), 76 n. 61.
21. In addition to the steady loss of territory, the militia's tendency to panic and bolt also resulted in the loss of significant quantities of arms and materiel. See the "Diario de Operaciones de la V Bandera," Martínez Bande, *Marcha,* 56–58 nn. 39-42.
22. Louis Fischer, *Politics,* 369, gives an eyewitness report on the chaos at the alcazar.
23. Orwell, *Catalonia,* 46; Louis Fischer, *Politics,* 370; Ehrenberg, *Eve of War,* 126-27.
24. Dolores Ibarruri, *Guerra y revolución en España. 1936-1939* (Moscow, 1966), 1:307.
25. Lister, *Guerra,* 64; Castro Delgado, *Hombres,* 375, 288-90.
26. The Communists in Spain, in addition to building up a paramilitary unit (MAOC), had actively sought party adherents among the officer corps of the regular army. They had at least some success in this program. See Martínez Bande, *Marcha,* 23; Castro Delgado, *Hombres,* 236; Payne, *Revolution,* 205; Bolloten, *Camouflage,* 223 n. 9.
27. Vidali entered the country ostensibly as a delegate of Socorro Rojo. He had previously worked as a Comintern agent in Argentina and the United States, but he arrived in Spain directly from Moscow. Castro Delgado, *Hombres,* 242-62, tells of a case where Vidali countermanded Vicente Uribe, a member of the politburo of the Communist party of Spain.
28. Castro Delgado, *Hombres,* 332, mentions a Frenchman who had been trained at the Frunze Military Academy in Moscow and a German who was referred to as "general" and was from the hierarchy of the German party (280-81). There can be no certainty about this man's identity, but it seems quite likely that it was Wilhelm Zeisser, who later commanded the XIII International Brigade under the *nom de guerre* General Gomez.
29. Lister, *Guerra,* 62.
30. Ibid, 54, 63-64; Ibarruri, *Guerra,* 1:296; Castro Delgado, *Hombres,* 412-13, 333-34. The party line on the necessity of a unified command and regular People's Army was stressed in a party manifesto as early as August 18, 1936. Ibarruri, *Guerra,* 1:307-8; *Communist International* 13, no. 10 (November-December 1936): 634.
31. *Vers la Liberté,* no. 6 (January 30, 1937), 1; Castro Delgado, *Hombres,* 399; Lister, *Guerra,* 74-75.
32. Koestler, *God That Failed,* 55; Jan Valtin, *Out of the Night* (New York, 1941), 484-88. Koestler, a member of the Communist party of Germany at the time, said that virtually the entire "red block" of Communist writers and artists with whom he had lived in Berlin prior to 1933 subsequently assembled on the left bank in Paris. Indeed the German Communist party continued to operate as a structural unit of the Comintern from headquarters in Paris.
33. Rosselli, *Oggi in Spagna,* 39; Randolfo Pacciardi, *Il Battaglione Garibaldi* (Lugano, 1938), 2; Regler, *Owl of Minerva,* 285.
34. *International Press Correspondence* 16, no. 35 (August 1936): 954. This official Comintern organ explained that the Workers Olympiad had been organized in protest

against the regular international olympics which were being held in Berlin that year. It called the Workers Olympiad a "great anti-fascist sports event."

35. *Garibaldini in Spagna* (Madrid, 1937); Max Wullschleger, ed., *Schweizer Kampfen in Spanien* (Zurich, 1939), 78.

36. Last, *Tragedy*, 53-54; Roselli, *Oggi in Spagna*, 11-14; Borkenau, *Cockpit*, 106-13; Pacciardi, *Garibaldi*, 18.

37. Nenni, *Guerre*, 261; *Communist International* 14, nos. 7-8 (August 1937): 1140-55.

38. Rosselli, *Oggi in Spagna*, 12-13; Orwell, *Catalonia*, 3; Borkenau, *Cockpit*, 72-73; Last, *Tragedy*, 170; Nenni, *Guerre*, 143-144.

39. Pat Sloan, ed., *John Cornford: A Memoir* (London, 1938), 199. Stansky and Abrahams, *Journey*, 317-19, offers a somewhat different explanation of why Cornford joined the POUM militia.

40. *Juventud Comunista* (December 17, 1936). This was a POUM organ. The statement was signed by Fritz Sandler.

41. Stansky and Abrahams, *Journey*, 340-41.

42. L'Amicale des Anciens Volontaires Francais en Espagne Republicaine, *L' Épopée D'Espagne: Brigades Internationales, 1936-1939* (Paris, 1956), 61; Wullschleger, *Kampfen*, 21-25.

43. Spanish Office of Information, *The International Brigades* (Madrid, 1952), 17.

44. *Épopée*, 61; Wullschleger, *Kampfen*, 26.

45. Keith Scott Watson, *Single to Spain* (London, 1937), 13-24. Watson, an Englishman who traveled across France and into Spain in September 1936, saw groups of men in France who were marshaled by what appeared to be "NCO's in mufti, to whom all gave the party salute."

46. *Épopée*, 43.

47. Spanish Office of Information, 17.

48. Theodor Balk, ed., *La Quatorzième* (Madrid, 1937), 216.

49. Pacciardi, *Garibaldi*, 7; Nenni, *Guerre*, 266.

50. Rosselli, *Oggi in Spagna*, 39; Pacciardi, *Garibaldi*, 5, 23. Rosselli had previously refused to affiliate his independent socialist Giustizia e Libertá party with the Italian version of the Popular Front because he wanted nothing to do with the Communists. See David J. Dallin, *Soviet Espionage* (New Haven, 1955), 208.

51. The use of the term centuria as a designation for the militia units seems to have been confined to those under Communist control. The Spanish generally used the word column. The use of centuria by the Communist units probably came from the standard Communist terminology for their paramilitary units in various places where they were called Red Hundreds. For the use of the term Red Hundreds in this context, see Valtin, *Out of the Night*, 437.

52. *Garibaldini in Spagna;* Ibarruri, *Guerra*, 2:113.

53. Wullschleger, *Kampfen*, 25-27.

54. Nenni, *Guerre*, 161; *Communist International* 14, no. 1 (January 1937): 805.

55. Nenni, *Guerre*, 161; Wullschleger, *Kampfen*, 24-34.

56. *Communist International* 14, no. 1 (January 1937): 803-6; *Boletín de Información*, no. 78 (December 1, 1937), in a eulogy of Beimler, said: "Beimler is for us a symbol of the fight of the revolutionary workers."

57. Ludwig Renn, *Der Spanische Krieg* (Berlin, 1955), 25-40, 66. Gustav Szinda, *Die XI Brigade* (Berlin, 1956), 23; Franz Dahlem, "The Military-Political Work of the Eleventh Brigade," *Communist International* 15, no. 5 (May 1938): 466.

58. Orwell, *Catalonia*, 75, 130-40.

59. Tom Mann was one of the founders of the Communist party of Great Britain. *Communist International* 13, no. 4 (April 1936): 259.

60. Esmond Romilly, *Boadilla* (London, 1937), 57; Thomas Wintringham, *English Captain* (London, 1939), 42-43; Watson, *Single to Spain*, 30-40.

61. Orwell, *Catalonia*, 38-39.

62. *Reconquista: Journal of the Thirty-fifth Division* (October 20, 1938), 10-11; Vincent Brome, *The International Brigades: Spain 1936-1939* (New York, 1966), 75-76, mentions a Polish General Wroblewski centuria and documents it from *Polacy Wojnie Hiszpanskiej*, ed., Michala Brona. The difficulty in pinning down the names of many of these early units is complicated by the fact that the names were in no way official or fixed. The various groups simply adopted a name. Sometimes the same group might have been called two or more different names by different people. In this same line, Hugh Thomas, *Spanish Civil War*, refers to a French Paris centuria (239). It seems in both these cases the units referred to are the same as the Dombrowsky and Commune de Paris.

63. *Za Mir a Svobody* (Madrid, 1937), as quoted in Arthur London, *España, España* (Prague, 1965), 180-81; *Nuestros Españoles* (Madrid, 1937).

64. Hard statistics do not exist, but in all the accounts by eyewitnesses and participants the numbers they mention bear out the cited estimates.

65. Rosselli, *Oggi in Spagna*, 251; Orwell, *Catalonia*, 130-40.

66. José Manuel Martínez Bande, *La intervención comunista en la guerra de España* (Madrid, 1965), 38.

67. The decision on whether a given foreign unit would join with the International Brigades sheds an interesting light on both the internal political situation in Popular Front Spain and the political nature of the International Brigades. The POUMists were anathema to the Communists and would not normally be accepted by them into their units even had the POUMists been willing to join them, which they were not. The Communists also did not welcome Anarchists, but Pacciardi, who was not a Communist, wanted Rosselli's unit to come into the Garibaldi battalion of the International Brigades because they were Italians. Rosselli, who was not an Anarchist and would perhaps have been acceptable to the Communists, refused to affiliate himself or his unit with the International Brigades because he realized it was a Communist-dominated outfit.

68. Luigi Longo, *Le Brigate Internazionali in Spagna* (Rome, 1956), 38-39; André Marty, "The International Brigades—Twelve Magnificent Months," *International Press Correspondence* 17, no. 45 (October 1937): 1014-15; *Un Año de las Brigades Internacionales* (Madrid, 1937). There are no official statistics on the International Brigades, but by putting together various bits of evidence, these figures would seem to be about right.

69. Longo, *Brigate*, 69, says they amounted to only some 150 to 200 men. Other figures for specific units do not differ greatly in total.

70. An example of this point of view is found in Colodny, *Struggle*, 58-59, 61.

CHAPTER 3

1. Marty Archives; Longo, *Brigate,* 30-45; Wullschleger, *Kampfen,* 20-30.
2. Nick Gillain, *Le Mercenaire* (Paris, 1938), 9-10; Longo, *Brigate,* 30; Spanish Office of Information, 60-61; Charlotte Haldane, *Truth Will Out* (New York, 1950), 87.
3. Browder, *Next Steps,* 15; Bill Lawrence, *Democracy's Stake in Spain* (New York, 1938), 23; *Communist International* 14, no. 2 (February 1937): 869; Haldane, *Truth,* 89-93, 98; on this see also Louis Budenz, Testimony, United States Subversive Activities Control Board (SACB), Docket No. 108-53, Herbert Brownell Jr., Attorney General of the U.S. vs. Veterans of the Abraham Lincoln Brigade, *Recommended Decision* (Washington, D.C., 1955), 20-25; William Z. Foster, *History of the Communist Party in the United States* (New York, 1952), 371-72; Krivitsky, *Secret Service,* 112; Hyde, *I Believed,* 60-64.
4. William Rust, *Britons in Spain: The History of the XV International Brigade* (London, 1939), 5-6. Rust put forth the theory of an organic continuity between the few foreigners fighting in the militias prior to the formation of the Brigades and the Brigades themselves.
5. As quoted in the *Boletín de Información,* December 12, 1937.
6. London, *España,* 177.
7. Browder, *Next Steps,* 3.
8. Lawrence, *Democracy's Stake,* 22-23; Louis Fischer, *Politics,* 405; Krivitsky, *Secret Service,* 112; Sandor Voros, *American Commissar* (Philadelphia, 1961); Edward Horan, Testimony, SACB, *Recommended Decision,* 26.
9. Dahlem, *Communist International* 15, no. 5 (May 1938): 449-50; see also Manuilsky's Report to the Eighteenth Congress of the CPSU, March 1939.
10. William J. Ryan, Testimony, U.S., Congress, House, 76th Cong., Un-American Activities Committee, *Hearings,* 1939, 11: 6811 (hereafter cited as HUAC, *Hearings*); George Alexson, *New York Times,* May 25, 1937, 1.
11. Reported to the United States Department of State by the American consul in Valencia in March 1937. *U.S. Diplomatic Papers, 1937,* 496. On the successful recruitment from labor unions, see Eby, *Bullet,* 5.
12. Louis Fischer, *Politics,* 379; Haldane, *Truth,* 87-93; Auguste Lecouer, *Le Partisan* (Paris, 1963), 60-62; Dallin, *Espionage,* 84.
13. Dahlem, *Communist International* 15, no. 5 (May 1938): 449-50.
14. Haldane, *Truth,* 93.
15. Horan, Testimony, SACB, *Recommended Decision,* 76.
16. Voros, *Commisar,* 269; Joseph Storobin, *The Life and Death of an American Hero: Dave Doran* (New York, 1938), 28.
17. Gladnick, Testimony, SACB, *Recommended Decision,* 23.
18. Haldane, *Truth,* 100; Rust, *Britons in Spain,* 12.
19. Krivitsky, *Secret Service,* 112; Eby, *Bullet,* 5-7.
20. Gillain, *Le Mercenaire,* 7-11.
21. *Nuestros Españoles,* 9.
22. Michala Brona, ed., *Polacy Wojnie Hiszpanskiej,* as quoted in Brome, *International Brigades,* 75-76.

23. Haldane, *Truth*, 100.
24. Peter Elstob, *Spanish Prisoner* (New York, 1939), 25-31.
25. John Sommerfield, *Volunteer in Spain* (New York, 1937), 3-5.
26. William Harris, Testimony, SACB, *Recommended Decision*, 27.
27. Horan, Testimony, SACB, *Recommended Decision*, 27.
28. Paul Brown was an alias for the Comintern agent whose real name was Alpi. He was a powerful figure behind the scenes in the American branch of the Comintern. Voros, *Commissar*, 272-74.
29. Herrick, Testimony, SACB, *Stenographic Record of Hearings*, 2:427. (These were not published but I was given access to them at the offices of the SACB in Washington. Since that agency no longer exists, I am told that the records of its hearings are available on microfilm through the Library of Congress).
30. Gladnick, Testimony, SACB, *Recommended Decision*, 23; Morris Maken, Testimony, SACB, *Stenographic Record*, 2:472.
31. William Ryan, Testimony, HUAC, *Hearings*, 1939, 11:6811; William McQuiston, Testimony, HUAC, *Hearings*, 1939, 11:6708.
32. Harris, Testimony, SACB, *Recommended Decision*, 27; Horan, Testimony, SACB, *Recommended Decision*, 26-27, and *Stenographic Record*, 4:1169.
33. Rust, *Britons in Spain*, 9-13; F. Jay Taylor, *The United States and the Spanish Civil War* (New York, 1956), 101-2.
34. Maken, Testimony, SACB, *Stenographic Record*, 2:725; Gates, *American Communist*, 43; Alvah Bessie, *Men in Battle* (New York, 1939), 11.
35. Haldane, *Truth*, 102-3. That this individual (whoever he really was) was in fact the chief of the IB organization in Paris must be doubted. He was more likely simply the highest authority with whom Haldane came into contact. Obviously the troika of Marty, Longo, and Vittorio, as well as other Comintern hierarchs involved in the enterprise, were above Max in authority.
36. Haldane said later that "Jack" was, in fact, Arnold Reid, former editor of the United States party publication, *New Masses*.
37. Haldane, *Truth*, 102-20, 296.
38. Ibid., 117-19; Krivitsky, *Secret Service*, 112-14.
39. Ruth Fischer, *German Communism*, 500. Fischer said that Walter Ulbricht, for example, performed this service, among others, for the NKVD.
40. Horan, Testimony, SACB, *Recommended Decision*, 26-27.
41. Romilly, *Boadilla*, 41; Krivitsky, *Secret Service*, 112-14.
42. Rust, *Britons in Spain*, 10; Haldane, *Truth*, 112-13.
43. Spanish Office of Information, 60; Balk, *Quatorzième*, 31.
44. Elstob, *Spanish Prisoner*, 32.
45. The raised arm and the clenched fist originated as the Communist party salute. It became the Popular Front salute and was widely adopted in Spain during the civil war. Its widespread use can be seen in numerous photographs from the period.
46. Elstob, *Spanish Prisoner*, 32-34.
47. Ibid., 36.
48. The Spanish word *salud*, meaning "health" became the common term of greeting among adherents of the Popular Front cause in Spain. Its constant use by persons of all nationalities, even when speaking and writing in their own language, shows that

the word took on a special connotation for them, that it was, in fact, one of the ritual paswords of the Popular Front in the civil war.

49. Elstob, *Spanish Prisoner*, 38-41.
50. Sommerfield, *Volunteer*, 6-18.
51. The term *International Column* was commonly used during the early period. *International Brigade* was not generally used until later, although the term brigade was used in the first official document signed by the foreign directors of the base at Albacete on October 28, 1936. A facsimile of this order can be seen in Spanish Office of Information, 70. The decision to call the organization by the term brigade was doubtless due to the fact that the "mixed brigade" was the Soviet, and therefore Comintern, idea for the best type of organizational structure for the Popular Front army. This concept, which meant that each "brigade" would be in effect a self-contained unit with its own auxiliary arms and services around a nucleus of four rifle battalions, was accepted by the Largo Caballero government about the end of December 1936, against the strong opposition of part of the Spanish military staff. See Madariaga, *Spain*, 512; Segismundo Casado, *Last Days of Madrid* (London, 1939), 59-60.
52. Ryan, Testimony, HUAC, *Hearings*, 1939, 11:6183; Bessie, *Men in Battle*, 202.
53. Actually, hard and reliable statistics on the Brigades are impossible to come by, but roughly correct figures are possible by putting various estimates and calculations together. The first two Brigades, those put together and in action in November 1936, numbered, by most accounts, about 3,000 each. Each was reinforced with new arrivals as the fighting of November and December took its toll in casualties; thus the estimate of 8,000 by late November seems about right. As to the numbers in the Brigades by February 1937, there is more room for error. The United States Consul in Barcelona reported on December 31, 1936, to Washington that according to best estimates some 4,000 volunteers had passed through Barcelona in the past week and that some 20,000 had done so since October 31. If this estimate was a good one, it would mean that a total of some 25,000 men had entered Spain by December 31. This would seem to agree with other estimates. Madariaga says he knows for certain that the Brigades numbered 22,000 men at one given time. Most observers agree that the number of foreign effectives in the Brigades reached a peak at about the time of the battle of the Jarama in February 1937 and that this was around 25,000 men. If we allow for high casualty rates sustained by the Brigades from their entry into the fighting in early November, a figure of 25,000 effectives in February would mean that something like 30,000 men had come into them since the first contingents arrived in October 1936. See U. S. *Diplomatic Papers*, 1936, 632; Madariaga, *Spain*, 506.

CHAPTER 4

1. Mikhail Koltsov, *Diario de la guerra de España* (Paris, 1963), 114.
2. Martínez Bande, *Marcha*, 113-15, 158 n. 157, says the Nationalists had only some 20,000 effectives at this point.
3. Nenni, *Guerre*, 52; Geoffrey Cox, *Defense of Madrid* (London, 1937), 22-24; Louis Fischer, *Politics*, 382; Ibarruri, *Guerra*, 2:133; R. Malinovski, *Bajo la bandera de la España republicana* (Moscow, 1969).

4. Georges Soria, "Preparations for the Defense of Madrid," *International Press Correspondence* 16, no. 46 (October 1936):1260; *Mundo Obrero*, Special Anniversary Edition (November 7, 1937); Last, *Tragedy*, 29-30. The Communist party of Spain had never, prior to the Popular Front era, been large or important. Its leaders did not stand high in the ranks of the Communist International and were thoroughly subservient to Comintern and Soviet control. See Castro Delgado, *Hombres*, Jesús Hernández, *Yo fuí un minestro de Stalin* (Mexico, 1953), and Valentín González, *Comunista en España y anti-Stalinista en Rusia* (Mexico, 1953). All are memoirs of high-ranking members of the Spanish party during the civil war who have since left the party and all agree that the party was simply a Comintern tool. Hernández, 59, tells of a meeting of the politburo of the Spanish Communist party in late July 1936, at which the following non-Spanish Comintern representatives were present: Togliatti, Duclos, Codovila, Stepanov, and Geroe. José Díaz, the chief of the Spanish party, essentially confirms this in his book *Tres años de lucha* (Toulouse, 1947), 127.

5. "No Pasarán—They Shall Not Pass," *Communist International* 13, no. 12 (December 1936):651, tells of a resistance meeting held in Madrid on November 11 at which José Díaz, Enrique Lister, Carlos Contreras, and Nicoletti spoke. Díaz was secretary of the Spanish Communist party, Lister was the top Spanish Communist military leader in the Fifth Regiment, Contreras was Vittorio Vidali, the Italian Comintern agent who was the chief political commissar of the Fifth Regiment, and Nicoletti (Giuseppe de Vittorio) was political commissar of the XI International Brigade.

6. *Estampa* (October 10, 1936), as quoted in Martínez Bande, *Marcha*, 119 n. 106.

7. Documentos Historicos, Ediciones del 5 Regimento, *Defensa de Madrid*, 19, as quoted in Ibarruri, *Guerra*, 1:162.

8. Ibarruri, *Guerra*, 1:128, 145-52; Castro Delgado, *Hombres*, 391; André Marty, "Madrid—The Verdun of Democracy," *International Press Correspondence* 16, no. 57 (December, 1936):1278. No pasarán was the Spanish equivalent of the French "Ils ne passeront pas," made famous at the battle of Verdun in 1916. Cox, *Madrid*, 51-52, says the radio carried continuous fervent speeches studded with the words "no pasarán, no pasarán" rising almost to a shriek.

9. Lister, *Guerra*, 84-85. For the best discussion of the flight of the government from Madrid and their attitude that the city was lost, see Bolloten, *Revolution*.

10. Lister, *Guerra*, 86; Malinovski, *Baja la bandera*, 87; Colodny, *Struggle*, 52; Louis Fischer, *Politics*, 395-98; Renn, *Krieg*, 78-79; Castro Delgado, *Hombres*, 395-405.

11. Lister, *Guerra*, 288; Castro Delgado, *Hombres*, 399-402.

12. There is some confusion as to the names of the Soviet military men in Spain since they used *noms de guerre* and made as little public display of themselves as possible. Malinovski, *Bajo la bandera*, refers to Berzin, who was in Valencia with the Loyalist government, as "the principal military advisor" (68); to Goriev, in Madrid, as the "Soviet military attaché in Spain" (66) and as the "military advisor to General Miaja" (14); and to Kulik as also being active in the Madrid defense of the winter of 1936-1937 (14-15).

13. Longo, *Brigate*, 71; Castro, *Hombres*, 393-94.

14. Colodny, *Struggle*, 75 n. 111.

15. Longo, *Brigate,* 36-37.
16. Ibid., 38-39.
17. Bolloten, *Camouflage,* 224 n. This information was supplied to Bolloten by Vidali.
18. Malinovski, *Bajo la bandera,* 266
19. Longo, *Brigate,* 39-40; *Un año de las Brigadas Internacionales* (Madrid, 1937), 1-20. It is impossible to correlate all the accounts of these early arrivals and come up with any completely consistent theory. The figures and dates cited here are Longo's, who should know. Information in the Marty Archives, such as it is, tends to bear this out. In fact, such inconsistencies as are present are of small consequence.
20. *Communist International* 13, no. 11 (December 1936):733-34.
21. Marty Archives; Dallin, *Espionage,* 47; Ypsilon, *Pattern for World Revolution* (Chicago, 1947), 219-20.
22. Ehrenburg, *Eve of War,* 167, suggests that Marty may have been mentally unbalanced. On some of Marty's disagreeable characteristics, see Louis Fischer, *Politics,* 389-90.
23. There are those who defend Marty's activities in Spain. For example, Colodny agrees with Marty that there were many spies, intelligence agents, and saboteurs in the Brigades. He also rationalizes the Trotskyist mania by agreeing that Trotskyist organizations were in fact infiltrated with Nazi and Fascist agents. He says in defense of Marty, "The task of transforming a collection of revolutionaries from thirty countries into a disciplined fighting force required a hand of iron." Colodny, *Struggle,* 63 and n. 109.
24. *Le Soldat de la République* (October 14, 1937); *Reconquista* (October 20, 1938).
25. Longo, *Brigate,* 152.
26. London, *España,* 184.
27. *Reconquista* (October 20, 1938); Longo, *Boletín de Información,* no. 231 (August 23, 1937); Marty Archives.
28. Ruth Fischer, *German Communism,* 500 n., states that Ulbricht was in charge of establishing an NKVD-controlled police apparatus for maintaining surveillance over the German-speaking members of the Brigades. A recent biographer, Stern, *Ulbricht,* 71 n., says that the evidence is lacking to establish just what Ulbricht's role in Spain was but that he was involved with the "political machines of the International Brigades" and those who supervised the German Communists fighting in Spain.
29. Valtin, *Out of the Night,* 356; Herrick, Testimony, SACB, *Recommended Decision,* 36-38. Herrick worked under Neumann's supervision in the censorship bureau of the International Brigades. He reports that Neumann sometimes boasted of the Trotskyites he had executed.
30. *Un año de las Brigadas Internacionales;* Marty Archives; *Boletín de Información,* no. 282 (October 17, 1937).
31. Louis Fischer, *Politics,* 386; Gillain, *Le Mercenaire,* 24; Wintringham, *English Captain,* 60-61; Pacciardi, *Garibaldi,* 42; *Le Soldat de la République,* no. 50 (October 8, 1937, 1.
32. *Boletín de Información,* no. 207 (July 31, 1937).
33. Spanish Office of Information, 69-71.

34. Romilly, *Boadilla,* 48-67; Louis Fischer, *Politics,* 401; *Boletín de Información,* no. 207 (July 31, 1937), offers a general view of this early organizational work as told by "Vidal."

35. Louis Fischer, *Politics,* 386-87. Fischer could hardly have been said to have "enrolled" in the Brigades. He went down to Albacete and helped out for as long as it suited him, though he continued to be an active partisan of the Loyalist cause throughout the war. Madariaga, *Spain,* 541, says that Fischer acted as chief purchasing agent for the Negrín government from a Paris headquarters. Fischer also wrote and spoke extensively for the Loyalists in the United States and contributed numerous articles to the *Nation.* See the pamphlet by Fischer, *The War in Spain.*

36. Louis Fischer, *Politics.* 387; Pacciardi, *Garibaldi,* 57; Watson, *Single to Spain,* 196; Romilly, *Boadilla,* 75-77; Sommerfield, *Volunteer,* 41; *Épopée,* 62.

37. Pacciardi, *Garibaldi,* 61.

38. Longo, *Brigate,* 51-52; Watson, *Single to Spain,* 107; Sommerfield, *Volunteer,* 23-24.

39. Dahlem, *Communist International* 15, no. 5 (May 1938):446.

40. Romilly, *Boadilla,* 61-62; Longo, *Brigate,* 54.

41. Watson, *Single to Spain,* 109-10; Adolfo Lizón Gadea, *Las Brigadas Internacionales en España* (Madrid, 1940); Sommerfield, *Volunteer,* 22-24.

42. Romilly, *Boadilla,* 42-43; Watson, *Single to Spain,* 105.

43. Longo, *Brigate,* 69.

44. Romilly, *Boadilla,* 67; Watson, *Single to Spain,* 69; Longo, *Brigate,* 69; Spanish Office of Information, 60, contains a photograph of this document.

45. *Boletín de Información,* no. 282 (October 17, 1937). This article was, interestingly, signed by Vidal's successor as base commander at Albacete, Maurice Lampe.

46. Longo, *Brigate,* 71.

47. Valtin, *Out of the Night,* 653; Renn, *Krieg,* 66-67; Alfred Kantorowicz, *Spanisches Tagebüch* (Berlin, 1948), 12-13; R. Hanmer, "Heroes of the Communist International," *Communist International* 13, no. 7 (July 1936): 503.

48. Renn, *Krieg,* 67; Valtin, *Out of the Night,* 241.

49. Renn, *Krieg,* 115; Regler, *Owl of Minerva,* 297; Barea, *Rebel,* 649; Ernest Hemingway, preface to Gustav Regler's *Great Crusade* (New York, 1940); Koestler, *God That Failed,* 24.

50. Kantorowicz, *Tagebüch,* 66; Balk, *Quatorzième,* 1-32; Regler, *Owl of Minerva,* 284-85, 311; Szinda, *XI Brigade,* 24-25; Dahlem, *Communist International* 15, no. 5 (May 1938):446. Dahlem states that the Brigade was "made up in its first months almost exclusively of Communists, mainly Party functionaries and Red Front fighters."

51. Balk, *Quatorzième,* 171; Sommerfield, *Volunteer,* 39.

52. Renn, *Krieg,* 67; Balk, *Quatorzième,* 176-79; Longo, *Brigate,* 69; *Épopée,* 62.

53. Longo, *Brigate,* 69; *Épopée,* 187, 193.

54. Balk, *Quatorzième,* 1-32.

55. Longo, *Brigate,* 70; Thomas, *Spanish Civil War,* 324; Spanish Office of Information, 77, and Brome, *International Brigades,* 80, all say that the Dombrowski battalion was commanded by a Pole named Tedeusz Oppman. None offer any documentation. It seems probable that Thomas and Brome took their information from the Spanish Office of Information (which was published first). I have found no other reference to

Oppman and therefore rely on Longo's account for the above names. Also London, *España*, 185, says the commander was Bolek Ulanovski and the political commissar was Matrizsiak.

56. *Nuestros Españoles*, 6; Sommerfield, *Volunteer*, 39.
57. Cox, *Madrid*, 184-87; Herbert Matthews, *Two Wars and More to Come* (New York, 1938).
58. *International Press Correspondence* 16, no. 57 (December 1938):1498.
59. Cox, *Madrid*, 184-87.
60. Krivitsky, *Secret Service*, 116-17; Pacciardi, *Garibaldi*, 42.
61. Krivitsky, *Secret Service*, 116.
62. Dallin, *Espionage*, 396.
63. Colodny, *Struggle*, 62 and n. 101, avers that in Kleber, the Red army was assigning one of its ablest officers to command the Internationals.
64. Longo, *Brigate*, 72; Pacciardi, *Garibaldi*, 59; Nenni, *Guerre*, 166.
65. Sommerfield, *Volunteer*, 44-50.
66. Ibid., 44-70; *Épopée*, 62-78. The original intention of the Madrid command was to use the Internationals in an attack on the Nationalist right flank near Vallecas, but this did not materialize and the Brigade was brought directly into Madrid. Martínez Bande, *Marcha*, 122 and Document 6.
67. Sommerfield, *Volunteer*, 72-83.
68. Cox, *Madrid*, 66-67.
69. Balk, *Quatorzième*, 180.
70. Barea, *Rebel*, 583.
71. Sommerfield, *Volunteer*, 84.
72. Units of the XI Brigade apparently saw action in several sectors within the next few days. According to most accounts, their first action was in the Casa de Campo, but the Madrid daily *Ahora*, in the November 9 edition, reported that the Internationals first entered combat in the Pozuelo area. Martínez Bande, *Marcha*, 127-30, and nn. 117, 118, offers a thorough discussion of this based on all the available documentation from the official records of the Loyalist army. See also Verle Johnson, *Legions of Babel* (University Park, Pa., 1967), 50 n. 23.
73. Renn, *Krieg*, 71-72; Cox, *Madrid*, 76.
74. Marty, "Twelve Magnificent Months," *International Press Correspondence* 17, no. 45 (October 30, 1937):1044; *Le Volontaire de la Liberté*, no. 28 (October 28, 1937); Longo, *Brigate*, 72-75; Renn, *Krieg*, 73.
75. Pacciardi, *Garibaldi*, 57; Renn, *Krieg*, 68.
76. Pacciardi, *Garibaldi*, 2.
77. Ibid., 4.
78. Einaudi, *Communism*, 210.
79. Pacciardi, *Garibaldi*, 4-7, 52-56; Longo, *Brigate*, 261.
80. Pacciardi, *Garibaldi*, 52-56; Dallin, *Espionage*, 208. Pacciardi commanded a unit in the allied armies during World War II and served as minister of defense in the postwar De Gasperi cabinet.
81. Longo, *Brigate*, 70; Giacomo Calandrone, *La Spagna Brucia* (Rome, 1962), 42.
82. Longo, *Brigate*, 261; Pacciardi, *Garibaldi*, 42.
83. Ibid.

84. Calandrone, *Spagna,* 21, 42.
85. Pacciardi, *Garibaldi,* 59; Regler, *Owl of Minerva,* 289; Ehrenberg, *Eve of War,* 174; Nenni, *Guerre,* 168.
86. Renn, *Krieg,* 5-18, 23-24, 67; Regler, *Owl of Minerva,* 173; Kantorowicz, *Tagebüch,* 13; Pacciardi, *Garibaldi,* 63.
87. Renn, *Krieg,* 25; *Communist International* 14, no. 1 (January 1937):803-6.
88. Renn, *Krieg,* 40-55, 64-68; Last, *Tragedy,* 88-89.
89. Koestler, *God That Failed,* 42-43.
90. Renn, *Krieg,* 65-75; Romilly, *Boadilla,* 68-74; Longo, *Brigate,* 75-77; Pacciardi, *Garibaldi,* 63; London, *España,* 185.
91. Renn, *Krieg,* 74-75; Romilly, *Boadilla,* 74.
92. In view of the large number of Frenchmen among the volunteers this could only have been explained by the fact that all the French with sufficient military or political experience must have been with the Commune de Paris battalion in the XI Brigade.
93. London, *España,* 76; Nenni, *Guerre,* 166; Ehrenberg, *Eve of War,* 171-76; Pacciardi, *Garibaldi,* 63; Louis Fischer, *Politics,* 388.
94. Renn, *Krieg,* 61-68.
95. Ehrenberg, *Eve of War,* 174; Regler, *Owl of Minerva,* 279, 297; Nenni, *Guerre,* 178.
96. *Communist International* 14, no. 9 (September 1937):656-58.
97. Ehrenberg, *Eve of War,* 173; Louis Fischer, *Politics,* 388.
98. Longo, *Brigate,* 76-77; Renn, *Krieg,* 75-77.

CHAPTER 5

1. Longo, *Brigate,* 137-38; Kantorowicz, *Tagebüch,* 195-96. Contrary to a widely held view, the XIII Brigade was not, originally, the Slavic Brigade. It became so only much later when the original XIII Brigade was disbanded and a new one, predominantly Slavic, replaced it.
2. Alfred Kantorowicz, *Tschapaiev: Das Battalion der 21 Nationen* (Madrid, 1938).
3. *Reconquista* (October 20, 1938), 10-11; Kantorowicz, *Tagebüch,* 197, 194-95.
4. Longo, *Brigate,* 138.
5. Lecouer, *Le Partisan,* 71; Kantorowicz, *Tagebüch,* 208; Dallin, *Espionage,* 75, 85-90, 364-66.
6. Kantorowicz, *Tagebüch,* 215-20.
7. Ibid., 196, 207; Longo, *Brigate,* 138.
8. There is much circumstantial evidence to support this contention. Louis Fischer, *Politics,* 427, confirms Largo Caballero's distrust of the Anarchists in December 1936. Colodny, *Struggle,* 94, 208 n. 13, states that he had firsthand information from absolutely reliable sources that the XIII Brigade was called to Valencia as an internal security measure.
9. Longo, *Brigate,* 140-41.
10. Kantorowicz, *Tagebüch,* 205-15; Longo, *Brigate,* 142-45; Wullschleger, *Kampfen,* 161-62.

11. Gillain, *Le Mercenaire,* 27; Spanish Office of Information, 60.
12. Marty Archives; *Reconquista* (October 20, 1938), 21.
13. Gillain, *Le Mercenaire,* 27; Balk, *Quatorzième,* 119; *Le Soldat de la République,* no. 1 (February 16, 1937); *Boletín de Información,* no. 282 (October 17, 1937).
14. Neal Wood, *Communism and the British Intellectuals* (New York, 1959), 167; Wintringham, *English Captain,* 82; *Communist International* 14, no. 2 (February 1937):869.
15. *Épopée,* 87.
16. Balk, *Quatorzième,* 94; Gillain, *Le Mercenaire,* 93, 110; Calandrone, *Spagna,* 210-11.
17. Gillain, *Le Mercenaire,* 92-93; Balk, *Quatorzième,* 79; Wintringham, *English Captain,* 75-76.
18. Balk, *Quatorzième,* 95-97; *Le Soldat de la République,* Special Edition (June 27, 1937); *Épopée,* 87.
19. Marty Archives; *Boletín de Información,* no. 282 (October 17, 1937).
20. Balk, *Quatorzième,* 76; Wintringham, *English Captain,* 66-67, 80-86; Brome, *International Brigades,* 278-79.
21. Balk, *Quatorzième,* 49.
22. Longo, *Brigate,* 151-52.
23. Ibid., 151-60; Balk, *Quatorzième;* Gillain, *Le Mercenaire,* 29–37; Wintringham, *English Captain,* 85-89.
24. *Le Livre de la 15eme Brigade Internationale: Nos Combats Contre le Fascisme* (Madrid, 1937), 15.
25. *Notre Combat,* no. 1 (March 3, 1937), 1; *Livre,* 134.
26. Wintringham, *English Captain,* 145-46, 191-92; Eby, *Bullet,* 54-59; Arthur Landis, *The Abraham Lincoln Brigade* (New York, 1967), 166-67; Steve Nelson, *The Volunteers* (New York, 1953), 99.
27. *Livre,* 135; *Notre Combat,* no. 25 (April 14, 1937), 1.
28. *Reconquista* (October 20, 1938), 16; *Notre Combat,* no. 25 (April 14, 1937), 1.
29. *Notre Combat,* no. 3 (March 17, 1937), 1. It is possible that some of the more unfortunate phrases were applied by overzealous editors of the Brigade press.
30. *Livre,* 136; Marty Archives; *Notre Combat,* no. 26 (April 23, 1937), 2.
31. *Notre Combat,* no. 28 (May 17, 1937), 2.
32. Wintringham, *English Captain,* 91; *Volunteer for Liberty* (November 7, 1938), 8; *Reconquista* (October 20, 1938), 14; *Communist International* 13, no. 2 (February 1936):126.
33. Rust, *Britons in Spain,* 29; Wintringham, *English Captain,* 92-100; *Livre,* 26.
34. Wintringham, *English Captain,* 95-112; Thomas, *Spanish Civil War,* 376.
35. Fred Copeman, *Reason in Revolt* (London, 1948). Copeman eventually rose to command in the battalion.
36. Wood, *Communism,* 58-59, 162-66.
37. Wintringham, *English Captain,* 166.
38. *Reconquista* (October 20, 1938), 14-15; Rust, *Britons in Spain,* 35.
39. *Volunteer for Liberty* (May 1, 1938), 2; *Reconquista* (October 20, 1938), 15; *Livre,* 202; Copeman, *Reason,* 80; Rust, *Britons in Spain,* 36.
40. *Livre,* 15, 34, 137, 202, 258; Marty Archives.

41. *Nuestros Españoles,* 6, 12; *Livre,* 15; Carlo Penchienati, *Brigate Internazionali in Spagna: Delitti della "Ceka" Communista* (Milan, 1950), 20.
42. Penchienati, *Spagna,* 18, 27; *Livre,* 82-84, 206.
43. *Nuestros Españoles,* 12; Penchienati, *Spagna,* 19; *Livre,* 22, 81, 206.
44. Earl Browder, *The Peoples Front* (New York, 1938), 128.
45. *The Hebrew and Jewish Tribunal* (January 1, 1937). This New York published newspaper states that about one-third of the Americans were Jews. On the ethnic makeup of the American contingent, see Eby, *Bullet,* 47 n. 9.
46. *Volunteer for Liberty* (November 7, 1938), 4.
47. Robert Merriman, "The Work of Americans in Spain," *Nuestro Combate* (December 1937–January 1938), 14.
48. Voros, *Commissar,* 269, 333-34; Eby, *Bullet,* 22-30.
49. Merriman, *Nuestro Combate* (Jauary 1938), 14; Eby, *Bullet,* 27; Voros, *Commissar,* 133. For an in-depth analysis of the composition of the American battalion, see Robert A. Rosenstone, *Crusade on the Left: The Lincoln Battalion in the Spanish Civil War* (New York, 1969).
50. Landis, *Brigade,* 27; Voros, *Commissar,* 333-50; Merriman, *Nuestro Combate* (January, 1937), 14; Eby, *Bullet,* 24-30.
51. *Notre Combat,* no. 7 (March 15, 1937), 1.
52. Testimony, SACB, *Recommended Decision,* 22; Eby, *Bullet,* 30, 204 n. 2.
53. Louis Fischer, *Politics,* 403; Voros, *Commissar,* 344-48; *Livre,* 209-10.
54. Eby, *Bullet,* 31 n. 6.
55. Voros, *Commissar,* 349. Voros got his facts on this from Merriman himself.
56. Eby, *Bullet,* 27.
57. Voros, *Commissar,* 349-53, does not make it clear whether he agrees that Harris was appointed by the party in New York or not. Witnesses say he was so appointed (SACB, *Recommended Decision,* 22). Landis, *Brigade,* 33, leaves it a mystery saying that "no reason exists for Harris' appointment." Most likely he was appointed military commander of the first contingent in New York due to his alleged army experience, something, it would seem, none of the other members of the contingent had. It is doubtful if this appointment was intended to be permanent since Harris had little stature in the party. Vidal would not likely have known this, since the American party's liaison with the Brigade hierarchy was poor at the time. See also Eby, *Bullet,* 30.
58. Merriman, *Nuestro Combate* (January 1938), 14; *Livre,* 22.
59. Voros, *Commissar,* 206.
60. Ibid.; Eby, *Bullet,* 39; *Livre,* 249.
61. Voros, *Commissar,* 352-54.
62. For a full discussion of this dispute, see Eby, *Bullet,* 38-48.
63. Voros, *Commissar,* 354-55; *Livre,* 99; Matthews, *Two Wars,* 221-22; *Volunteer for Liberty* (November 7, 1938), 1-2.

CHAPTER 6

1. The XII Brigade moved into the University City fighting directly after experiencing its first taste of combat (and a sound beating) resulting from its attack on

the Nationalist right flank at Cerro de los Angeles (Cerro Rojo). This entire affair had demonstrated, at the price of numerous killed and wounded, that the Brigade and its component units were in no condition to carry out the complex task of an offensive operation. As the Soviet general Batov, who served as adviser to the XII Brigade during the operation, put it, with some understatement: "The course of the combat already had begun to reveal the defects of our improvised organization." *Pravda* correspondent Koltsov said it more precisely: "A day of disillusionments and great sorrows. The attack achieved nothing.... Artillery preparation was lamentable. The new combatants, poorly instructed, advanced with indifference and, on approaching Cerro de los Angeles they were disconcerted before the enemy fire and stuck to the earth.... This failure was hard." The abortive attack led Pacciardi, commander of the Italian Garibaldi battalion, to feel a certain distrust of the high command. "One does not attack a fortress with the bayonet," he thought. And Pacciardi was not alone. In the wake of the debacle, Marty sent the German Communist Gustav Regler to the XII Brigade as a "special commisar." He told Regler pointedly that he had full powers, clearly meaning that if Regler felt it expedient to have a few men shot to restore discipline he had Marty's blessing. Regler found XII Brigade commander General Lukacs a tired and sad man. "We were ordered to take that place without adequate artillery preparation," he said. "Naturally we were beaten." On this entire operation, see Regler, *Owl of Minerva*, 279-89; Pacciardi, *Garibaldi*, 64-71; Romilly, *Boadilla*, 104-17; Watson, *Single to Spain*, 110-25; Renn, *Krieg*, 75-80; Malinovski, *Bajo la bandera*, 335; Koltsov, *Diario*, 224-25; Longo, *Brigate*, 75-85.

2. Martínez Bande, *Marcha*, 144-45.

3. José Manuel Martínez Bande, *La lucha en torno de Madrid* (Madrid, 1970), 48-50; Longo, *Brigate*, 130-31; Pacciardi, *Garibaldi*, 105-6.

4. Renn, *Krieg*, 113-18; Longo, *Brigate*, 117, 130-31; Szinda, *XI Brigade*, 29; Dahlem, *Communist International* 15, no. 5 (May 1938):115.

5. Following this action the XI Brigade, reduced to some 600 effectives, was withdrawn to Murcia in southern Spain for rest, reinforcement, and reorganization.

6. Esmond Romilly's *Boadilla* offers a firsthand account of the XI Brigade in this action.

7. Koltsov, *Diario*, 273; Colodny, *Struggle*, 105, estimates Nationalist casualties at 15,000.

8. López Muñiz, *Batalla*, 99.

9. Lister, *Guerra*, 100; Malinovski, *Bajo la bandera*, 116.

10 Lister, *Guerra*, 100; Vicente Rojo, *España Heróico* (Buenos Aires, 1942), 70-71; Martínez Bande, *Lucha*, 95-100.

11. There are numerous accounts of the Pingarron debacle. Among those chiefly relied on here were Voros, *Commissar*, 355-58; Wintringham, *English Captain*, 254-57; Matthews, *Two Wars*, 223-24; Maken and Gladnick, Testimony, SACB, *Stenographic Record;* Eby, *Bullet*, 40-65.

12. Renn, *Krieg*, 225-26.

13. Nenni, *Guerre*, 50, 106; Louis Fischer, *Politics*, 46-47.

14. For a brief period between the end of the Jarama campaign and the end of the Brunete offensive the old XII Brigade had been split into two Brigades: the XII (Garibaldi) and the CL. Shortly thereafter the CL was disbanded.

15. Pacciardi, *Garibaldi*, 255; Calandrone, *Spagna*, 114; Penchienati, *Spagna*, 91. The *New York Times* reporting on the decreasing role of the Internationals on October 24, 1937, gave the figure of 7,000 to 8,000 still on active duty.
16. Voros, *Commissar*, 410.
17. Thomas, *Spanish Civil War*, 488, states that by the end of 1937 the Nationalist army numbered 600,000 men. At about the same time, he says (493), the Loyalist army numbered some 450,000 men.

CHAPTER 7

1. The designations *People's Army* or *Popular Army* were used more or less indiscriminately in referring to the new government army created by the Loyalist regime.
2. *Boletín de Información*, no. 302 (November 7, 1937), 4.
3. *Communist International* 15, no. 5 (May 1938): 445-46.
4. "Our Army Is a People's Army," *Volunteer for Liberty* 1, no. 2 (June 1, 1937), 1; *Communist International* 14, no. 2 (February 1937): 869.
5. *Soldat de la République*, no. 44 (August 17, 1937), 3.
6. *Ecole des Commissaires de Guerre*, Theme 9, Marty Archives.
7. David T. Cattell, *Communism and the Spanish Civil War* (Berkeley, 1955), 211; Payne, *Revolution*, 374. Something of this nature did occur at the very end of the war when Communist and non-Communist units of the Loyalist army fought a small-scale civil war between themselves. By that time, however, the International Brigades no longer existed. Had they done so, they would surely have been on the Communist side of the barricades. On this episode see Payne, *Revolution*, 355-58.
8. *Communist International* 14, no. 3 (March 1937): 179; also an article by "Nicoletti," *Communist International* 13, no. 11 (November 1936): 741.
9. *Ecole des Commissaires de Guerre*, Theme 9, Marty Archives.
10. *Boletín de Información*, no. 280 (October 15, 1937), 6-8.
11. *Frente Rojo*, as quoted in the *Boletín de Información*, no. 283 (October 10, 1937), 4; *Mundo Obrero* (November 7, 1937).
12. Browder in a speech to an enlarged politburo meeting in November 1937, as reported in the *Communist* (December 1937).
13. *Boletín de Información*, no. 344 (December 28, 1937), 2.
14. *Communist International* 14, no. 2 (February 1937): 869; *Nuestro Combate*, no. 35 (December 1937-January 1938), 5.
15. *Communist International* 15, no. 5 (May 1938): 454-55; ibid., 14, no. 2 (February 1937): 866.
16. *Boletín de Información*, no. 280 (October 15, 1937), 6-8; *Communist International* 14, nos. 5 and 6 (June 1937): 1072. See Louis Fischer's report (405) on his interview with Comintern chief Dimitroff in which Dimitroff voiced the hope that an American Popular Front could be forged from the Americans fighting in the International Brigades.
17. Robert Minor, *Report to the Tenth Convention of the Communist Party of New York*, May 1938.

18. Maken, Testimony, SACB, *Stenographic Record,* 2:752, stated that in the Lincoln battalion, commissars adopted the slogan "Every member of the Brigade a member of the Communist Party." John Little, *Report to the Tenth Convention of the Communist Party of New York,* May 1938.
19. Harry Pollitt, *Communist International* 14, no. 2 (February 1937): 860
20. *Boletín de Información,* no. 283 (October 1937), 1.
21. *Volunteer for Liberty* 2, no. 2 (January 18, 1938), 4.
22. Marty, *Volunteer for Liberty* 1, no. 21 (November 1, 1937), 11; *Communist International* 17, no. 3 (March 1940): 182; Bill Lawrence, *Democracy's Stake,* 22.
23. *Communist* (December 1937), 1082-83. On the United States party's treatment of Nelson, see the *Daily Worker* (November 10, 1937), "Steve Nelson an Exemplary Political Commissar in the International Brigades." British battalion commander Fred Copeman was also rewarded for his services in Spain with co-option into the central committee of the Communist party of Great Britain. Both Auguste Lecouer and Rol Tanguy rose into the top echelons of the French party following their work in Spain and almost the entire hierarchy of the Italian Communist party which emerged after World War II was composed of ex-International Brigaders.
24. A clear indication of the fact that the Comintern, and not the Loyalist government, controlled the Brigade chiefs was the recall of Marty himself to Moscow on one occasion and before the hierarchy of the French party on another to account for his direction of the Brigades. Marty's absences from Spain on these occasions were not publicized but there are various accounts of them. It would seem that in the summer of 1937 he was absent and that his place had been taken by François Billoux. Colodny, *Struggle,* 106, states that Moscow recalled Marty, and Lecouer, *Le Partisan,* refers to Marty's recall.
25. Krivitsky, *Secret Service,* 112, says some 500 such men went to the International Brigades. Krivitsky avers that these foreign Communists living in the Soviet Union were dispatched to Spain by Stalin partly to furnish reliable cadres for the Brigades and partly to relieve himself of their unwanted presence in Russia where the great purges were under way.
26. Dallin, *Espionage,* 40, 54, 84, 87, 140.
27. Longo, *Brigate,* 188-90; Calandrone, *Spagna,* 43-44; Nenni, *Guerre,* 167.
28. Marty Archives, handwritten notes on Barontini. He is also discussed by Longo, Calandrone, Pacciardi, and Penchienati.
29. Longo, *Brigate,* 364-70; Nenni, *Guerre,* 235-37.
30. Penchienati, *Spagna,* 50.
31. Testimony, SACB, *Recommended Decision,* 88-89. The two major functions of the Friends of the Abraham Lincoln Brigade (FALB) were propaganda and fund raising. According to White the FALB raised over $425,000. *Volunteer for Liberty* (January 1940). The *Volunteer for Liberty* was the official publication of the veterans of the Lincoln Brigade. *Time* magazine (April 18, 1938), 21, said the FALB, organized in April 1937, had over 25,000 dues-paying members. It reported collections of $115,701.42 as of that date. The FALB also took charge of the veterans upon their leaving Spain. David Leeds, financial secretary of the Communist party in New York directed the repatriation of American Brigade men. He operated from Paris using the name David Ameriglio. McCuiston, Testimony, HUAC, *Hearings,* 6725.

32. Voros, *Commissar,* 316-17.
33. Gates, *American Communist,* 50; Lecouer, *Le Partisan,* 97.
34. Alexander Foote, *Handbook for Spies* (London, 1953); Dallin, *Espionage,* 184; Haldane, *Truth,* 287-88.
35. Gladnick, Testimony, SACB, *Recommended Decision,* 49.
36. As quoted in SACB, *Recommended Decision,* 51-52. Indeed, according to the NKVD chief in Spain, Alexander Orlov, he and a Russian staff under his command organized and operated the guerrilla warfare operations of the Loyalists. Orlov Memo.
37. Renn, *Krieg,* 145. Lister, *Guerra,* 277, corroborates this situation. He says that both Largo Caballero and later Prieto, as well as most of the high command of the Loyalist army, opposed the organization of guerrilla warfare and resisted efforts to do so. The Communists on the other hand favored this approach and "took certain practical steps" to organize that type of operation, including the operation of schools for guerrilla warfare.
38. Renn, *Krieg,* 145-50.
39. Voros, *Commissar,* 326-27
40. Penchienati, *Spagna,* 35; Marty Archives; Koltsov, *Diario,* 100, says that Togliatti was among the Comintern delegation that organized the Brigades in October 1936.
41. Lecouer, *Le Partisan,* 79.
42. Voros, *Commissar,* 307-10.
43. The Soviet officers "Colonel Valois" and Petrovitch were involved in the earliest stages of the Brigades' organization at Albacete. Kleber, a Red army officer himself, operated under the direct orders of Goriev during the defense of Madrid; Lukacs had the Soviet general Batov ("Fritz") as his permanent adviser; Kahle enjoyed the constant services of the Soviet officer called "Loti." On the whole subject of the Soviet military mission in Spain, see Malinovski, *Bajo la bandera;* Ehrenburg, *Eve of War;* Krivitsky, *Secret Service.*
44. By the summer of 1937 ex-International Brigade commanders Walter, Gall, Kleber, and Kahle commanded the People's Army divisions that incorporated the various International Brigades.
45. Balk, *Quatorzième,* 143-44; Longo, *Brigate,* 325; Gillain, *Le Mercenaire,* 103-4; *Le Soldat de la République,* no. 23 (April 14, 1937).
46. *Le Soldat de la République,* no. 24 (April 22, 1937).
47. Marty Archives. Sagnier had served with Dumont in that unit since its origins in October 1936 and had acted as provisional commander during Dumont's occasional absences. Balk, *Quatorzième,* 140-42, 156, 192-93. Vittori had once served three years in a French prison in Madagascar. Upon his release and return to France he had served as secretary of the Secours Rouge, the French branch of that important Communist-front organization. He had arrived in Spain in January 1937.
48. Gillain, *Le Mercenaire,* 104-12; on the general problem, see Balk, *Quatorizième,* 156.
49. The British battalion also went through a thorough reorganization in the wake of the Jarama battle. Wintringham, wounded in the Jarama fighting, had no further direct contact with the battalion. When he returned to duty in June 1937, it was to replace the American Merriman as chief English-speaking instructor at the Interna-

tional Brigade's officer training school. During the subsequent hard fighting Jock Cunningham took effective command of the battalion and remained in command until wounded in a skirmish in March. Cunningham later returned to duty as a major attached to the Brigade staff. Fred Copeman replaced Cunningham in command of the battalion, a post he held until April of 1938. Wintringham, *English Captain*, 229-30, 272-95; Copeman, *Reason*, 104-10; Rust, *Britons in Spain*, 57.

50. *Volunteer for Liberty* (May 1, 1938), 14, announced these changes. British party writer Rust draws the usual smoke screen of vagueness over this transaction saying merely, "from Britain there came three new commissars." This purposefully vague way of saying things was developed to a fine art by Communist writers. The great value of it was that it told the initiated quite clearly what the writer intended to tell them and told the uninitiated reader little or nothing about the concrete role of the party in these operations. Rust, *Britons in Spain*, 56.

51. Thomas, *Spanish Civil War*, 465. He cites George Aitkin as his source for this.

52. Copeman, *Reason*, 136-40. Copeman fails to specify just which of the British commissars were in favor of the death penalty.

53. Ibid., 136-40.

54. For a full discussion of Johnson and this entire episode, see Eby, *Bullet*, 105-16. Landis, *Brigade*, also deals with this, but less satisfactorily.

55. Voros, *Commissar*, 270-72; Steve Nelson, *The Volunteers;* Landis, *Brigade*, 164-65; Eby, *Bullet*, 105. Nelson went on to become XV Brigade commissar and, later, a member of the top echelon of the United States party. Men in the American unit who received command positions directly from the party in the United States won the sobriquet "ninth floor generals," a reference to the ninth floor of the party's New York headquarters where the politburo met. On the party's deciding whether a functionary should go to Spain or not, see Joseph Starobin, *The Life and Death of an American Hero*, 78.

56. Among this contingent was Rol Tanguy.

57. Lecouer, *Le Partisan*, met this man again in 1946 as the military attaché to the Polish Embassy in Paris, 70 n.

58. Ibid. 69-71.

59. These can be seen in various editions of the *Volunteer for Liberty* and also in Kantorowicz, *Tagebüch*, 296 ff.

60. *Communist International* 14, no. 9 (September 1937):659. At some point during the Brunete campaign of July 1937 the XIII Brigade underwent a crisis from which it never recovered. Just what happened or the exact sequence of events remains unclear. But the results leave no room for doubt as to the seriousness of the event. The XIII Brigade was dissolved as a unit and its men were scattered into other Brigades. Simultaneously the Dombrowski Brigade dropped the CL designation and assumed the number XIII itself, thus helping to cover up the fact of the dissolution of the original XIII Brigade. Nothing of this appears in Communist accounts of the Brigades. That there was some trouble in the XIII Brigade, however, was alluded to by various sources (Lecouer, *Le Partisan*, 91-97; Kantorowicz, *Tagebüch*, 489-90). Even the *Volunteer for Liberty* mentioned that one unit, unnamed, "yielded to panic." August 9, 1937. For a vivid, if questionable, account of the "mutiny" of the XIII and its dissolution, see Gillain, *Le Mercenaire*, 150-55.

61. Longo, *Brigate,* 261-63.

62. Following the battle of Guadalajara the XII Brigade was reorganized into two separate brigades. One, commanded by Pacciardi, remained the XII (Garibaldi) and consisted of Italians and Spaniards only. It was joined in April by Italians from the XV Brigade and from the old Giustizia e Libertá column which had been with the Anarchist militia in Aragon since the beginning of the war. The other included the Poles of the Dombrowski, the Franco-Belgian André Marty battalion, and a newly formed Slavic-Hungarian battalion named for the Hungarian Communist Rakosi. The new Brigade took the name "Dombrowski" and the number CL. Both the Garibaldi and the Dombrowski brigades remained under the overall command of General Lukacs. Following this reorganization and due to the command appointments made by Pacciardi, the three battalions of the Garibaldi Brigade were commanded respectively by Battistelli, a Republican; Marvin, a Communist; and Penchienati, a nonparty man. That command structure, with Pacciardi as Brigade commander, made the Garibaldis unique among the International Brigades in having a predominantly non-Communist military command. Francesco Leone, "The International Brigades Yesterday and Today," *Communist International* 14, nos. 5 and 6 (June 1937): 1070; Balk, *Quatorziéme,* 175-76; Penchienati, *Spagna,* 31-32, 57-59; Renn, *Krieg,* 153-54; Pacciardi, *Garibaldi,* 213; Calandrone, *Spagna,* 150-52.

An early example of Pacciardi's attitude toward running his own Brigade was the case of Captain Morelli, adjutant of the second battalion. Morelli, a Communist, had printed a circular in which he attacked and libeled several of the non-Communist officers attached to Pacciardi's staff. Pacciardi's immediate arrest of Morelli threw the Communist politicos into a dither. Their hearts were with Morelli, but they were unable to pressure Pacciardi into reversing his course. Penchienati, *Spagna,* 59; Calandrone, *Spagna,* 144.

63. Longo, *Brigate,* 263-65; Calandrone, *Spagna,* 175-85; Penchienati, *Spagna,* 59, 90-91.

64. Longo, *Brigate,* 330-34.

65. Lecouer, *Le Partisan,* 82; Louis Fischer, *Politics,* 428; Orwell, *Catalonia,* 175; John McGovern, *Terror in Spain* (London, 1938).

66. Orwell, *Catalonia,* 196-232; Borkenau, *Cockpit,* 244-57.

67. Lecouer, *Le Partisan,* 82-83; "Treason Is the Only Name for Treason," *Our Fight,* no. 39 (May 10, 1937); *Le Soldat de la République,* no. 34 (June 20, 1937); no. 44 (August 17, 1937); no. 45 (August 29, 1937); Longo, *Brigate,* 330-33.

68. *Volunteer for Liberty* 1, no. 1 (May 24, 1937); Departmental Note No. 6540 as published in the *Boletín de Información,* July 28, 1937.

69. Pacciardi, *Garibaldi,* 224-27; Penchienati, *Spagna,* 60-61.

70. Johnson, *Legions,* 108-9.

71. Longo, *Brigate,* 332-41; Nenni, *Guerre,* 177. For contemporary Spanish voicing of mistrust of the government and the Communists, whom they called "Stalinist reactionaries," see *Juventud Obrero,* a POUM newspaper (which was subsequently suppressed by the government).

72. On July 11 Lukacs, Pacciardi, Gerassi (commander of the Dombrowski Brigade), Gustav Regler, and "Fritz" (Lukacs's Soviet adviser), proceeded down a road near the front. Nationalist artillery opened up and hit one of the three cars, killing

Lukacs and seriously injuring both Regler and "Fritz." Petrof, Lukacs's vice-commander, assumed command and the operation proceeded.

73. Pacciardi, *Garibaldi,* 234-39.
74. Ibid., 240-44; Penchienati, *Spagna,* 70; Calandrone, *Spagna,* 157.
75. Pacciardi, *Garibaldi,* 140-42, 240-44. The divisional commander was Kleber, the Comintern general who had commanded the Brigades during the defense of Madrid in November-December 1936.
76. Calandrone, *Spagna,* 182; Nenni, *Guerre,* 181; Longo, *Brigate,* 390-91.
77. Penchienati, *Spagna,* 91; Calandrone, *Spagna,* 182; Nenni, *Guerre,* 181. While basically noncommittal on the quarrel Nenni seems largely to agree with Pacciardi. The Brigade, he said, after ten months of combat, was demoralized and needed a long period of rest and reorganization. Calandrone says (183-84) that the commissariat agreed to a period of leave outside Spain for those who wanted it and that the Spanish government refused to allow it. This is doubtful. In fact, Brigade men left Spain whenever the commissariat saw fit. It is also unlikely that the minister of war, Prieto, would have objected. Certainly the Communists could have arranged it if they had so desired.
78. Calandrone, *Spagna,* 182.
79. Penchienati, *Spagna,* 90-92.
80. Nenni, *Guerre,* 181. Apparently trying to steer a middle course, Nenni merely says that Pacciardi went to Paris to expose the situation and on his return was assigned to division staff. He also says, without comment, that this "crisis in command" caused grave repercussions in the Brigade.
81. Penchienati, *Spagna,* 94-95; Calandrone, *Spagna,* 183-84. Despite the knowledge that he had been ousted by the communists, Pacciardi would do nothing to hurt the cause of Loyalist Spain. When he left Spain in the winter of 1937 he went on a propaganda tour for the government. He also subsequently wrote a book about the Garibaldis in Spain in which he said virtually nothing against the Communists.
82. Some 2,000 volunteers were already in Albacete with more on the way. Longo, *Brigate,* 40-45; André Marty, "Twelve Magnificent Months," *International Press Correspondence* 17, no. 45 (October 1937): 1014-15.
83. Longo, *Brigate,* 42-44.
84. André Marty, "Twelve Magnificent Months," 1014-15; Longo, *Brigate,* 44-45; *Épopée,* 50.
85. Longo, *Brigate,* 262-65.
86. Nenni, *Guerre,* 166-67. Nenni is often erroneously referred to as a member of the Brigades.
87. Longo, *Brigate,* 254-55.
88. Ibid., 252-56.
89. Ibid., 254-57.
90. André Marty, "The International Brigades," *International Press Correspondence* 18, no. 24 (May 1938): 586; Dahlem, *Communist International* 15, no. 5 (May 1938): 450.
91. "Some New Problems and Their Solutions," *Boletín de Información,* no. 283 (October 24, 1937), 7-8. Later, long after the Spanish war, when Longo wrote his book on the Brigades he recalled that the situation was not made easier by the attitude of many of the Internationals themselves who exaggerated the role of the Brigades in the

war and who felt it was impossible to assimilate the Spanish conscripts who were "worthless."
92. *Il Garibaldino*, no. 8 (August 16, 1937), 1; "Nuevos Combatientes," *Le Soldat de la République*, no. 49 (September 24, 1937), 1.
93. Longo, *Brigate*, 255-56.
94. *Volunteer for Liberty*, no. 20 (November 1, 1937); Calandrone, *Spagna*, 228-29.
95. Ibid., 229—31.
96. The Communists' chief weapon in their vendetta against Prieto was to call him a "pessimist" and "defeatist." For fuller discussions of this, see Indalecio Prieto, *Cómo y por qué salí del Ministerio de Defensa Nacional* (Paris, 1939); Cattel, *Communism;* Payne, *Revolution.*
97. Penchienati, *Spagna,* 118; Calandrone, *Spagna,* 279.

CHAPTER 8

1. Indeed it was the Communist Fifth Regiment which served as the nucleus of that army, forming its first six Brigades. An article in the *Volunteer for Liberty,* "Our Army Is a People's Army," no. 2 (June 1, 1937), 1, emphasized the role of the Fifth Regiment and the Communist party in the creation of the People's Army and in the institution of the political commissar system throughout that army. For the best account of the Loyalist commissar system, see Bolloten, *Revolution.*
2. Some have suggested that Alvarez del Vayo was in fact a "crypto-Communist." For example, Payne, *Revolution,* 167. On the formation and role of the commissariat from the Communist point of view, see Ibarruri, "The Time Has Come to Create a Single Party for the Proletariat," *Communist International* 14, no. 9 (September 1937): 642; also *Communist International* 14, nos. 5-6 (June 1937): 1091.
3. Louis Fischer, *Politics,* 455, recounts a conversation in which Prieto, then minister of war, said that he had lost trust in the Communists mainly because of the way they had "tried to get control of the army through the officers and commissars." When Fischer observed that "at the front the commissars improve the morale of the troops," Prieto countered, "But why must the vast majority of them be Communists?"
4. Dahlem, *Communist International* 15, no. 5 (May 1938): 450; Marty, *Heroic Spain,* 14-15; Marty, *Communist International* 14, nos. 5-6 (June 1937): 1090.
5. "Our Army Is a People's Army," 1.
6. Marty, "Twelve Magnificent Months," 1044; *Communist International* 15, no. 5 (May 1938): 450.
7. *Frente Rojo* (April 17, 1937), 1.
8. Enrique Castro Delgado, "La fortaleza de nuestro ejército reside en la consciencia política de sus soldados," *Le Soldat de la République,* no. 41 (July 27, 1937), 1. In this article Castro Delgado also points out that in its role as animator and political guide of the army, the political commissariat published 57 periodicals, edited 1,235 wall newspapers, maintained 490 libraries with 5,438 volumes, and sent 1,299,000 periodicals to the front.
9. From the official organ *El Comisario,* as quoted in *Ecole des Commissaires de Guerre,* Theme 10, Marty Archives.

10. *Bulletin of the Political Commissars of the International Brigades,* no. 3 (September 1937).
11. Marty, *Heroic Spain,* 14-15; Castro Delgado, "La fortaleza de nuestro ejército reside en la consciencia política de sus soldados," 1; Marty, "The International Brigades," 586; Dahlem, *Communist International* 15, no. 5 (May 1938): 448-50.
12. *Livre,* 146.
13. Enrique Castro Delgado, "Las relaciones del Comisario con el Mando," *Nuestro Ejército* (October 1938).
14. "Les devoirs des Commissaires," *Ecole des Commissaires de Guerre,* Theme 10, Marty Archives.
15. *Our Fight,* no. 13 (March 20, 1937), 2.
16. *Il Garibaldino,* no. 6 (August 1, 1937), 1.
17. Ibid., no. 7 (August 7, 1937), 7.
18. *El Comisario* (organ of the General Commissariat of War), as quoted in *Ecole des Commissaires de Guerre,* Theme 11, Marty Archives.
19. "Le Commissaire de Guerre, Facteur Essentiel de L'Armée Populaire," translated and extracted from *El Comisario, Ecole des Commissaires de Guerre,* Theme 11, Marty Archives.
20. *Ecole des Commissaires de Guerre,* Themes 11 and 12, Marty Archives.
21. Ibid.
22. Martínez Bande, *Lucha,* 25 n. 1.
23. An example of this was the conflict between Penchienati, when he commanded the Dimitroff battalion of the XV Brigade, and the battalion commissar, a German party fanatic recently arrived from Russia named Furman. When Furman sought to undermine Penchienati's authority, General Gall told Penchienati to have Furman shot if he gave him any further trouble. Gall could take such a position with assurance not because he was Brigade commander but because he was powerfully connected with the party. Penchienati, *Spagna,* 24-25.
24. *Livre,* 160-62.
25. Longo, *Brigate,* 240-43; Voros, *Commissar,* 321; Penchienati, *Spagna,* 33.
26. Dahlem, *Communist International* 15, no. 5 (May 1938): 450.
27. *Ecole des Commissaires de Guerre,* Theme 10, Marty Archives.
28. Longo, *Brigate,* 54-55.
29. *Ecole des Commissaires de Guerre,* Theme 10, Marty Archives.
30. Ibid.
31. Longo, *Brigate,* 285-86; Calandrone, *Spagna,* 94-95; Pacciardi, *Garibaldi,* 178.
32. Regler, *Owl of Minerva,* 305.
33. Longo, *Brigate,* 289.
34. "Propaganda behind Enemy Lines—A Task for our Political Commissars," *Volunteer for Liberty* 1, no. 10 (August 1937), 6.
35. "Organization of Propaganda at the Front," *Ecole des Commissaires de Guerre,* Theme 10, Marty Archives; Longo, *Brigate,* 250; Calandrone, *Spagna,* 187.
36. Dolores Ibarruri, "Employ All Means to Defend and Consolidate the People's Front," *Communist International* 15, no. 2 (February 1938): 282-85; ibid., 14, no. 9 (September 1937): 659; *Ecole des Commissaires de Guerre,* Theme 10, Marty Archives; Dahlem, *Communist International* 15, no. 5 (May 1938): 450.

37. Horan, Testimony, SACB, *Recommended Decision,* 43; also Herrick, ibid; *Le Soldat de la République,* no. 30 (June 1, 1937), 1.
38. Rust, *Britons in Spain,* 31; Voros, *Commissar,* 319; *Le Soldat de la République,* no. 2 (February 20, 1937), 1.
39. Maken, Testimony, SACB, *Recommended Decision,* 36; Last, *Tragedy,* 36; Landis, *Brigade,* 618 n. 3.
40. Marty, "Twelve Magnificent Months," 1044.
41. Shipman, Testimony, SACB, *Stenographic Record,* 8:3042; Wintringham, *English Captain,* 113-14; Regler, *Great Crusade,* 22; *Communist International* 15, no. 5 (May 1938): 449; Gates, *American Communist,* 47.
42. Johnson, *Legions,* 184 n. 14. This phrase was used in a letter to Johnson from Gates.
43. Voros, *Commissar,* 321-40, 410; Penchienati, *Spagna,* 331; Gates, *American Communist,* 62; Eby, *Bullet,* 185-88, 227-28. There are many firsthand accounts of death sentences being pronounced. See Gillain, *Le Mercenaire,* 215; Regler, *Owl of Minerva,* 279, 292, 324-25; Penchienati, *Spagna,* 112; Lecouer, *Le Partisan,* 72-79.
44. Voros, *Commissar,* 322.
45. "Bureaucracy and the Commissar," *Bulletin of the Political Commissars of the International Brigades* (September 1937), 16-17.
46. Voros, *Commissar,* 322. YCL was the Young Communist League; Last, *Tragedy,* 35, says of this situation in the XI Brigade to which he transferred from a Spanish unit in the summer of 1937, "Even in sexual matters the new puritanism of the Soviet Union was imitated. Wherever the International Brigades were garrisoned, the brothels were closed."
47. Gates, *American Communist,* 55.
48. By an anonymous British volunteer as quoted in Voros, *Commissar,* 328.
49. *Mundo Obrero* (July 22, 1936), 1; Ibarruri, *Guerra,* 1, 302; Lister, *Guerra,* 64; Castro Delgado, *Hombres,* 288-90; Longo, *Brigate,* 56.
50. Rust, *Britons in Spain,* 30.
51. Watson, *Single to Spain,* 82-83.
52. For example, Beimler, "Nicoletti," Longo, Dahlem, Regler.
53. Marty, "The International Brigades," 586; Dahlem, *Communist International* 15, no. 5 (May 1938): 449.
54. Ibid., 454.
55. For example, the lead article in *Il Garibaldino,* no. 14 (September 30, 1937), 1, stressed the necessity for strong discipline in all military units. But, it assured its readers, it was not referring to that "oppressive discipline of the bourgeois armies of the world."
56. Voros, *Commissar,* 311-32; Last, *Tragedy,* 33-34; Gillain, *Le Mercenaire,* 58; "Las Brigadas Internacionales bajo el terror Stalinista," *Juventud Obrero* (November 30, 1937).
57. This is from documents located in the Marty Archives on the International Brigades medical service. The Brigades maintained their own separate medical service which included at least three hospitals, named La Pasionaria, Universidad, and Casa Roja. Doctors and nurses came from various countries; most of the menial work was performed by Spaniards. Interestingly, in July 1937 the Spanish employees at one of

the hospitals tried to demand higher wages. The Communists blamed this on the Anarchists and Troyskyists.

58. Luigi Longo, "Some New Problems and Their Solution," *Boletín de Información*, no. 283 (October 24, 1937), 1; Dahlem, *Communist International* 15, no. 5 (May 1938): 447.

59. Luigi Longo, "Soldados Activistas," *Reconquista* 1, no. 1 (August 1, 1938), 7; Szinda, *XI Brigade*, 81–82; "Work of the Activists," *La Marsellesa*, no. 4 (August 25, 1938), 1; "The Activist Pledge," *Volunteer for Liberty* 2, no. 25 (July 19, 1938), 2.

60. *Le Soldat de la République*, no. 2 (February 20, 1937), 1. Discipline, declared the same source later that year, is "the first principle for the army," and, it continued, it is not the role of the military officer but of the political commissar to inculcate this discipline. Ibid., no. 30 (June 1, 1937), 1; "Discipline in Our Republican Army," *Our Fight*, no. 4 (March 8, 1937), 1.

61. *Our Fight*, no. 73 (June 21, 1937), 1.

62. "What Is a Salute," *Nuestro Combate*, no. 35 (December 1937), 7; *Reconquista* (October 20, 1938), 16.

63. *Bulletin of the Political Commissars of the International Brigades* (September 1937), 29–30; *Boletín de Información*, no. 70 (November 21, 1937), 3.

64. "The Fifth Column," *Bulletin of the Political Commissars of the International Brigades* (September 1937), 13; "The Conference of Political Commissars in Albacete," *International Press Correspondence* 17, no. 20 (May 1937): 477; *Le Commissaire* (June 12, 1937).

65. Marty, "Twelve Magnificent Months," 1044; Longo, *Brigate*, 55; "Vigilance," *Le Soldat de la République*, no. 45 (August 29, 1937), 1.

CHAPTER 9

1. Calandrone, *Spagna*, 54–55; Kantorowicz, *Tagebüch*, 98–99; see Kantorowicz, passim, for reprints of the original articles on the XIII Brigade.
2. Longo, *Brigate*, 244.
3. Ibid; *Vers la Liberté*, no. 8 (February 1, 1937).
4. *Livre*, 153–60.
5. Longo, *Brigate*, 250.
6. Maken, Testimony, SACB, *Recommended Decision*, 34–35.
7. *Boletín de Información* (December 31, 1937). In accordance with the commissariat's order of December 27, 1937, publication was suspended on December 31.
8. Longo, *Brigate*. 250; *Boletín de Información*. no. 260 (September 24, 1937), 8.
9. Penchienati, *Spagna*, 48–50. *Volunteer for Liberty* 2, no. 32 (September 17, 1938), 1; ibid., (November 7, 1938), 12.
10. *Nuestros Españoles* (Madrid, 1937).
11. Calandrone, *Spagna*. 224–26; Kantorowicz, *Tagebüch*, 520.
12. *Boletín de Información*, no. 299 (November 2, 1937), 8.
13. Francisco Anton, "Trotskyism—The Mortal Enemy of the People's Front," *Communist International* 15, no. 1 (January 1937): 87. See also Francisco Anton,

"Trotskyists in Spain—Open Agents of Fascism," *Imprecor,* Special Edition on Spain, 18, no. 24 (May 17, 1938), 548-52.

14. From a speech by José Díaz to the Plenum of the Communist party of Spain, Valencia, 1937, Marty Archives.

15. Le procès du centre parallèle Trotzkiste deviant le Tribunal Supreme de l'URSS," *Vers la Liberté,* no. 9 (February 2, 1937), 2.

16. "Les Trotzkystes, enemis jurés du peuple, de la liberté et de la democratie," *Le Soldat de la République,* no. 1 (February 16, 1937), 2.

17. "Fascismo y Trotzkismo," *Le Soldat de la République,* no. 44 (August 17, 1937), 6.

18. *Ecole des Commissaires de Guerre,* Theme 10, Marty Archives. Among the many other articles run on the subject of Trotskyism were "Franco's Trotskyist Allies against International Solidarity," *Boletín de Información,* no. 242 (August 5, 1937), 4; André Marty, *Heroic Spain* (New York, 1937); "More Poumists Nabbed as Spies," *Volunteer for Liberty* 1, no. 10 (August 16, 1937), 3; "Vigilance," *Le Soldat de la République,* no. 45 (August 29, 1937), 1; "Exterminate the Trotskyists," *Our Fight,* no. 39 (May 10, 1937), 2; *Notre Combat,* no. 28 (May 17, 1937), 1.

19. Numero Extrodinario, "XX Aniversario de la Unión Soviética," (November 7, 1937); *Boletín de Información,* no. 290 (October 27, 1937), 6-10; ibid., no. 284 (October 21, 1937), 7-8; ibid., no. 265 (October 22, 1937), 8; ibid., no. 280 (October 14, 1937), 8.

20. Among the many examples of this were A. Golubev, "A Soviet Military Specialist on the Significance of the Jarama Battles," *Volunteer for Liberty* 1, no. 3 (June 8, 1937); "The Policy of British Imperialism," ibid., 1, no. 4 (June 15, 1937); *Boletín de Información,* no. 310 (November 18, 1937), 6; Marcel Cachin, "Staline," ibid., no. 307 (November 11, 1927), 3; and "The Economic Progress of Soviet Industry," *Vers la Liberté,* no. 2 (January 25, 1937), 1.

21. *Boletín de Información,* no. 327 (December 9, 1937), 2; ibid., no. 325 (December 7, 1937), 5; ibid., no. 286 (October 23, 1937), 6; ibid., no. 299 (November 2, 1937), 8.

22. *Volunteer for Liberty* 1, no. 2 (June 1, 1937), 2; *Le Soldat de la République,* no. 7 (May 2, 1937), 1; ibid., no. 9 (May 5, 1937), 1.

23. *Boletín de Información,* no. 279 (October 13, 1937), 8.

24. *Le Soldat de la République,* no. 36 (July 1, 1937), 1; *Volunteer for Liberty* 1, no. 4 (June 15, 1937), 6; *Boletín de Información,* no. 315 (November 23, 1937), 7; *Nuestros Españoles; Boletín de Información,* no. 213 (August 7, 1937), 5; "Thaelmann in Paris—1932," ibid., no 294 (October 30, 1937), 7-8; "Hommage à Notre Grand Ami Ernst Thaelmann," *Vers la Liberté,* no. 30 (April 21, 1937), 1; *Boletín de Información,* no. 317 (November 25, 1937), 5-6, offers Browder's analysis of recent American political developments. Ibid., no. 330 (December 12, 1937), 12; ibid., no. 319 (November 28, 1937), 3; "Maurice Thorez Apporte à la 12e Brigade le Salut du Front Populaire Francais," *Vers la Liberté,* no. 11 (February 5, 1937), 1; ibid., no. 13 (February 9, 1937), 1; ibid., no. 4 (January 27, 1937), 1; ibid., no. 5 (January 28, 1937), 1; ibid., no. 6 (January 30, 1937), 1.

25. *Boletín de Información,* no. 285 (October 19, 1937), 6; *Volunteer for Liberty* 1, no. 1 (May 24, 1937), 5; *Boletín de Información,* no. 239 (September 2, 1937), 5.

26. *Il Garibaldino*, no. 18 (October 28, 1937), 7, carried a full-page message to the Italians in the Brigade from the Italian Communist party. *Volunteer for Liberty* 1, no. 4 (June 15, 1937), 8; *Boletín de Información*, no. 233 (August 27, 1937), 7.
27. *Notre Combat*, no. 11 (March 25, 1937), 1; *Our Fight*. no. 15 (March 22, 1937), 1; *Volunteer for Liberty* 1, no. 4 (June 15, 1937), 6.
28. *Boletín de Información*, no. 315 (November 23, 1937), 7-8.
29. *Volunteer for Liberty* 1, no. 5 (June 22, 1937), 1, discusses the proposed meeting, including a message from Dimitroff, and photographs of the Comintern delegation, Longo, Dahlem, Thorez, Cachin, Díaz; "Towards United Action," ibid., no. 7 (July 12, 1937), 1; ibid., no. 6 (June 29, 1937), 6.
30. *Le Soldat de la République*, no. 25 (April 27, 1937), 1; ibid., no. 48 (September 20, 1937), 1.
31. Ibid., no. 46 (September 1, 1937), 4. This was addressed to Comrade de Brouckere and signed "The Belgian Comrades of the XIV Brigade."
32. Ibid. This was signed "Vittori, Political Commissar, XIV Brigade and Dumont, Commander, XIV Brigade."
33. *Volunteer for Liberty* 1, no. 4 (June 15, 1937), 6; André Marty, *Heroic Spain;* Franz Dahlem, "The Communist International in the Fight for International Unity," *Imprecor*, Special Edition (October 1937), 586-90. This article is devoted to a summary of the Comintern's efforts to "achieve solidarity and unity of action" with the Socialist and Labor organizations. It shows clearly that the Comintern put a great deal of effort into the attempt toward getting these groups fully to support the Communist Popular Front line in Spain and their disillusionment in failing to do so.
34. *Boletín de Información*, no. 242 (August 5, 1937), 4.
35. Georgi Dimitroff, "The United Front of the Struggle for Peace," *Communist International* 13, no. 5 (May 1936): 20; ibid., 3, "The Struggle for the Anti-Japanese People's Front in China."
36. *Boletín de Información*, no. 321 (December 2, 1937), 6.
37. "Can China Beat Japan?" ibid., no. 292 (October 30, 1937), 7-8 (including an analysis by Mao Tse-Tung as quoted from Edgar Snow's *Red Star over China*).
38. *Boletín de Información*, no. 230 (August 24, 1937), 7-8.
39. "Treason Is the Only Name for Treason," *Our Fight*, no. 40 (May 11, 1937), 1; "Long Live the Popular Front," *Volunteer for Liberty* 1, no. 1 (May 24, 1937), 4. These were among a flood of articles on the general subject of Trotskyism and uncontrollables following the events in Barcelona of May 1937.
40. This was consistently stressed in the Brigade press; for example, *Il Garibaldino*, no. 9 (August 24, 1937), 1; *Vers la Liberté*, no. 6 (January 30, 1937), 1.
41. The best discussion of the Communists versus Largo Caballero conflict is in Bolloten, *The Spanish Revolution*. see also Largo Caballero, *Mis Recuerdos* (Mexico, 1954). Prieto, *Comó y por qué;* Marty, *Heroic Spain*, 24; Marty, "Spain Is Waiting," *Boletín de Información*, no. 306 (November 12, 1937), 6; *Volunteer for Liberty* 1, no. 1 (May 24, 1937), 1-5; ibid., 1.
42. *Ecole des Commissaires de Guerre*, Marty Archives.
43. *Communist International* 17, no. 3 (March 1940): 179; ibid., 13, no. 11 (November 1936): 741.
44. *Boletín de Información*, no. 283 (October 19, 1937), 4.

45. *Il Garibaldino,* no. 18 (October 28, 1937), 4-5; *Boletín de Información,* no. 210 (August 3, 1937), 2.
46. *Notre Combat,* no. 27 (May 1, 1937), 9; *Le Soldat de la République,* no. 49 (September 27, 1937), 4-5; Departmental Notice 6553, Albacete, July 22, 1937, as printed in the *Boletín de Información,* no. 204 (July 28, 1937), 12.
47. Louis Fischer, *Politics,* 406.
48. *Boletín de Información,* no. 344 (December 28, 1937), 2.
49. Robert Minor, *Report to the Tenth Convention of the Communist Party of New York,* May 1938; *Boletín de Información,* no. 282 (October 17, 1937), 6.
50. *Communist International* 14, no. 2 (February 1937): 866; ibid., nos. 5-6 (June 1937): 1077; *Boletín de Información,* no. 280 (October 19, 1937), 6.
51. *Tagesnachrichten der Internationalen Brigaden,* no. 281 (October 16, 1937), 3.
52. *Nuestro Combate,* no. 35 (December 1937-January 1938), 5.
53. *Boletín de Información,* no. 282 (October 17, 1937), 7.
54. Ibid., no. 260 (September 24, 1937), 8.
55. Louis Fischer, "Madrid's Foreign Defenders," *Nation* (September 4, 1937), 235-37; Martha Gellhorn, "Men without Medals," *Collier's* (January 15, 1938), 49.
56. Matthews, *Two Wars,* 220; Vincent Sheean, *Not Peace but a Sword* (New York, 1939), 70, 269.
57. *Ecole des Commissaires de Guerre,* Theme 9, Marty Archives.
58. Barea, *Rebel,* 643.
59. *Vers la Liberté,* no. 11 (February 5, 1937), 1; ibid., no. 13 (February 9, 1937), 1.
60. *Boletín de Información,* no. 332 (December 10, 1937), 2.
61. Ibid., no. 283 (October 9, 1937), 4.
62. *Volunteer for Liberty* 1, no. 7 (July 12, 1937), 2, 6.
63. *Notre Combat,* no. 28 (May 17, 1937), 3; *Volunteer for Liberty* 1, no. 7 (July 12, 1937), 4-6; Haldane, *Truth,* 124-31.
64. *Notre Combat,* no. 7 (March 15, 1937), 3.
65. *Our Fight,* no. 3 (March 7, 1937), 1; ibid., no. 36 (May 7, 1937), 1; *Boletín de Información,* no. 328 (December 10, 1937), 4; Gates, *American Communist*, 56-57.
66. *Boletín de Información,* no. 315 (November 23, 1937), 2.
67. *Volunteer for Liberty* 2, no. 33 (October 6, 1938), 1.
68. Herrick, Testimony, SACB, *Report and Order,* 19. The FALB raised over $450,000. *Volunteer for Liberty* (January 1940). The FALB metamorphosed into the Veterans of the Abraham Lincoln Brigade after the Spanish war and continued to publish a paper called the *Volunteer for Liberty.* The VALB was also a party-controlled organization.
69. Haldane, *Truth,* 98-99, 141.
70. *Nuestros Españoles,* 9.
71. *Boletín de Información,* no. 28 (October 28, 1937), 7; an article in *Il Garibaldino* informed the Italian volunteers how word of their activities in Spain was beamed into Italy. "Le repercussioni in Italia di un anno di lotta della Brigata," no. 18 (October 28, 1937), 6. The same was true of Yugoslavia. *Nuestros Españoles* "Lo que decimos al mundo de nuestra lucha," 43.
72. *Boletín de Información,* no. 253 (September 16, 1937).

73. *Volunteer for Liberty* (June 29, 1937), 8.
74. Ibid. (August 23, 1937), 1.
75. Kantorowicz, *Tagebüch,* 433-34; Renn, *Krieg,* 294, 318-19; Ehrenburg, *Eve of War,* 183; *Boletín de Información,* German Edition, no. 291 (October 27, 1937), 4; Regler, *Owl of Minerva,* 314-15; Nenni, *Guerre,* 229; Last, *Tragedy,* 232; *Notre Combat,* no. 29 (June 3, 1937), 5.
76. Ibid, no. 11 (March 25, 1937), 1; *Boletín de Información,* no. 269 (October 3, 1937), 2.
77. *Volunteer for Liberty* 2, no. 20 (May 25, 1938), 12; Marcel Acier, ed. *From Spanish Trenches* (New York, 1937); Joe Dallet, *Letters from Spain* (New York, 1938); FALB, *Letters from Spain* (San Francisco, 1937); *Letters from the Trenches from our Boys in Spain* (New York, n.d.). Letters also appeared in various sympathetic periodicals. "With the International Brigade in Spain," *Nation* (May 8, 1937).

CHAPTER 10

1. Orlov Memo; Krivitsky, *Secret Service,* 104.
2. Borkenau, *Cockpit,* 239-41.
3. Orwell, *Catalonia,* 175-79.
4. Ibid., 146-47.
5. The notoriety of the Cheka operating as an autonomous force was mentioned as one factor causing an anti-Communist reaction among many Spaniards in an interesting political analysis sent to the State Department by an American diplomatic officer in October 1937: Doc. 852100/6955, *Foreign Relations of the U.S., 1937,* 236.
6. Orwell, *Catalonia,* 174-75; John McGovern, *Terror* 1-20.
7. Elstob, *Spanish Prisoner,* 55-110.
8. Olaf DeWet, *The Patrol Is Ended* (New York,1938), 320-30.
9. Orwell, *Catalonia,* 196, 216-17; the POUM newspaper carried an article on Smillie's death entitled "Un crimen horrendo del que debe responder el Gobierno Negrín." *Juventud Obrero* (July 12, 1937), 2.
10. Last, *Tragedy,* 276.
11. Payne, *Revolution,* 346-47. This includes a verification of the complete autonomy of the Brigade SIM from the official government SIM by a onetime chief of the government SIM, Manuel Ulibarri. Ulibarri referred to the Brigade police as "a direct offshoot of the GPU and off limits to us."
12. Penchienati, *Spagna,* 39.
13. "Las Brigadas Internacionales bajo el terror Stalinista," *Juventud Obrero* (November 30, 1937). This article is based on the statement of a British deserter from the Brigades in which he tells of being arrested and incarcerated by the Brigade Cheka in the prison at Albacete. He tells of the many other Brigade comrades imprisoned there.
14. Late in 1938 certain Loyalist officials did attempt to intervene in the autonomous police powers of the Brigades. By that time, however, the government was almost ready to disband the Brigades. Penchienati, *Spagna,* 121-23.
15. Gillain, *Le Mercenaire,* 220-25; Honeycomb, Testimony, HUAC, *Hearings,* 7747-48.

16. Penchienati, *Spagna*, 40-41; Ruth Fischer, *German Communism*, 500; Last, *Tragedy*, 276; Krivitsky, *Secret Service*, 104.
17. Penchienati, *Spagna*, 42.
18. Ibid., 39; Ruth Fischer, *German Communism*, 500 (on the difficulties of pinning down Ulbricht's role in the Spanish war, see Stern, *Ulbricht*. 71-72 n.).
19. Valtin, *Out of the Night*, 356.
20. Testimony, SACB, *Recommended Decision*, 36-37. Neumann was among the many Comintern stalwarts who, when recalled from Spain back to Moscow, fell victim to the purges there. Perhaps he was even accused of Trotskyism.
21. McGovern, *Terror*, 5-10.
22. Valtin, *Out of the Night*, 308-13; Richard Krebs, Testimony, HUAC, *Hearings*, May 27, 1941, 8517.
23. Liston Oak, Testimony, HUAC, *Hearings*, March 21, 1947, 72; Liston Oak, "Alert," *New Leader* (March 15, 1947).
24. Valtin, *Out of the Night*, 313; Liston Oak, Testimony, HUAC, *Hearings*, March 21, 1947, 73. The murder of Nin became something of a cause célèbre. The story was later told by the top Spanish Communist Jesús Hernández that in fact Nin had been imprisoned by Cheka agents and tortured. Later, under the direction of Vidali, a contingent of German International Brigade men posing as Gestapo Agents, had staged a jail break to liberate Nin, following which they murdered him. Hernández, *Minestro de Stalin*, 126.
25. Dallin, *Espionage*, 409, from an article by Liston Oak in the Socialist journal *The Call*, December 18, 1937; ibid., 409, as quoted from the testimony of William McCuiston before the HUAC; ibid., as quoted from the testimony of Maurice L. Malkin before the HUAC.
26. Budenz, *Men without Faces*, 35-37. Nelson later played a key role in the Soviet espionage apparatus connected with getting atomic bomb intelligence in the United States and was among those convicted and imprisoned under the Smith Act. On Nelson's background and activities, see Dallin, *Espionage*, 467-68.
27. For example, Auguste Lecouer was assigned by Marty to the XIII Brigade political commissar post. Rol Tanguy eventually became political commissar of the XIV Brigade and, much later, led the Communist attempt to take over Paris before the Allies or General de Gaulle could arrive. See Larry Collins and Dominique Lapierre, *Is Paris Burning?* (New York, 1965).
28. Lecouer, *Le Partisan*, 79; Copeman, *Reason*, 107-11.
29. *U. S. Diplomatic Papers, 1937*, 482.
30. *Notre Combat*, no. 7 (March 15, 1937); "Attention Aux Agents de Franco," *Le Soldat de la République*, no. 20 (April 4, 1937), 1.
31. Gillain, 195; *U. S. Diplomatic Papers, 1937*, 482; Honeycomb, Testimony, HUAC, *Hearings*, 7747-50. There was not, except in the peculiar case of the Italians who entered the International Brigade through the original Garibaldi group, any written commitment on the part of anyone. The terms of agreement set down in the document drawn up by the Italian Popular Front committee in Paris did specifically state the six-month term.
32. Numerous such cases are documented in *The Red Dominion in Spain* (Madrid, 1961).

33. *U. S. Diplomatic Papers, 1937,* 556-57. It is doubtful if these men were executed. The more common practice was to sentence would-be deserters to labor or discipline companies and to assign these units to dangerous sectors of the front.

34. Edward Knoblaugh, *Correspondent in Spain* (New York, 1937), 227.

35. *New York Times,* May 25, 1937, 1. The correspondent was George Axelsson. This particular recruit actually deserted while in France, having decided on the trip that he had made a mistake. This case fits the same pattern as that of William Ryan who also was recruited through the ads for skilled workers run by the Society for Technical Aid to Spanish Democracy.

36. Henry Scott Beattie, Letter to Editor, *Canadian Forum* (April 1938).

37. "Las Brigadas Internacionales bajo el terror Stalinista," *Juventud Obrero* (November 30, 1937). That this man wrote such an article and that it appeared in a POUM newspaper would have clearly put him in the category of Trotskyist and have marked him for liquidation so far as the Communists were concerned.

38. Stephen Spender, *World within World* (New York, 1951), 220-21.

39. Ibid., 224.

40. Bessie, *Men in Battle,* 170-95, on the passionate desire of the large majority of men of the American battalion to leave Spain by the time of the official withdrawl in late 1938. See Edwin Rolfe, *The Lincoln Battalion* (New York, 1939), 245-46, on the drying up of the stream of new recruits by mid-1938 and the numerical weakness of the American contingent by then.

41. Bessie, *Men in Battle,* 149.

42. Regler, *Owl of Minerva,* 325.

43. Longo, *Brigate,* 258-60.

44. Penchienati, *Spagna,* 91; Gillain, *Le Mercenaire.* 196-97.

45. Honeycomb, Testimony, HUAC, *Hearings,* 7745-55; Gillain, *Le Mercenaire,* 196-97.

46. *U. S. Diplomatic Papers, 1937,* 491-531.

47. Lecouer, *Le Partisan,* 77-79; Gillain, *Le Mercenaire, 230-47.*

48. Marty Archives.

49. McCuiston, Testimony, HUAC, *Hearings,* 6708-25.

50. Herrick, Testimony, SACB, *Recommended Decision,* 121; Voros, *Commissar,* 472.

51. Haldane, *Truth Will Out,* 127, 137.

52. Valtin, *Out of the Night,* 717.

53. Willy Brandt, *My Road to Berlin* (London, 1960); Erich Wollenburg, "Der Apparat: Stalin's Funfte Kolonne," *Ostprobleme,* no. 19 (1951), as quoted in Stern, *Ulbricht;* Orwell, *Catalonia,* 207.

54. Maken, Testimony, SACB, *Stenographic Record,* 4:840-49; Voros, *Commissar,* 232.

55. Horan, Testimony, SACB, *Recommended Decision,* 39; Voros, *Commissar,* 286; Borkenau, *Cockpit,* 255-56, related a similar case and said, "In general the political commissars of the International Brigades are in the habit of supposing that every man who leaves the Brigade in order to take up work in another capacity—not under direct Communist control—is a deserter, and treat him accordingly."

56. Herrick, Testimony, SACB, *Recommended Decision,* 38.

57. Gladnick, Testimony, SACB, *Recommended Decision*, 38-39; Johnson, *Legions*, 108-9; Penchienati, *Spagna*, 114-20; Copeman, *Reason*, 136-47, on executions in the British battalion.

58. Gillain, *Le Mercenaire*, 215; Voros, *Commissar*, 410-11; Penchienati, *Spagna*, 112-13.

59. Lecouer, *Le Partisan*, 72; Louis Fischer, *Politics*, 400-405; Regler, *Owl of Minerva*, 179, 292, 324-25; Penchienati, *Spagna*, 119.

60. Martínez Bande, *Intervención comunista*, 110; Lecouer, *Le Partisan*, 79; Louis Fischer, *Politics*, 404-5.

61. Marty Archives. In the 1950s he was expelled from the party, but that had nothing to do with his work in Spain.

62. Ernest Hemingway, *For Whom the Bell Tolls* (New York, 1939), 417-26.

63. Maken, Wolff, Testimony, SACB, *Recommended Decision*, 168.

64. Marty Archives.

Bibliographical Essay

Since I have used a wide variety of primary sources in this study, especially the official Comintern press and the press of the International Brigades themselves, my chapter notes provide a better and more thorough indication of this type of material than could any formal bibliography. In this essay, therefore, I will discuss only the more important books and documentary sources that I found to be valuable in this study of the International Brigades.

The standard general work in English on the civil war in Spain as a whole, both military and political, is Hugh Thomas, *The Spanish Civil War* (New York, 1961). A revised and expanded edition of this work was published in 1977. An excellent analysis of the immediate background to the war, emphasizing the internal chaos of the left and the radicalization and polarization of politics that led to the *pronunciamiento* is R.A.H. Robinson, *The Origins of Franco's Spain* (Pittsburgh, 1970). Solid works on the political role of the Communists and the Soviet Union during the civil war are David T. Cattell, *Communism and the Spanish Civil War* (Berkeley, 1955) and *Soviet Diplomacy and the Spanish Civil War* (Berkeley, 1957).

The best and most indispensable works on the internecine struggles of the left during the war and on the methods by which the Communists succeeded in dominating the Loyalist regime are Burnett Bolloten, *The Grand Camouflage* (New York, 1961) and his later expansion of the same theme, *The Spanish Revolution* (Chapel Hill, N.C., 1979). Excellent also is Stanley Payne, *The Spanish Revolution* (New York, 1970).

The memoirs and accounts of participants and firsthand observers of events in Spain are numerous. Among the more useful are George Orwell, *Homage to Catalonia* (New York, 1952), which offers an excellent insight from both a participant and an acute observer into the actual political situation on the left during the first year or so of the war. It was among the first to cut through the propaganda smoke screen that depicted the Loyalists as united defenders of the Republic. Another work that did somewhat the same thing, but from a more detached point of view, was Franz Borkenau, *The Spanish Cockpit* (London, 1937). Useful insights into much that went on in Madrid from the perspective of a Spanish Socialist who worked in the censorship bureau there are to be found in Arturo Barea, *The Forging of a Rebel* (New York, 1946). An important inside look at these events by one who was an active participant is Pietro Nenni, *La Guerre de Espagne* (Paris, 1960). Nenni was chief of the Italian Socialist party, an active advocate of the Popular Front and of Loyalist Spain, and a political collaborator of both the Spanish Socialists and the Communists. Other useful accounts by firsthand observers are Geoffrey Cox, *Defense of Madrid* (London, 1937), by a British Communist correspondent; Ilya Ehrenburg, *Eve of War 1933–1941* (London, 1963) by a knowledgeable Russian; and Mikhail Koltsov, *Diario de la guerra de España* (Paris, 1963) by the *Pravda* correspondent (and a leading Soviet agent) in Spain during the war. Louis Fischer, *Men and Politics* (New York, 1941) is an important source from a pro-Loyalist American who was well placed and connected to know much of what went on in Spain during the war.

The recollections of several Loyalist army officers are of some interest. José Martín Blásquez, *I Helped to Build an Army* (London, 1940), on the problems of creating the Loyalist People's Army; Seigismundo Casado, *Last Days of Madrid* (London, 1939), by the Loyalist officer who led the anti-Communist forces in the showdown within the Loyalist camp at the end of the war; and Vicente Rojo, *España heroica* (Buenos Aires, 1942), by the chief of staff of the Loyalist army indicate something of the political relationships within the Loyalist government and army.

Some of the leading politicians of the left have contributed their accounts. Manuel Azaña, *La velada en Benicarlo* (Buenos Aires, 1939), offers the postwar reflections of the president of the Republic. From the Socialists we have Fransicso Largo Caballero, *Mis recuerdos* (Mexico, 1954), and Indalecio Prieto, *Cómo y por qué salí del minesterio de defensa nacional* (Paris, 1939). From leading Spanish Communists we have accounts from both those who remained in the party and those who left. Among the former are Dolores Ibarruri, *Guerra y revolución en España 1936-1939* (Moscow, 1966); Enrique Lister, *Nuestra guerra* (Paris, 1966); and José Díaz, *Tres años de lucha* (Toulouse, 1947), all of whom defend and justify the role of the party during the war. Among the latter are Enrique Castro Delgado, *Hombres made en Moscú* (Barcelona, 1965); Valentín González, *Communista en España y anti-Stalinista en Rusia* (Mexico, 1953); and Jesús Hernández, *Yo fui un minestro de Stalin* (Mexico, 1953). These are to a large extent exposés of the role of puppet of the Soviet Union and Comintern played by the Spanish Communists.

On the general theme of Soviet and Comintern policy and strategy during the Popular Front era and the application of that to the Spanish conflict, Arthur Koestler, *Invisible Writing* (New York, 1954) and his essay in Richard Crossman ed., *The God That Failed* (New York, 1950) are especially valuable since he was a party activist and knowledgeable insider at the time. A solid secondary work on this subject is K. E. McKenzie, *The Comintern and World Revolution* (New York, 1964). On the American party Theodore Draper, *The Roots of American Communism* (New York, 1957), and Lewis Coser and Irving Howe, *The American Communist Party* (New York, 1962) are good general works, while Louis Budenz, *Men without Faces: The Communist Conspiracy in the USA* (New York, 1948) is by a leading party defector, and William Z. Foster, *History of the Communist Party in the United States* (New York, 1952) is the party line by a leading member.

For European Communist parties, M. Einaudi, *Communism in Western Europe* (Ithaca, N.Y., 1951); Franz Borkenau, *World Communism* (London, 1939); Hilton W. Young, *The Italian Left* (London, 1949); Carola Stern, *Ulbricht: A Political Biography* (New York, 1964); and Ruth Fischer, *Stalin and German Communism* (Cambridge, Mass., 1948) are all good. For England, Philip Toynbee, *Friends Apart* (London, 1954) by a one-time party adherent and Douglas Hyde, *I Believed* (New York, 1950) by a party activist during the Popular Front era who later defected are revealing. Neal Wood, *Communism and the British Intellectuals* (New York, 1959) is an excellent study of particular value in providing biographical background to many British Communists who participated in the International Brigades. Charlotte Haldane, *Truth Will Out* (London, 1949) is valuable as a firsthand account of the Comintern recruitment

Bibliographical Essay 219

efforts and the operations in Paris by a British Communist who later left the party. Also of interest on this subject are Pat Sloan, ed., *John Cornford: A Memoir* (London, 1938), and Peter Stansky and William Abrahams, *Journey to the Frontier* (New York, 1966). Works particularly useful in furnishing hard-to-find information on individuals involved in Comintern activities in Spain and elsewhere, and into some of their activities prior to the Spanish war, are Walter Krivitsky, *In Stalin's Secret Service* (New York, 1939), written by a general in the Soviet army intelligence service in western Europe in the 1936–1937 period who later defected; David J. Dallin, *Soviet Espionage* (New Haven, Conn., 1955); Alexander Orlov, *The Secret History of Stalin's Crimes* (New York, 1953) by the chief Soviet NKVD agent in Spain; Jan Valtin, *Out of the Night* (New York, 1941) by an ex German Communist; and J. Rindl and J. Gumpery (pseud. Ypsilon), *Pattern for World Revolution* (Chicago, 1947). For the Soviet military personnel in Spain (at least those deemed mentionable at the time of publication), Rodin Malinovski y otros, *Bajo la bandera de la España republicana* (Moscow, 1969). This is the official Soviet account of the role of their army officers in Spain. Also helpful in pinning down individuals are the publication of the Spanish Office of Information, *The International Brigades* (Madrid, 1952), and José Manuel Martínez Bande, *La intervención comunista en la guerra de España* (Madrid, 1965).

On the military aspects of the war as a whole, the only treatment in English is Hugh Thomas, *The Spanish Civil War* (New York, 1961, 1977). On the battles for Madrid, Robert Colodny, *The Struggle for Madrid* (New York, 1958) is useful. The standard Spanish military history of the war is Manuel Aznar, *Historia de la guerra de España* (Madrid, 1958). But more useful are the series of monographs on various campaigns and operations by José Manuel Martínez Bande, *La marcha sobre Madrid* (Madrid, 1968), and *La lucha en torno de Madrid* (Madrid, 1970). Martínez Bande, an officer in the Spanish army, had access to the archives of the army's Servicio Historico Militar, an advantage other historians lack.

On the attitudes and activities of the non-Communist Italians in the Spanish militia, Carlo Rosselli, *Oggi in Spagna, Domani in Italia* (Paris, 1938) is interesting. Other works on the non-Communist foreigners in the militia are George Orwell, *Homage to Catalonia* (New York, 1952), and Jef Last, *The Spanish Tragedy* (London, 1937).

The works dealing with the International Brigades specifically can be categorized in various ways. There are the official publications of the Brigade Commissariat itself. Among the more important of these are *Año de las Brigadas Internacionales* (Madrid, 1937); Theodor Balk, ed., *La Quatorzième* (Madrid, 1937); *Le Livre de la 15eme Brigade Internationale* (Madrid, 1937) and its English language equivalent *The Book of the XV Brigade* (Madrid, 1938); *Garibaldini in Spagna* (Madrid, 1937); Alfred Kantorowicz, *Tschapaiev: Das Bataillon de 21 Nationen* (Madrid, 1938); and *Nuestros Españoles* (Madrid, 1937). All of these are naturally highly slanted to show the Brigades in the most favorable light and follow the standard Communist and Popular Front line. Their chief value for the historian is in the many names and the biographical information they provide on individuals in the various units, and in the many details on at least some of the activities and attitudes prevalent among those in charge of the Brigades.

A second category would be the semi-official works written by party functionaries and activists and published under party auspices. These include L'Amicale des Anciens

Volontaires Français en Espagne Republicaine, *L'Èpopèe d'Espagne: Brigades Internationales 1936–1938* (Paris, 1956); Alfred Kantorowicz, *Spanisches Tagebüch* (Berlin, 1948); Steve Nelson, *The Volunteers* (New York, 1953); Joe North, *Men in the Ranks* (New York, 1939); Marcel Acier, ed., *From Spanish Trenches* (New York, 1937); William Rust, *Britons in Spain: The History of the XV International Brigade* (London, 1939); Gustav Szinda, *Die XI Brigade* (Berlin, 1956); and Max Wullschleger, *Schweizer Kampfen in Spanien* (Zurich, 1939). These adhere to basically the same standards as the first group and are of value in about the same way.

A third category includes those books written by participants in the Brigades as individuals rather than under party control. These vary greatly as to approach, range of view, and knowledgeability of the writers. By far the single most important primary source book written on the entire subject of the political side of the Brigades is Luigi Longo, *Le Brigate Internazionali in Spagna* (Rome, 1956). Although Longo adheres strictly to the party line, it is the party line from a particularly authoritative source. Longo's position and role in the Comintern, in the Brigades, and later (at the time his book was published, for example), the Communist party of Italy all make him a key witness. His book covers the entire picture of the Spanish war and of the International Brigades from beginning to end. It deals with virtually all the political issues and questions involved. Thus it offers the historian a prime source for an authoritative statement of the Communist position on all these matters. Another source from the Italian contingent is Giacomo Calandrone, *Spagna Brucia* (Rome, 1962). This account by a party member and close collaborator of Longo's while in Spain basically echos Longo's book but is valuable in furnishing details and also as an example of the Communist position on many of the controversial issues within the XII Brigade. Two other essential sources from the Italians are Randolfo Pacciardi, *Il Battaglione Garibaldi* (Lugano, 1938); and Carlo Penchienati, *Brigate Internazionali in Spagna: Delitti della "Ceka" Communista* (Milan, 1950). Pacciardi's book is somewhat disappointing in its lack of discussion on the political issues in the Brigade. Published while the war in Spain was still in progress, Pacciardi presumably did not wish to do or say anything that might weaken or embarrass the Loyalist camp: thus his silence on matters of importance. Still his book offers the best source for his own attitudes toward what he thought he (and the other Italians) were, or should be, doing in Spain. Penchienati's book is quite a different matter. Written long after the event by a nonpolitical who served in the Brigades from beginning to end, and who was a top-ranking officer in the Garibaldi unit, Penchienati's book is a thorough exposé of the political machinations of the Communist hierarchy of the Brigades, of their vendetta against Pacciardi, and of the operations of the political police apparatus in the Brigades. It is also a valuable source for the identification and background of many of the Italians in Spain.

Among the American contributions are Alvah Bessie, *Men in Battle* (New York, 1939). Bessie, an American party member and writer, was a late arrival in Spain. His book reflects in general the party line on Spain and the Brigades, but there are a few places where he sheds light on some of the less positive aspects of things. The book, like many of the more personal accounts, deals heavily with the combat experience. Another of this same type is Edwin Rolfe, *The Lincoln Battalion* (New York, 1939) by the onetime editor of the *Volunteer for Liberty* in Spain. From a somewhat different perspective but still completely favorable to the Brigades is John Gates, *The Story of an American Communist* (New York, 1958). Written long after the Spanish war by one who rose to become XV Brigade commissar and who, much later, left the party and seeks to explain it all in this book, Gates's comments on his experience in the Brigades are strangely reticent. He still felt, even after losing faith in the party, that his Brigade experience was the high point in his life. It seems he was still unwilling, or unable, to disturb that memory with a very searching analysis. Sandor Voros, *American Commissar* (Philadelphia, 1961) on the other hand is a thoroughgoing critique of the Communist policy in Spain and of the Brigades themselves. Voros, who was a party activist at the time of his tour in Spain, offers a good many insights into the working of the American party toward the Spanish war and the Brigades and, from the political side, is quite a valuable source.

Nick Gillain, *Le Mercenaire* (Paris, 1938), written by a nonpolitical who served as an officer in the XIV Brigade, takes a critical view of the Communists' role but is mainly a personal memoir. It provides numerous interesting details about individuals and events. Auguste Lecouer, *Le Partisan* (Paris, 1963) is a much more valuable source on the political side of things. He was an activist in the French party and was sent to Spain to serve as a politically reliable cadre in the Brigades. He was given several political assignments by Marty and, in general, was a knowledgeable insider. He wrote this book after leaving the party.

The fullest account from a German who was in a position to know much of what was going on is Ludwig Renn, *Der Spanische Krieg* (Berlin, 1955). Renn deals mainly with the military campaigns of the Brigades but offers insights into numerous other matters. Gustav Regler, *Owl of Minerva* (New York, 1960) is much more valuable from the political side. Regler, a member of the German party, sometime political commissar of the XII Brigade, and an articulate spokesman for the Communists in Spain, wrote this book after leaving the party. Its view of the Brigades is interesting when compared with his earlier fictionalized account in the novel *The Great Crusade* (New York, 1940).

From the English participants John Sommerfeld, *Volunteer in Spain* (London, 1937), Keith Scott Watson, *Single to Spain* (London, 1937), and Esmond Romilly, *Boadilla* (London, 1937) are personal accounts of the experiences of rank and filers in the Brigades. Thomas Wintringham, *English Captain* (London, 1939) is by a more highly placed and knowledgeable participant. Wintringham, a party member and writer, commanded the British battalion in its opening combat experience. While uncritical and mainly concerned with the military side, much factual information is included on the early development of the Brigades. More valuable from the political point of view is Fred Copeman, *Reason in Revolt* (London, 1948). Copeman served in the British battalion throughout and rose to command it. He later left the party and his book reflects his disillusionment with the Communists. Jef Last, *The Spanish Tragedy* (London, 1937) is by a Dutch Communist who served in both the Spanish militia and the Brigades. He later left the party and offers a critical view of its operations in Spain.

The only scholarly secondary work on the Brigades as a whole is the interesting but slim book by Verle Johnson, *Legions of Babel* (University Park, 1967). Popular treatments are Vincent Brome, *The International Brigades: Spain 1936–1939* (New York, 1960); Jacque de Bayac, *Les Brigades Internationales* (Paris, 1968); and Adolfo Lizón Gadea, *Las Brigadas Internacionales en España* (Madrid, 1940). The most massive secondary work on the American contingent is Arthur Landis, *The Abraham Lincoln*

Brigade (New York, 1967). It, unfortunately, is basically a rerun of the standard party line in every respect and is badly flawed by errors of both commission and omission. Robert A. Rosenstone, *Crusade on the Left: The Lincoln Battalion in the Spanish Civil War* (New York, 1969) focuses chiefly on the motivation of the American participants. By far the best and most penetrating study of the American battalion is Cecil Eby, *Between the Bullet and the Lie* (New York, 1969).

Perhaps the best, most complete, and most authoritative source for the Communist position on the Popular Front, the war in Spain, the International Brigades, and other concerns is the official party press. The most useful are the official Comintern organs, the *Communist International,* and *International Press Correspondence (Imprecor).* Also useful are the party newspapers, *Mundo Obrero* and *Frente Rojo* in Spain, the *Daily Worker* in Britain and the United States, and *L'Humanité* in France.

For the position of the Brigade leadership the best source is the Brigade press. I found the *Volunteer for Liberty, Le Soldat de la République, Nuestro Combate, Reconquista,* and the *Boletín de Información de las Brigadas Internacionales* especially valuable.

The volumes of the *Foreign Relations of the United States, Diplomatic Papers* (Washington, D.C., 1954, 1955, 1956) for the years of the Spanish Civil War offer occasional worthwhile insights into certain events in Spain, especially the efforts of American Brigade men to get out of the country. The testimony of certain witnesses before the United States Congress, House Committee on Un-American Activities, regarding the experience of American participants in the International Brigades is also a valuable source for certain aspects of the story which would otherwise be lacking. A source of even more value to the study of the Brigades is the hearings of the United States Subversive Activities Control Board on the Veterans of the Abraham Lincoln Brigade organization. Numerous men who had served in the Brigades gave testimony at these hearings that ran to twelve volumes and many thousands of pages that compose the Stenographic Record of the hearings. A synopsis of the testimony and the findings of the board were printed in U.S. Subversive Activities Control Board, Docket no. 108–153, Herbert Brownell Jr., Attorney General of the United States, Petitioner v. The Veterans of the Abraham Lincoln Brigade, Respondent, *Recommended Decision* (Washington, D.C., 1955). A second, and even more condensed, synopsis of the findings was printed as the *Report and Order of the Board* (Washington, D.C., 1955).

The Marty Archives are disappointingly scant and sketchy. They contain a collection of largely irrelevant or redundant material so far as the Brigades, or Marty's role in them, is concerned. The one item of significant value in them is a copy of the instructors' manual used in the International Brigade school for political commissars. This document is one of the best firsthand sources for the programs and policies of the Brigade political hierarchy and of the thoroughgoing Communist orientation provided for fledgling political commissars in the Brigades.

The Orlov Memo comprises the answers given by Alexander Orlov, the chief Soviet NKVD man in Spain, to a set of questions posed to him by Stanley Payne. Orlov had by that time defected from the USSR and was thus free to speak the truth. There is little or nothing in this about the Brigades themselves, but it is firsthand evidence of some of the operations of the NKVD in Spain. A copy of this document was kindly furnished to me by Professor Payne.

Bibliographical Essay 223

A major bibliographical source for the entire Spanish Civil War is R. de la Cierva y colaboradores, *Bibliografia sobre la guerra de España (1936–1919) y sus antecedentes* (Madrid, 1968). The most thorough and easily available bibliography in English is in Burnett Bolloten, *The Spanish Revolution* (Chapel Hill, N.C., 1979). Others are in Hugh Thomas, *The Spanish Civil War* (New York, 1961, 1977); Stanley Payne, *The Spanish Revolution* (New York, 1970); and, specifically on the Brigades, Verle B. Johnson, *Legions of Babel* (University Park, Pa., 1967).

The fullest available collection of the Brigade newspapers is in the Hemeroteca Municipal in Madrid. Other major sources on the Spanish Civil war in Spain are to be found at the Unidad de Estudios sobre la Guerra de España, the Biblioteca Nacional, and the army's Servicio Histórico Militar. All of these are located in Madrid. In the United States the largest collections of material on the Spanish war are at the Hoover Institution at Stanford University (Bolloten collection), the University of California (Southworth collection), and the Library of Congress. There is also the David McKelvy White collection at the New York city public library which contains a very complete file of the *Boletín de Información* published by the Brigade commissariat. The Marty Archives are held by the Widener Library at Harvard University.

Index

Aalto, William, 96
Abraham Lincoln battalion: recruitment of, 34-35, 38-41; organization of, in Spain, 76-80; ethnic composition of, 76, 101-2, 198 nn.45, 49; political composition of, 76-78, 92-96, 98, 101-2, 127, 138, 201 n.18; poor leadership of, 77-78, 198 n.57; first combat of, 85-95; CPUS views as party achievement, 92-94, 150; internal problems of, dealt with by CPUS, 101-2; political commissars of, appointed by CPUS, 78, 101-2, 203 n.55; cheka activity in, 164-66, 173-74; drying up of stream of recruits for, 169, 215 n.40. *See also* International Brigade, XV
Abraham Lincoln Brigade. *See* Abraham Lincoln battalion; International Brigade, XV
Adler, Fritz, 144, 145
Aitken, George, 74, 99-100
Albacete, 50-56
Albacete Commissariat. *See* Political Commissariat, International Brigade
Alvarez del Vayo, Julio, 4, 118-19, 206 n.2
American battalion. *See* Abraham Lincoln battalion
American Society for Technical Aid to Spain, 34, 39, 215 n.35
Ameriglio, David. *See* Leeds, David
Anarchist, 3, 6, 14; attitude toward the militia and the People's Army, 17-18; militia columns, 17, 18, 26; Communist attitude toward, 20-21, 104-5, 140, 147-48; attitude toward the Loyalist government, 69-70, 196 n.8; attitude toward the Communists, 69-70, 107; attitude toward the International Brigades, 70, 107, 188 n.67; bring revolution to Aragon, 185 n.17
Anarchosyndicalist. *See* Anarchist
André battalion, 56, 59, 60, 82

André Marty battalion, 66-67, 82
Anillo, Giorgio, 76
Araquistain, Luis, 4
Arsenovitch, 76
Ascaso column, 26
Attlee, Clement, 154
Azaña, Manuel, 4, 110, 181 n.2
Azzi, Arnaldo, 64, 86

Bahnick, William, 95
Balk, Theodor, 139
Barcelona: revolution in, 6; militia in, 20, 23-29; Workers Olympiad in, 23, 186 n.34; May crisis in, 104-6
Bard, Phil, 77
Barea, Arturo, 60, 152
Barontini, 95, 107, 109, 201 n.28
Barthel. *See* Chaintron, Jean
Bates, Ralph, 29, 38, 154
Batov, General (Fritz), 198 n.1, 202 nn.43, 72
Battistelli, 204 n.62
Beimler, Hans, 23, 27, 52, 65, 82, 186 n.32, 187 n.56
Berchtold, Eugene, 40
Berghe, Van der, Captain, 101
Berzin, General Jan, 12, 14, 192 n.12
Bessie, Alvah, 41, 152, 175, 215 n.40
Bianco, Vincenzo (Krieger), 71
Bielov, Colonel, 53, 67
Billoux, Francois, 52, 201 n.24
Birch, Lorrimer, 28-29
Bocchi, 71
Boletín de Información de las Brigadas Intercionales, 137-38
Borkenau, Franz, 6, 28, 159, 185 n.17, 215 n.55
Brandt, Willy, 173
Brigade commissariat. *See* Political Commissariat, International Brigade
British battalion: recruitment of, 32, 35-36; political composition of, 35; organization of, in Spain, 73-75; first combat of, 83; internal problems dealt with by the CPGB, 99-101,

Index

202 n.49, 203 n.50; political commissars of, appointed by the CPGB, 100-1
Brodsky, George, 77
Browder, Earl, 8, 10, 32, 38, 42, 92, 94
Brown, Fred, 35, 78. *See also* Brown, Paul
Brown, Paul (Alpi), 38, 190 n.28. *See also* Brown, Fred
Broz, Joseph (Tito), 31, 36
Brunete offensive, 88-89
Budenz, Louis, 165

Calandrone, Giacomo, 63, 117, 131, 138, 205 n.77
Canadian battalion. *See* MacKenzie-Papineau battalion
Castro Delgado, Enrique, 21, 48-49, 120, 181 n.1, 185 n.14, 206 n.8
Centuria: origins and activities of, 22-23; origin of the term, 187 n.51; names of, unofficial, 188 n.62; relationship to the International Brigades, 29-30, 188 n.69. *See also* Commune de Paris; Dombrowski; Gastone-Sozzi; militia; Thaelmann; Tom Mann
Chaintron, Jean (Barthel), 73
Chapaiev battalion, 68-70
Checa, Pedro, 48
Cheka, 161, 163, 164, 172, 213 nn.5, 11, 14, 214 n.24. *See also* NKVD; SIM
Codovila, Vittorio (Medina), 52, 184 n.44, 192 n.4
Colodny, Robert, 193 n.23, 195 n.63, 196 n.8, 201 n.24
Comintern: as fount of Popular Front propaganda, 9; interpretation, policy, and actions toward the Spanish conflict, 9-15; agents in Spain, 16, 21, 184 n.44, 186 n.2, 192 n.4; relationship to the Fifth Regiment, 21-22, 186 n.28; recruitment of the International Brigades, 31-46, 189 nn.4, 11, 190 nn.35-36; and the defense of Madrid, 48-49, 82-84, 88-89; agents form directorate of the International Brigades, 51-52, 202 n.40; cadres staff International Brigade hierarchy, 51-52, 56-59, 67-76, 82, 94-97, 194 n.50, 201 nn.24,

25, 28, 203 n.55, 214 nn.20, 26, 27; staffs and controls International Brigade military command, 67, 98, 195 n.63, 202 n.44; generals command People's Army divisions, 84, 88-89, 202 n.44, 205 n.75; attitude toward and control of the International Brigades, 90-118, 149-52, 190 n.39, 193 n.28, 200 n.16, 201 nn.18, 23, 24, 203 nn.50, 55, 205 n.77, 212 n.71, 213 n.4; attitude toward the Second International, 144-46, 211 nn.29, 33; relationship to the CPS, 192 n.4. *See also* Communist; Communist party, France (CPF); Communist party, Germany (CPG); Communist party, Great Britain (CPGB); Communist party, Spain (CPS); Communist party, United States (CPUS); Soviet Union
Commune de Paris battalion, 57, 59, 82
Commune de Paris centuria, 26, 29, 30
Communist: attitude toward bourgeois democracy, 8; party line during the Popular Front era, 10; party line toward the Spanish conflict, 13-14; attitude toward military discipline, 19-21, 130; parties as recruitment agencies for the International Brigades, 31-40; attitude toward the International Brigades, 90-94, 149-51; attitude toward other proletarian parties, 105, 148; attitude toward the Loyalist government, 113-18; attitude toward and domination of the Loyalist political commissar system, 119-21; party members rewarded for work in Spain and the International Brigades, 201 n.23. *See also* Comintern
Communist party: Bulgaria (CPB), 71, 75, 76; Czechoslovakia (CPC), 41; France (CPF), 26, 31-36, 41-43, 57, 70-71, 75, 92, 96, 102, 143, 153, 190 nn.35, 36, 201 nn.23, 24, 202 n.47, 214 n.27; Germany (CPG), 7, 9, 23, 27, 56, 64, 65, 73, 92, 143, 182 n.32, 186 nn.28, 32, 187 n.56, 193 n.28; Great Britain (CPGB), 11, 29, 32, 35-37, 41-42, 70, 100-101, 143, 190 nn.35, 36, 201 n.23,

203 n.50; Italy (CPI), 12, 27, 71, 76, 201 nn.23, 24; Spain (CPS), 3, 7-9, 12-13, 16-18, 22, 47-48, 50, 185 n.14, 186 nn.26, 30, 192 n.4; United States (CPUS), 8, 10, 32, 34-35, 38-40, 77-78, 92, 94, 95, 98, 101-2, 143, 165, 189 n.11, 198 n.57, 201 nn.23, 31, 203 n.55, 214 n.26, 215 n.35; Yugoslavia (CPY), 36, 72, 75, 103, 138
Contreras, Carlos. *See* Vidali, Vittorio
Copeman, Fred, 74, 99-101, 197 n.35, 201 n.23, 202 n.49, 203 n.52
Copic, Vladimir, 52, 72-73
Cornford, John, 6, 19, 24, 25, 28
Cox, Geoffrey, 58, 60, 153
CTV, 86
Cunningham, Jock, 74, 100, 202 n.49

Daduck, Stephen, 79
Dahlem, Franz, 52, 54, 90, 92, 95, 115, 119, 120-21, 128, 132, 194 n.50, 211 n.29
de Brouckere, Louis, 144
Delasalle, Colonel, 71-72
de Madariaga, Salvador, 181 n.1
DeMaio, Tony, 44, 173
Denz, Albert, 82
Dependents Aid Committee, 155-56
de Rosa, Fernando, 24
de Vittorio, Giuseppe (Nicoletti), 27, 31, 59, 82, 95, 192 n.5
DeWet, Olaf, 160-61
Díaz, José, 9, 22, 48, 50, 105, 140-41, 192 nn.4, 5, 211 n.29
Dimitroff, Georgi, 8, 33, 34, 93, 139, 150, 200 n.16, 211 n.29
Dimitroff battalion, 75-76, 83, 86
Dombrowski battalion, 57, 82, 195 n.55
Dombrowski centuria, 57
D'Onofrio, Edoardo, 138
Doran, Dave, 102, 129, 134
Dorf, Arthur, 56
Duclos, 192 n.4
Dumont, Jules, 26, 57, 99, 202 n.47
Durbecq, 75

Elstob, Peter, 37, 45, 160

Fifth Regiment: organization of, by the Communists, 19-21; an example of meshing of Comintern apparatus in Spain, 21; discipline in, 21; provides nucleus of the People's Army, 22, 206 n.1; as a Comintern political instrument, 22; absorbs PSUC militia units, 26; and the defense of Madrid, 48; relationship to the International Brigades, 50-51. *See also* Castro Delgado, Enrique; Lister, Enrique; Vidali, Vittorio
Fischer, Louis, 20-21, 33, 53, 87, 150, 152, 194 n.35, 196 n.8, 200 n.16, 206 n.3
Fischer, Ruth, 43, 190 n.39, 193 n.28
Foote, Alexander, 96
Fort, Captain, 75, 86
Fox, Ralph, 70, 71
Franco-Belge battalion. *See* André Marty battalion
Friends of the Abraham Lincoln Brigade (FALB), 34, 39, 40, 96, 155, 201 n.31, 212 n.68
Front organizations, Communist, 9, 10, 11, 12. *See also* American Society for Technical Aid to Spain; Dependents Aid Committee; Friends of the Abraham Lincoln Brigade; VALB
Furman, 75, 76, 207 n.23

Galicz, Janos (Gall, General), 72, 73, 80, 84, 85, 89, 202 n.44, 207 n.23
Gall, General. *See* Galicz, Janos
Galli, 75, 86
Gallo. *See* Longo, Luigi
Garibaldi battalion, 61-64, 76, 82, 86, 95, 103-7, 204 n.62, 205 nn.77, 80
Garibaldi Brigade. *See* International Brigade, XII
Gastone-Sozzi centuria, 26, 27, 29, 30, 57, 64
Gates, John, 41, 96, 128, 129, 134, 173-74
Gayman. *See* Vidal
Geilhorn, Martha, 152
George Washington battalion, 76. *See also* Abraham Lincoln battalion; International Brigade, XV
Geroe, Erno, 184 nn.44, 45, 192 n.4
Gillain, Nick, 36, 162, 174
Gil Robles, José María, 5, 181 n.2

Index

Giustizia e Libertá, 23, 187 n.50, 204 n.62. *See also* Rosselli, Carlo
Gladnick, Robert, 38
Golssenau, Arnold Vieth von. *See* Renn, Ludwig
Gomez, General. *See* Zeisser, Wilhelm
Goriev, General, 12, 49, 192 n.12, 202 n.43
Gottwald, Clement, 31
Grebenaroff, 75, 76, 85
Guadalajara, battle of, 86-87
Guerilla warfare, 96-97, 202 nn.36, 37
Guimple, Boris, 71

Haldane, Charlotte, 32, 35, 41-44, 154, 172, 190 nn.35, 36
Harris, Jim, 78, 79, 80, 198 n.57
Harris, William, 39
Hemingway, Ernst, 153, 175-76
Henri Vuillemin Battalion, 68
Herman, Irving, 40
Hernández, Jesús, 16, 214 n.24
Herrick, William, 38, 155
Heusler, Andre, 70
Honeycomb, 162
Horan, Edward, 40, 43
Hourihan, Martin, 101
L'Humanité, 7, 10, 26

Ibarruri, Dolores (La Pasionaria), 17, 18, 22, 48, 120, 130
ILP (Independent Labour party), 24, 29
International Brigade: origins of, 6, 14-15, 185 n.54; relationship to foreigners in militia units, 29-30, 188 nn.67, 69; recruitment of, 31-46, 189 nn.4, 11, 190 n.35, 215 n.35; transportation of, into Spain, 44-47; numbers of troops in, 46, 88-89, 191 n.53, 193 n.19, 200 n.15; concentration and organization of, at Albacete, 50-56, 202 n.40; Comintern staffs the political commissariat of, 50-52, 82, 94, 110-14; political and military hierarchy of, staffed by Comintern, 51-52, 56-59, 67-76, 82, 94-97, 194 n.50, 201 nn.24, 25, 28, 203 n.55, 214 nn.20, 26, 27; uniforms and equipment of, 53-54; military and political discipline in, 54, 79, 98-102, 109, 130-35, 193 n.23, 203 n.52, 207 n.23, 208 nn.43, 55, 209 n.60, 215 nn.33, 55; political composition of, 54, 57, 59, 60, 61, 63, 64; and the defense of Madrid, 59-61, 83, 87, 195 nn.66, 72, 198 n.1, 199 n.6; cadres arrive from the Soviet Union for, 75, 76, 78, 94-95, 107, 201 nn.25, 28; first Americans in, 76-78, 85, 198 n.45; military role and significance of, 81, 88-89; military command of, 82, 83, 84, 89, 98; casualties of, 83, 85-86, 199 n.5; change in role and significance of, after spring 1937, 88-89, 200 nn.15, 17; become heavily Spanish in personnel, 89, 205 n.91, 215 n.40; political significance of, to the Comintern, 90-94, 147-49; Soviet army officers in, 94-95, 202 n.43; Communist parties reward members for service in, 94, 201 n.23; Comintern authority in, 95-101, 203 n.50, 207 n.23; Soviet army advisers to, 98, 202 n.43; military command of, 98, 202 n.44; internal problems of, dealt with by Comintern, Communist parties, 98-103, 203 nn.52, 60, 205 nn.77, 78, 79; Communist parties appoint political commissars in, 98, 102, 214 n.27; Spanish conscripts in, 108, 114-16, 133, 205 n.91; training schools in, 116, 122-23, 147-49, 202 n.49; political commissars in, 119-35, 209 n.60; party cell structure in, 131-32; hospitals of, 132-33, 208 n.57; press and propaganda of, 136-58, 212 n.70; Communist nature of press and propaganda of, 139-49, 211 n.39; attitude toward Trotskyism of, 140-41, 148, 193 n.23, 211 n.39; attitude toward the Soviet Union and Comintern of, 141-44, 147-49, 208 n.46; attitude toward other proletarian parties of, 143-46, 148-49, 157; Communist indoctrination of political commissars in, 147-49; as symbol of proletarian solidarity, 149-58; intellectuals in, 157-58; SIM (Cheka) activities in, 159-72, 213 nn.11, 13, 14; desertion from,

165-72, 214 n.31, 215 nn.33, 35, 40, 55
International Brigade, XI, 56-61, 81-89, 97, 195 n.72, 199 n.5
International Brigade, XII, 61-67, 81-83, 86, 89, 103-4, 107, 108-10, 116, 198 n.1, 199 n.14, 204 n.62, 205 nn.77, 78, 79
International Brigade, XIII, 68-70, 89, 102-3, 196 nn.1, 8, 203 n.60
International Brigade, XIV, 52, 70-73, 83, 89, 98-99, 202 n.47
International Brigade, XV, 71-80, 83, 85, 89, 204 n.62
International Brigade, CL, 199 n.14, 203 n.60, 204 n.62
International Column, 191 n.51. *See also* International Brigade
Italian Legion, 26, 62, 63, 64
Italian Popular Front Committee, 62, 63, 187 n.50, 214 n.31
Ivanov, General, 87

"Jack." *See* Reid, Arnold
Jarama, Battle of the, 83-86
Johnson, Alan, 78, 101
Jones, David, 101

Kahle, Hans, 56, 57, 65, 82, 87, 202 nn.43, 44
Kantorowicz, Alfred, 103, 136-39
Katz, Otto (André Simon), 12
Kerrigan, Peter, 74, 100
Klaus, Lt. Colonel, 73, 85
Kleber, General Emilio, 52, 57, 58, 59, 69, 70-72, 82, 89, 195 n.63, 202 nn.43, 44, 205 n.75. *See also* Stern, General Lazar
Koestler, Arthur, 7, 8, 9, 10, 12, 186 n.32
Koltsov, Michael, 12, 14, 47, 83, 184 nn.45, 47, 185 n.54, 198 n.1, 202 n.40
Kopp, George, 19
Krause, Hans, 172
Krieger. *See* Bianco, Vincenzo
Krivitsky, General Walter, 13, 43, 58, 159, 201 n.25
Kulik, General, 192 n.12

Labour party, British, 143, 144, 157
Lampe, Maurice, 194 n.45

Landau, Kurt, 173
La Pasionaria. *See* Ibarruri, Dolores
Largo Caballero, Francisco, 3, 4, 13, 16, 17, 26, 47-50, 57, 62, 97, 104-6, 110, 119, 196 n.8, 202 n.37
Last, Jef, 161, 183 n.34, 208 n.46
Law, Oliver, 101
Lawrence, Bill, 38, 94-97
Le Boucher de Albacete. *See* Marty, André
Lecouer, Auguste, 96, 98, 102, 103, 165-66, 171, 201 nn.23, 24, 203 n.57, 214 n.27
Leeds, David, 201 n.31. *See* Ameriglio, David
Lincoln battalion. *See* Abraham Lincoln battalion
Lincoln-Washington battalion. *See* Abraham Lincoln battalion
Lister, Enrique, 16, 21, 48-50, 84, 192 n.5
Little, John, 93
Litvinov, Maxim, 7
Locatelli, 71
Longo, Luigi (Gallo): early activities in Spain, 26, 27, 188 n.69; role in original organization of the International Brigades, 31, 49, 50, 52, 63, 64, 67, 70, 72, 82, 90, 93, 95, 211 n.29; differences with Pacciardi on nature of the Brigades, 103-4, 109; attitude toward the May crisis in Barcelona, uncontrollables, Largo Caballero, 105; on the non-Communist Loyalist military staff, 105; on the significance of the International Brigades connection with the Comintern, 111; on the nature and role of the International Brigades, 113; on the Comintern as guide to the Popular Front and the war in Spain, 113; on the importance of training and indoctrinating the Spanish troops in the Brigades, 115, 205 n.91; as chief political commissar of the Brigades, 124; on key role of the political commissars, 124-30; on discipline, 131; on the Activist program, 133; as International Brigade press and propaganda chief, 136-39

Index

Loti, 202 n.43
Loyalist government, 112, 114-15, 182 n.14; relationship of, to the International Brigades, 98, 100-101, 110-11, 116-18
Lukacs, General, 52, 67, 69-70, 198 n.1, 202 n.43, 204 nn.62, 72. *See* Zalka, Mate
Lutz, Fred, 101

Macartney, Wilfred, 72
McCuiston, William, 39
McGovern, John, 163-64
MacKenzie-Papineau battalion, 76
Madrid, defense of, 47-67, 81-89, 184 n.47, 192 nn.5, 9, 12, 195 nn.66, 72; 198 n.1
Maken, Morris, 38, 41, 85
Mallozzi, 95, 107
Mann, Tom, 188 n.59
Marlowe, Inver. *See* Scott, John
Martínez Barrio, Diego, 111
Marty, André; early activities of, regarding Spain, 31, 46, 48, 50; biographical sketch of, 51-52; as organizer of the International Brigades, 56, 61, 71, 72, 78, 79; on the significance of the International Brigades, 90, 93, 115; paranoia of, 101-3, 193 nn.22, 23, 198 n.1; on key role of political commissars, 120, 128-29, 131, 135; as Le Boucher de Albacete, 163, 174-75, 198 n.1; defenders of, 193 n.23; recall of, 201 n.24
Marvin, 204 n.62
Matthews, Herbert, 152
Matuczacz, 57, 194 n.55
Medina. *See* Codovila, Vittorio
Merriman, Robert, 78-80, 85-86, 95, 202 n.49
Miaja, General José, 49
Militia: failure of, to stop Nationalists, 14, 47; Communist and Socialist parties create, before war, 16; war brings proliferation of, 16; reflect different ideologies of Popular Front, 16-26; revolutionary aims of, 17; lack of military efficiency of, 18-20, 186 n.21; foreigners in, 22-30; relationship to the International Brigades, 30

Mills, Saul, 102
Mink, George, 163-64
Minor, Robert, 42, 93, 96, 98, 127, 150, 154
Modetti, Maria, 21
Monmousseau, Gaston, 11
Moquet, Prosper, 97
Morandi, Aldo, 71
Morelli, 204 n.62
Munzenburg, Willi, 9, 10, 11, 12

Nanetti, Nino, 24
Nathan, George, 71, 73
Negrín, Juan, 105-7, 118
Nelson, Steve, 94, 102, 164-65, 201 n.23, 203 n.55, 214 n.26
Nenni, Pietro, 5, 26-27, 52, 62, 87, 110-12, 205 nn.77, 80
Neumann, Heinz, 52, 263, 193 n.29, 214 n.20
Nicoletti. *See* de Vittorio, Giuseppe
Nin, Andres, 214 n.24
NKVD, 12, 43-44, 52, 58, 159-60, 184 n.48, 190 n.39, 193 n.28, 213 nn.5, 11, 214 n.24
Noce, Teresa (Estella), 138, 139
Nonintervention agreement, 183 n.35

Oak, Liston, 164, 182 n.14
Olympiad, Workers, 186 n.34
Oppman, Tedeusz, 194 n.55
Orlov, Alexander, 12, 159, 184 n.48, 202 n.37
Orwell, George, 6, 17, 18-20, 28, 160

Pablo, General. *See* Pavlov, General
Pacciardi, Randolfo, 23, 25, 26, 58, 61, 64, 86; conflict with the Communists, 103-10, 188 n.67, 195 n.80, 198 n.1, 204 nn.62, 72, 205 nn.77, 80; 81
Parovic, Blagoie (Schmidt), 36, 103, 139
Pavlov, General (Pablo), 84
Paynter, William, 100
Penchienati, Carlo, 76, 104-10, 117, 204 n.62, 207 n.23
People's Army: Communist role in origins and formation of, 17-18, 22, 191 n.51, 206 n.1; relationship to the International Brigades, 88, 90-91, 98, 202 n.44; Prieto's efforts to curb Communist predominance in, 116;

229

political commissar system in, 119, 206 nn.1, 2, 3; ex-International Brigade generals command divisions of, 202 n.44; Soviet army officers attached to, 202 nn.43, 44, 205 n.75
Perchuk, Harry, 173
Petrovich, 71, 202 n.43
Picelli, Guido, 95
Platone, Felice, 107
Political Commissariat, International Brigade: key personnel of, 52-53; as direct extension of Comintern, 94-95, 100-103, 107, 111-14; relationship to International Brigade military command, 98; demands severe disciplinary regime, 99-100; problems with Pacciardi, 103-10; and the Barcelona May crisis, 104-6; as nexus between the International Brigades and the Loyalist government, 110-18; resists efforts to assimilate International Brigades into the People's Army, 112-18; attitude toward Loyalist government, 112-15; reliance on political commissar system, 120-24, 131; controls International Brigade press and propaganda output, 137-39; use of "cheka" (SIM) to police Brigades, 161-65
Political Commissars, International Brigade: party stalwarts, 54, 100-103, 126-27, 131, 208 n.52; appointed by Communist parties, 98, 102, 203 n.50, 214 n.27; and indoctrination of Spanish conscripts, 116; functions of, 121-35; relationship to military command, 121-23; training schools for, 122-23, 126; as direct extension of the authority of the International Brigade political commissariat and the Comintern, 124; as ideological mentors of International Brigade troops, 124-25, 126-27; as propagandists toward enemy forces, 124-26; duty to propagate Communist ideology and party line to the troops, 126; effectiveness of, 127-30; control International Brigade press and propaganda output, 127, 136; and censorship, 127; as key to inculcation and maintenance of discipline, 130-35, 209 n.60; as political police agents, 135, 165; Communist indoctrination and training of, 147-49. *See also* Fifth Regiment; People's Army
Pollitt, Harry, 11, 32, 92, 101, 154
Popular Army. *See* People's Army
Popular Front: Spanish, 4; as a Soviet strategy, 1-11; dilemma posed by Spanish conflict to, 10; Italian, 187 n.50
POUM: attitude toward the Communists, 14, 204 n.71; attitude toward militia and People's Army, 17-18; militia, 24-29; Communist vendetta against, 138; 140, 185 n.6, 188 n.67, 204 n.71
Pozas, General Sebastián, 48
Prieto, Indalecio, 4, 109-10, 116, 118-19, 202 n.37, 205 n.77, 206 nn.3, 96
Profintern, 11
Proletarian parties, Spanish, 3, 4, 5, 6, 182 n.13, 185 n.6
PSUC, 24-28, 50, 65
Putz, Colonel, 71, 99

Raimondi, 95, 107
Rebiere, Pierre, 56, 86, 110-11
Red Army. *See* Soviet Army
Red Front Fighters, 54, 56, 65, 194 n.5
Regler, Gustav, 22, 23, 65, 82, 128, 140-41, 153, 174, 185 n.54, 198 n.1, 204 n.72
Reid, Arnold, 42, 190 n.36
Rein, Mark, 172
Renn, Ludwig, 27-28, 62-67, 82, 87, 97
Republic, Spanish, 3-6, 181 nn.2, 6, 9
Republican party, Italian, 23, 62
Revolution, Spanish, 3-6, 182 nn.13, 14, 185 nn.5, 14, 17
Roasio, Antonio, 64
Robeson, Paul, 154
Rojo, General Vicente, 123
Rolfe, Edwin, 138, 152, 215 n.40
Romilly, Esmond, 46
Rosenberg, Marcel, 12, 14
Rosselli, Carlo, 23, 25, 26, 187 n.50, 188 n.67
Roten Front Kämpfer Bund. *See* Red Front Fighters

Index

Rust, William, 32, 44, 127, 130, 152, 203 n.50
Ryan, William, 39, 215 n.35

Sagnier, Marcel, 99, 202 n.47
Salud, 190 n.48
Salute, Popular Front, 190 n.45
Schevenels, Louis, 144-45
Schindler, 69
Schmidt. *See* Parovic, Blagoie
Schuster, Louis. *See* Vehlov, Fritz
Scott, John, 79
Seacat, John, 39
Seacord, Douglas, 79, 85
Second International, 11, 95, 111, 144. *See also* Socialist party, Italian; Socialist party, Spanish
Sheean, Vincent, 152
SIM, 161, 172-75, 213 n.11. *See also* Cheka; NKVD
Simon, André. See Katz, Otto
6 Fevrier battalion, 75, 86
Smillie, Robert, 161, 213 n.9
Socialist party, Italian, 5, 62
Socialist party, Spanish, 3-4, 9, 16
Sommerfield, John, 37, 38, 46, 53, 54, 61
Soviet Army: officers and the defense of Madrid, 49, 84, 85, 89, 184 n.47; officers in the International Brigades, 50, 75, 76, 78, 94-95, 107, 195 n.63, 201 nn.25, 28, 202 n.44; advisers to the International Brigades, 94-95, 98, 202 n.43; advisers to the People's Army, 192 n.12. *See also* Batov, General; Berzin, General Jan; Galicz, Janos; Goriev, General; Kleber, General Emilio; Lukacs, General; Pavlov, General; Soviet Union; Walter, General
Soviet Union: adoption of Popular Front strategy, 6-8; reaction to the Spanish conflict, 10-14, 183 n.32, 33, 34; military mission to Spain, 12-14, 22, 50, 192 n.12, 202 n.43; makes decision to create International Brigades, 54, 185 n.54. *See also* Comintern; International Brigade; Madrid, defense of; NKVD; Soviet Army
Springhall, D. F., 74, 85, 100

Staimer, Richard, 82
Stalin, Joseph, 10, 47, 201 n.25
Stember, Sam, 78, 79, 101
Stepanov, 184 n.44, 192 n.4
Stern, General Lazar. *See* Kleber, General Emilio
Stern, Marvin, 173
Stomatov, 71
Suardi, Emilio, 118
Sukulov, Victor, 95
Swierczewski, General Karol. *See* Walter, General

Tabakoff, 76
Tanguy, Rol, 201 n.23, 203 n.56, 214 n.27
Tapsell, Walter, 100-101, 172
Thaelmann battalion, 64-66, 82
Thaelmann centuria, 27-30, 65-66, 69
Thorez, Maurice, 14, 92, 102, 153, 211 n.29
Tisa, John, 138
Tito. *See* Broz, Joseph
Togliatti, Palmiro (Ercoli, Alfredo), 12, 52, 97, 184 n.45, 192 n.4, 202 n.40
Tom Mann centuria, 28, 57
Toynbee, Philip, 183 n.41
Trotskyism, 7, 140-41, 145, 148, 159, 193 nn.23, 29, 210 n.18, 211 n.39

Ulanovski, Bolek, 57, 194 n.55
Ulbricht, Walter, 9, 52, 163, 190 n.39, 193 n.28
Ulibarri, Manuel, 213 n.11
Uncontrollables, 105, 106, 140, 148. *See also* Anarchists; POUM; Trotskyists
University City. *See* Madrid, defense of
Uribe, Vicente, 186 n.27

VALB (Veterans of the Abraham Lincoln Brigade), 176, 212 n.68
Valois, Colonel, 202 n.43
Valtin, Jan, 164, 172
Vehlov, Fritz (Schuster), 66, 82
Vidakovitch, 76
Vidal, 52, 53, 78, 79, 80, 198 n.57
Vidali, Vittorio (Contreras), 16, 21-22, 47, 50, 52, 120-22, 163, 186 n.27, 195 n.5
Vittori, 99, 202 n.47
Volunteer for Liberty, 136-38
Voronov, General, 84

Voros, Sandor, 89, 97-98, 101-2, 129, 138, 174

Wallach, Albert, 173
Walter, General, 52, 70, 72, 84, 89, 99, 202 n.44
Watson, Keith Scott, 28
White, David McKelvey, 95, 96
White, Paul, 173

Williams, Bert, 100
Wintringham, Tom, 74, 86, 128, 153, 202 n.49
Wisniewski, Stephen, 110-11

Zalka, Mate. See Lukacs, General
Zanoni, Arturo, 117-18
Zeisser, Wilhelm (Gomez), 52, 68, 69, 186 n.28